S0-BIX-969

CROWELL'S HANDBOOK OF
GILBERT AND SULLIVAN

BY THE AUTHOR

Crowell's Handbook of World Opera

Crowell's Handbook of Gilbert and Sullivan

Crowell's Handbook of

GILBERT AND SULLIVAN

Compiled by

FRANK LEDLIE MOORE

Introduction by Dorothy Raedler
Producer-Director, The American Savoyards

THOMAS Y. CROWELL COMPANY

New York, Established 1834

MT
100
S9747
M7

45339

Copyright © 1962 by Thomas Y. Crowell Company
All rights reserved. No part of this book may
be reproduced in any form, except by a reviewer,
without the permission of the publisher.
Library of Congress Catalog Card No. 62-12817
Designed by Laurel Wagner
Manufactured in the United States of America
1 2 3 4 5 6 7 8 9 10

INTRODUCTION

Many books have been written on the subject of Gilbert and Sullivan and the timeless comic operas upon which they collaborated. As a matter of fact, a selected bibliography is included in this volume. However, I do not believe that a more complete or useful compilation of Gilbert and Sullivan material than *Crowell's Handbook of Gilbert and Sullivan* can be found.

The student of Gilbert and Sullivan seeking concise, easily readable information, the Gilbert and Sullivan "fan" interested in learning more about the operas, and particularly the librarian who is required to answer endless questions on a variety of subjects will find this handbook a one-volume answer and ready reference for almost any question which might be asked concerning the operas; the biographies of Gilbert, Sullivan, and D'Oyly Carte; other works by Gilbert and Sullivan; or the identity of the original members of the Savoy Opera Company. There is an alphabetical list of the opera roles, and even (a great boon for librarians!) an alphabetical list of first lines and famous lines. Here indeed is a book which belongs in every school and public library, as well as on the bookshelf of every Gilbert and Sullivan enthusiast.

DOROTHY RAEDLER
Producer-Director
The American Savoyards

PREFACE

Crowell's Handbook of Gilbert and Sullivan is, primarily, a book of facts, arranged in look-up form so that you can get a little more out of the operas than you may have before. The Victorian age is definitely over in most parts of the world and it is becoming difficult to make out all the meanings that must have been apparent to first-nighters. Many of these nuances have been set straight here.

There is something more, not so explicit but quite important. Though Gilbert and Sullivan worked in an age of overwhelming sentimentality, rigid (some would say unnatural) morality, and frustrating inhibitions; though their operas are in old-fashioned forms, with simple structures, devoid of the complexities of our modern, anxious era, their work remains a classic of musical theater. The good operas stand as archetypes of a unity in construction that should be a lesson to modern producers. Every word of Gilbert's comes through clearly because of Sullivan's musical support, and yet the melodic line—whatever you think of its musical style—is beautifully formed. Likewise every movement on the stage contributes to the effect of its moment in the play. Every scene balances with every other scene.

This is a remarkable achievement. We have nothing that quite compares with it except in a few—very few—operas. It would be stretching things too far to compare our two authors with Sophocles in any other respect, but it is possible to say that in Gilbert and Sullivan we see a unity that *suggests* the unity in Sophocles' tragedies.

F. L. M.

CONTENTS

Thespis

OR, THE GODS GROWN OLD

First performed at the Gaiety Theater, London,
23 December 1871

TWO ACTS

CAST

Gods

JUPITER, *aged chief of the gods*
APOLLO, *aged god of the sun*
MARS, *aged god of war*
DIANA, *aged goddess of the moon*
MERCURY, *not so aged god of thieves and messenger of the gods*

Thespians

THESPIS, *theatrical manager*

SILLIMON, *actor*

TIMIDON, *actor*

TIPSEION, *actor*

PREPOSTEROS, *actor*

STUPIDAS, *actor*

SPARKEION, *actor*

NICEMIS, *actress*

PRETTEIA, *actress*

DAPHNE, *actress*

CYMON, *actor*

Chorus of the stars

SETTING

ACT I: Ruined temple on the summit of Mount Olympus.
ACT II: The same, but the ruins have been restored.

SONGS AND CHORUSES

Note: The only music of *Thespis* that remains consists of the following:

ACT I

Chorus with dance: Climbing over Rocky Mountain (*Thespians*)
Song: Little Maid of Arcadee (*Sparkeion*)

SYNOPSIS

ACT I

High on the misty peak of Mount Olympus lie the beautiful ruins of the ageless temple of the gods, where young and vigorous deities of classic Greece once gambolled and loved. Now the kindly green hand of Nature has garlanded these fallen stones with soft leaves and tender grasses, decorating their antiquity with nostalgic beauty. But the gods themselves, being immortal, are by no means dead. They live on and on, sick and tired of the details and rigmarole of their official positions. Apollo has grown seedy in spite of his attempts to keep his hair blond and his belly potless. Diana, goddess of the moon, cannot go out at night without wrapping herself in layer upon layer of dismal woolens to keep out the damp and drafts. Glorious youth has left them forever. Gout and the ague are the chief topics of their conversation as they go about their tasks. Only Mercury, ever active, keeps his youth.

It is morning. Diana has just come from night duty and Mercury returns from a profitable evening of stealing the cosmetics and beauty aids each of the gods needs from earth, but which are no longer delivered by means of votive sacrifice.

The oldest, wisest, and most to be respected of them all is Jupiter. This aged deity is seriously concerned about the poor state of things on Olympus, particularly in the matter of the offerings from below. Once they were plentiful and of fine material; indeed, there was a time in the very ancient past when the altars gave up human sacrifices, but those glorious days seem to have withered away completely. What comes up now from the badly tended temples below is more often something like canned beef. Something must be done about it.

Suddenly there is a frightening sound, one never before heard on the sacred heights of Olympus. A herd of noisy mortals can be seen clambering up the slopes toward the temple. The gods barely have time to slip away into their shadowy ruins before Sparkeion and Nicemis arrive, far ahead of their friends. It is their wedding day (the ceremony takes all day in Greece) and this is the first brief moment that they have been able to be alone together.

They are actors, members of the troupe managed by Thespis. Before this nuptial celebration—which is only half over: the official pronouncement has not yet been spoken—they had each enjoyed affairs of love with other members of the troupe. Sparkeion had once been engaged to Daphne, and Nicemis once allowed the suit of Thespis himself. Jealousy is thus still possible, and the marriage may have to be halted if the two principals should decide not to go through with it.

At last the others arrive, climbing over the rocks. They are a preoccupied lot, full of little resentments and urgings which not one of them suppresses. They argue about everything, especially Preposteros who is, on stage, the villain of the company. By day he is bitter. But these bickerings are routine. What is much worse just now is that Daphne has arranged to be seated next to Sparkeion for the picnic. Nicemis, in high dudgeon, then takes up loudly with Thespis, hoping to remind Sparkeion that she is not to be treated so shabbily. It must be noted that the manager is not happy with this arrangement, since it tends to bridge that gap of hierarchy which he considers must be maintained between a theatrical manager and his tools.

At this point the Olympian gods have had enough of the interlopers. In their most awe-inspiring full costume of authority they mount the broken columns around the picnic site and command these presumptuous mortals to leave forthwith.

The actors are not dismayed. Thespis introduces himself. Jupiter, realizing who he is, steps down to ask some technical advice of this theatrical expert. Would Thespis help the gods discover why they seem to have lost their influence on earth? Would he, perhaps, teach them a technique for again appearing as impressive as they did in days long gone? Thespis is quite agreeable. He then makes the happy suggestion that the gods should, for a beginning, disguise themselves and travel for a year among the people of the world, to find out what the true state of things may be. While they are away the actors will take their places on Olympus, to give the illusion that all is quite well with celestial affairs and that the gods are in their abode. Jupiter thinks this an admirable scheme and he agrees to it. Leaving Mercury to keep an official eye on things while they are gone, the gods depart for their sabbatical year of research.

Thespis takes the place of Jupiter, Sparkeion becomes Apollo, Nicemis is Diana, Timidon becomes the god of war, and Daphne takes the part of Calliope, the muse of fame.

ACT II

A year has passed. The most obvious change the Thespians have wrought upon the summit of the mountain is immediately visible, and very impressive. The new Olympian Temple of the Gods is a splendid, indeed a magnificent, edifice, in perfect repair and with an elegant throne for Thespis to occupy as he plays his role of substitute Jupiter. The marbles and fine stonework of the building are, of course, only an illusion created by masterful stage designers, but the effect is all that really matters—and the effect is stupendous.

All is not, however, running smoothly. The actors have run into unforeseen difficulties in playing their parts. Pretteia, as Venus, is required by the genealogy of the gods to love Vulcan, played by her own grandfather, an obscure actor named Presumptios. A mature actress should not be troubled by the intrusion of mere reality, but should play her part perfectly under any conditions. Unfortunately Pretteia is too young and too much a neophyte for that. To love her own grandfather is difficult for her. And Diana, played by Nicemis, makes her rounds at night not alone, but with her lover Sparkeion. This is doubly disturbing, because Sparkeion is cast as Apollo, the sun, who never should be seen at night. Cupid is also played by a mortal, one with excellent taste for pretty girls. He has made a complete botch of his role by shooting his potent arrows only at the most beautiful of them, never aiming at a bachelor, so that:

While ev'ry young man is as shy as a hermit,
Young ladies are popping all over the place!

With twelve months gone, it is time for the annual reckoning, time for Mercury to present the accumulated complaints received from earth during the year past. In this case, since Jupiter is still absent, Thespis must preside over the heavenly court. Mercury goes to summon the other substitute gods who must attend.

While he is away Daphne, as Calliope, brings her own, private complaint, saying that her former lover Sparkeion (Apollo) has married Nicemis. Thespis wonders why this must be brought up now. Daphne points out that she, playing Calliope the goddess of fame, is custodian of the Olympian library. In it she has come across a book which delineates the Olympian peerage, and in which, in the list of the wives of Apollo, the name Calliope appears in the final position. Thus it is established that there exists a bigamous situation which Daphne insists be cleared up.

The court is called into session. Seated among the spectators are the real gods of Olympus, disguised so that only Thespis and Mercury know who they are. In order to quell any suspicions, Thespis introduces them to the assembly as members of the press. When the complaints from earth have been brought out and heard, however, it is entirely too much for the real gods to take in silence. They rise to depose Thespis and take over again the reins of the world's government. In punishment for the terrible chaos into which the substitute gods have thrown everything, Jupiter condemns the Thespians as a group to be:

eminent tragedians
Whom no one ever, ever goes to see!

HISTORICAL NOTE

All that remains of the music for *Thespis* are a song and a chorus. The song is "Little Maid of Arcadee," the chorus "Climbing over Rocky Mountain," which was later used in *The Pirates of Penzance.* The Gilbert and Sullivan Opera Company of New York tried to reconstruct *Thespis* with music by Frank Miller in 1953, but the original remains only as a play script.

One wonders why. The play is not much worse than the average successful work of the collaboration. There are disturbing inconsistencies in it. The puns and twists of meanings are just about on a par with, for instance, those of *Iolanthe* or *Ruddigore*. But *Thespis* ran not more than sixty-four performances before disappearing from the stage forever. Perhaps it was not that the music was bad or that it didn't, in general, fit the story. Although German Reed had asked Gilbert and Sullivan to work together on a one-act operetta as early as 1870, *Thespis* was the first actual collaboration between these two. Later they had great difficulty getting together. Perhaps at this early stage it took considerable experiment to find the way to begin. It was easy enough for Gilbert to work with Frederick Clay and turn out a potboiler that would be moderately successful, and for Sullivan to take up the poetry of Tennyson for an oratorio or a set of songs. But when they worked together, there must have been a general disarrangement of their creative processes, caused by their personalities, a raising of the sights which made a more distant target possible but difficult at the same time. Perhaps when they first worked together, whether they intended to continue or not, they spent their effort on discovering the *modus vivendi* rather than on the stuff of the drama itself. Perhaps their technique of sending samples to each other by mail began even this early, but did not—because they did not know each other—permit a real meeting of minds.

The basic rhythm of the production must surely have missed a few beats. *Ages Ago*, Gilbert's collaboration with Clay, ran more or less smoothly because it was unified in its time structure. Probably Gilbert wielded far more power over his composer in this than he could at the beginning over Sullivan. *Thespis* could not have been so unified. If it had been it would not have failed so permanently. I speak of the underlying structure of drama. One can feel its presence when it works; there is a marvelous exhilaration in good *ensemble* of creation. But when it is missing, drama drags.

All that is theory and conjecture. The facts will never be known, not for *Thespis*. One doubts whether the effort of discovering the truth would really be worth while, considering that it would at best supply a reason for the play's closing after two months.

The play was put on stage in three weeks' time with a company of actors who did not know each other and were not known by the director (as were the members of the D'Oyly Carte company, founded later). The part of Mercury was played by a woman, Nellie Farren. Fred Sullivan, the composer's brother, played Apollo. One of the sopranos sang the opening performance consistently sharp. Gilbert directed, as he had already learned to do for his other plays. He had developed his technique to such a point that he knew exactly how he wanted each actor to make each gesture and speak each line of his dialogue. With a new company this became a source of argument and friction. Why *Thespis* should have suffered and failed because of it, when Gilbert's other plays succeeded under the same conditions, is yet a mystery.

But there were innovations with which other productions did not have to deal. Gilbert insisted that the chorus be active on stage, that they not just stand and sing like so many stumps in a forest. In this he anticipated Bizet, who required the same thing from the chorus of *Carmen* four years later. Bizet even ordered that the girls smoke cigarettes! In each case precedent was smashed and in each case the opening night was uneasy. *Thespis* also suffered from inadequate rehearsal. It must have been a shabby affair. But it did last sixty-four nights, time enough to have been brought into shape had a basic structure been shapely enough.

Oddly, the only other bad failure in the collaboration of Gilbert and Sullivan was *The Grand Duke*, their last, which, like *Thespis*, opens with a marriage between members of an acting company and deals with the experiment of actors ruling a world. Perhaps, like modern Broadway plays that cannot free themselves of self-conscious obsessions with actors' dreams and actors' intellects, *Thespis* and *The Grand Duke* just did not reach the outside world with a message of symbolic importance.

Trial by Jury

A DRAMATIC CANTATA

First performed at the Royalty Theater, London, 25 March 1875   ONE ACT

CAST

THE LEARNED JUDGE	Bar
THE PLAINTIFF, ANGELINA	S
THE DEFENDANT, EDWIN	T
COUNSEL FOR THE PLAINTIFF	Bar
USHER	Bar or B
FOREMAN OF THE JURY	B
ASSOCIATE	Silent
FIRST BRIDESMAID	
Chorus of Bridesmaids	

SETTING

A court of justice.

SONGS AND CHORUSES

Chorus: Hark, the hour of ten is sounding (*Chorus*)
Solo: Now, Jurymen, hear my advice (*Usher*)
Song: When first my old, old love I knew (*Defendant*)
Chorus: All hail, great Judge (*Chorus*)
Song: When I, good friends, was called to the bar (*Judge*)
Chorus: Comes the broken flower (*Bridesmaids*)
Solo: O'er the season vernal (*Plaintiff*)
Aria: With a sense of deep emotion (*Counsel for the Plaintiff*)
Song: Oh, gentlemen, listen, I pray (*Defendant*)
Duet: I love him—I love him—with fervour unceasing (*Plaintiff and Defendant*)
Finale: Oh joy unbounded (*Ensemble*)

{ 7 }

SYNOPSIS

The scene is a court of Justice. The Jury is all ready, nay, thirsty for the case. Barristers and attorneys dot the room with their snowy wigs. It is ten o'clock, time for the case of Edwin, sued by Angelina for breach of promise. The Usher steps forward to advise the Jury that this is the hall of justice, and that therefore, in accordance with the ancient tradition of Anglo-Saxon law, they must sternly control their emotions, remain free from any hint of bias, and maintain a judicial frame of mind.

Oh, listen to the plaintiff's case;
Observe the features of her face—
The broken-hearted bride.
Condole with her distress of mind;
From bias free of every kind
This trial must be tried!

And when, amid the plaintiff's shrieks,
The ruffianly defendant speaks—
Upon the other side;
What he may say you needn't mind—
From bias free of every kind,
This trial must be tried!

Into this spider's web, so well woven to snare him, steps the Defendant. As soon as he tells them who he is, the Jury, as a man shouts:

Monster, dread our damages!

And they shake their fists furiously. The Defendant insists that they should at least hear a statement from him. Agreed. They all arise, step out of the jury-box and gather around him while he sings:

I was a love-sick boy!

He pleads that he was very young and unprepared for constancy in love when the trouble that forms the body of this case arose. The jurymen know well that a young man cannot be trusted, but since they are one and all older men now, and completely respectable, they are unanimously devoid of sympathy for him. Back they snap to the jury-box, ready for the trial to commence.

Enter the Learned Judge, to a chorus of praise—ecstatic praise—from everyone present. He accepts this as a man in his station must, and takes a moment to tell them the most interesting story of how he became a judge.

When I, good friends, was called to the bar,
I'd an appetite fresh and hearty,

But I was, as many young barristers are,
An impecunious party.

Though poor, he had the right clothes to make an impression. But he got nowhere so long as he persisted in being a hard-working barrister. At last a new path opened to him. He fell in love with the daughter ("who might pass for forty-three, in the dusk with the light behind her") of a rich attorney. Bright were his prospects. He clambered, rung upon rung, up through the levels of court until he, too, became rich and famous. Having achieved everything important, he threw over the elderly daughter of the rich attorney, caring no more for her father's anger. And now he is ready to try a case of breach of promise as a highly respected judge,

And a good judge, too!

The trial opens with the swearing-in of the Jury. This peculiar ceremony requires its candidates to kneel in their places inside the jury-box until they are entirely hidden behind its solid oak front while the Usher recites the formula of the oath to empty space. In response to his command, their disembodied hands are raised, but the jurymen remain invisible until the process is done. The Usher then calls in the Plaintiff, who enters, preceded by a chorus of bridesmaids in their finery.

Comes the broken flower—
Comes the cheated maid.

At first the Judge falls in love with the first Bridesmaid and sends her a note. But when the pretty Plaintiff comes into view he quickly sends his Usher after that note and transfers it to her, saying,

Oh, never, never, never, since I joined the human race
Saw I so exquisitely fair a face.

He is not alone in his pleasure. The Jury is smitten by the beauty of the bevy of bridesmaids. Counsel for the Plaintiff opens:

With a sense of deep emotion,
I approach this painful case;
For I never had a notion
That a man could be so base.

In words of tenderness and shocked delicacy he retails the events that led this affair into the tragedy of open court. The sweet, innocent girl smiled upon this traitor. The world became all beautiful to her:

An existence à la Watteau.

But when she tried to set a definite date this scoundrel endeavored to avoid it. Imagine! She had actually bought her trousseau, but this heartless villain did not marry her. The jury is deeply moved.

Cheer up, cheer up, we love you!

The dear, fragile maiden feels faint. The Foreman begs her to recline on his shoulder. The learned Judge outranks the Foreman of the Jury and wins the prize. By this time the fury of the Jury is boundless. The Defendant states his side of the case. He does not deny that he once loved this girl, or that he later changed his mind and fell in love with another. But Nature herself is changeable:

Consider the moral, I pray,
Nor bring a young fellow to sorrow.
Who loves this young lady today,
And loves that young lady tomorrow.

He suggests a possible resolution of this suit of breach of promise, if the court will permit;

I'll marry this lady today
And I'll marry the other tomorrow!

The Judge thinks this not a bad solution; in fact he considers it a most practical proposal, quite reasonable. He takes it under consideration. But the Counsel for the Plaintiff, diligently reading from an ancient book of law, points out that:

In the reign of James the Second
It was generally reckoned
As a very serious crime
To marry two wives at one time.

This dilemma, then, must be submitted in due form to the Jury. In a final statement, the Plaintiff impresses the twelve sympathetic men with the sincerity of the love she once had for the ungrateful Defendant. Surely such devotion is worth high damages? For his rebuttal the Defendant tries to prove that she could not possibly have ever been in love with him, for:

I smoke like a furnace—I'm always in liquor—
A ruffian—a bully—a sot;
I'm sure I should thrash her, perhaps I should kick her,
I am such a very bad lot!

This is a nasty difficulty for the Jury to assess. The Judge tentatively suggests they test the truth of his statement by plying him with liquor on an experimental basis. But this is rejected. Forthwith the Learned Judge renders his decision, without bothering to consult the jury for theirs:

> *Put your briefs upon the shelf,*
> *I will marry her myself!*

And he prances down from the bench to kiss Angelina with all the court to witness.

HISTORICAL NOTE

Trial by Jury is less than forty minutes long, just under the limit of comfort for an audience sitting in one place without intermission. There have been longer single acts in the history of opera. Indeed, there is one well-known modern work composed as one act but lasting nearly three hours. It represents a remarkable exception rather than the rule. *Trial by Jury* also contains no spoken dialogue. It is the only such work of the Gilbert and Sullivan series. It seems very interesting, when one considers their entire output of comic operas, that their first successful work, one of the most popular, was so economically written and composed, so tightly put together. All the other operas contain moments that are not quite as finely conceived and exposed as we would wish. Sometimes a theatrical contrivance stands in the way, or we feel a slippage for a moment because we have momentarily lost our belief in the magical world on the stage. *Trial by Jury*, by its very form, prevents that loss. We are caught up immediately into a courtroom in a crazy world within which everything happens not only logically—within its madness—but also quickly and abso-lutely, without time being wasted in down-to-earth explanation. The work is just long enough to allow a real exploration into this madness, but not so long that fatigue reminds us of our own unfortunate sanity.

Richard D'Oyly Carte was a young man, hired to manage a small theater in the Soho district of London. He had visions of the grandeur of being a great impresario some day. Perhaps, even so early, he realized that the road to such fame lay along the way of developing an English opera, English musical plays. But at the moment he had a perfectly prac-tical problem. Offenbach's *La Périchole* was on the bill but did not fill an evening. Carte needed another work. Gilbert dropped in to see Carte about this time, probably on other business. He was already a very suc-cessful playwright, one whom Carte might ask for advice or help in this situation. As it happened, Gilbert not only was willing to do something for Carte, but had an unused manuscript of a little piece he had worked up for the prima-donna Parepa-Rosa, and which her husband, Carl Rosa, was to have set to music. Madame Rosa had recently died, leaving Gilbert with an unclaimed little libretto.

They talked it over. Carte was a shrewd enough young man to think that Carl Rosa was not the only composer who might be interested. If they could get Arthur Sullivan to work with them, the growing national fame that that serious musician enjoyed would certainly help at the box office. Gilbert liked this suggestion and drove around to see Sullivan one uncomfortable morning in March, shortly thereafter. Opening the new manuscript, Gilbert read it through anxiously and hurriedly, as if he actually detested it. When he came to the end he shut it with a bang and waited, apparently expecting an unfavorable reaction. It seemed totally to have escaped his attention that Sullivan had been laughing uproariously throughout the reading. When it dawned on Gilbert that his audience of one had liked his libretto, the agreement was promptly signed. Thus began the collaboration that was to continue precariously, but fruitfully, for many years.

It took three weeks to compose the score, with rehearsals conducted simultaneously, which is pretty good time for such a well-conceived work, without the composer's having had time to mull it over. On the 25th of March *Trial by Jury* was brought before the public and made an immediate hit. The fact that England's serious oratorio composer had written a comic-opera success may have shocked a few, but the audiences who heard it were unanimously pleased with the fine job he did. Musical comedy in England had been in a very low state for a long time. Orchestras were sloppy in their technique, composers wrote what they thought would match continental models such as Offenbach. But Sullivan came out with an uncompromising gem of good music, wedded to a hilarious but equally carefully made script. The effect upon opera and musical comedy in Britain was not long in making itself evident. Incidentally *La Périchole* did not withstand the onslaught. Soon after *Trial by Jury* opened as second on the bill, the Offenbach had to be surreptitiously dropped. An ordinary English musical farce took its place.

At first, because of the importance of his name, Sullivan was considered as the creator of *Trial by Jury*. Posters called it a dramatic cantata by Arthur Sullivan. The librettist was of little importance; in fact, on the first night's program his name was incorrectly listed as W. C. Gilbert. But it must be admitted now that the elegant format of *Trial by Jury* was Gilbert's conception. The fact that it was so readily understood and implemented by Sullivan is a further compliment to the author's ability. In all the other operas one can trace the effect of what must have been Sullivan's suggestions for rhythms and shapes. But *Trial by Jury* was all Gilbert's.

The first performance in the United States took place at the Eagle Theater in New York, 15 November 1875. It was unauthorized; the authors got not one red cent from it. But they were doing well enough. Their own production had come to an end after 128 nights, and then only because the leading man, the Learned Judge, played by the composer's brother Fred Sullivan, was taken off stage by illness. Credit for the immediate success of the work was due in no small measure to his gift for comedy. In 1884, *Trial by Jury* was revived by the D'Oyly Carte Company for the first time, to replace *Princess Ida*, which had begun to do badly. Since it first opened, *Trial by Jury* has perhaps had as many performances, all told, as any other work by Gilbert and Sullivan. Certainly its miniature format has helped make that possible. But one must not forget that college and other amateur productions of older works are repeated not only because they are short and easy to understand, but because they continue to please. *Trial by Jury* is practically indestructible.

The Sorcerer

*First performed at the Opéra Comique, London,
17 November 1877*   TWO ACTS

CAST

SIR MARMADUKE POINTDEXTRE, *an elderly baronet*	B
ALEXIS, *of the Grenadier Guards, his son*	T
DR. DALY, *Vicar of Ploverleigh*	Bar
NOTARY	B
JOHN WELLINGTON WELLS, *of J. W. Wells & Co.,* *Family Sorcerers*	Bar
LADY SANGAZURE, *a lady of ancient lineage*	C
ALINE, *her daughter, betrothed to Alexis*	S
MRS. PARTLET, *a pew-opener*	C
CONSTANCE, *her daughter*	S
Chorus of Villagers	

SETTING

ACT I: Exterior of Sir Marmaduke's mansion, midday.
ACT II: The same, midnight.

SONGS AND CHORUSES

ACT I

Chorus: Ring forth, ye bells (*Villagers*)
Aria: When he is here (*Constance*)
Ballad: Time was when Love and I were well acquainted (*Dr. Daly*)
Chorus: With heart and with voice (*Girls of the Village*)
Aria: Oh, happy young heart! (*Aline*)
Duet: Welcome joy, adieu to sadness! (*Sir Marmaduke and Lady Sangazure*)
Ballad: Love feeds on many kinds of food, I know (*Alexis*)
Song: Oh! My name is John Wellington Wells (*Wells*)
Incantation: Sprites of earth and air (*Wells*)
Aria: Let us fly to a far-off land (*Aline*)

{ 14 }

Chorus: Now to the banquet we press (*Villagers*)
Brindisi: Eat, drink, and be gay (*Sir Marmaduke*)

ACT II

Trio: 'Tis twelve, I think (*Alexis, Aline, Wells*)
Aria: Dear friends, take pity on my lot (*Constance*)
Ballad: Thou hast the power thy vaunted love (*Alexis*)
Quintet: I rejoice that it's decided (*Alexis, Aline, Sir Marmaduke, Mrs. Partlet, Dr. Daly*)
Duet: Hate me! I drop my H's—have through life! (*Wells, Lady Sangazure*)
Song: Oh, my voice is sad and low (*Dr. Daly*)
Duet: Alas! that lovers thus should meet (*Aline, Dr. Daly*)
Finale: Or I or he must die (*Ensemble*)

SYNOPSIS

ACT I

> *Ring forth, ye bells,*
> *With clarion sound—*
> *Forget your knells,*
> *For joys abound.*
> *Forget your notes*
> *Of mournful lay,*
> *And from your throats*
> *Pour joy today.*

Thus the villagers celebrate the betrothal of Alexis and Aline. There is only one who is unhappy: Constance. She will not confess the reason, not even to her mother, until the chorus discreetly leaves them by themselves. When everyone else has gone, the poor girl confides her secret.

She is in love, and grief-stricken because of it. Whom does she love? Why, Dr. Daly, the vicar, that delicate man whom we see passing by at this very moment musing on his past. When he was a very young man, he tells us, he was the object of every girl's most beckoning attention. But now—ah, times have changed!

In the most round-about fashion Mrs. Partlet brings the lithesome girl and the vicar together and then she delicately raises the general subject of the bliss of matrimony. The reverend gentleman does not take the hint easily. He declares that his amorous days, unfortunately, are done, and that although it would be pleasant to have someone around the house to keep it warm and cheery, he is quite sure he will end his days in sorry bachelorhood.

Determined not to be put off by this temporary set-back, Mrs. Partlet takes her daughter away as the middle-aged man waits to greet Sir Marmaduke and the about-to-be-betrothed Alexis. They have come together to have a meeting with the young man's fiancée. She is not due yet. The father takes a moment to explain to his boy that his madly rapturous expressions of love, which the father cannot help hearing from time to time, are not well advised. When *he* was a young man and in love with the Lady Sangazure, conversations were quite restrained, as is only proper. But here comes the prospective bride, announced by a chorus of village maidens.

> *With heart and with voice*
> *Let us welcome this mating;*
> *To the youth of her choice,*
> *With a heart palpitating,*
> *Comes the lovely Aline!*

Alexis greets her, but can hardly maintain the dignified tone of conversation his father had recommended. Sir Marmaduke, for his part, has caught sight of Aline's mother, the very Lady Sangazure of whom he had just been speaking. Suddenly he is seized by a strong emotion. So is the lady. But both repress themselves while their children meet.

ALEXIS: *Oh, my adored one!*
ALINE: *Beloved boy!*
ALEXIS: *Ecstatic rapture!*
ALINE: *Unmingled joy!*

The Lady Sangazure and Sir Marmaduke, having failed to keep their composure, sing a duet which each intends to keep on a quite formal plane, but in which each gives voice to repressed passion. Aloud they sing most proper and polite greetings, but behind the hand:

> *Wild with adoration!*
> *Mad with fascination!*

Ardent love, though years have passed since they last met. While this ceremony throbs on, the Notary has arrived with a marriage contract drawn up, ready to be signed by Alexis and Aline. In a twinkling of an eye the deed is done and the two are irrevocably bound for marriage. Their love is true, there can be no doubt of it, for they spend half their time together telling each other how it has been tried, tested, and found perfect under the most extreme stresses during the short intervals when they are apart. Not for money do they love, nor for rank nor any other ulterior purpose. It is for love of love alone.

Aline cannot but admire her fiancé's high principles. Not only does he believe that their love has benefited them exceedingly, but in true aristocratic benevolence he has arranged for a reputable firm of sorcerers to have a love potion distributed among the villagers so that even the lowly may taste the purity of the emotion their betters feel. There shall be no more distinction of age or wealth. All who drain the philtre will be thrust headlong into love. Such a forced harmony cannot but be beneficial to society as a whole. The Sorcerer, who has just arrived, is a very busy man:

> *Oh! my name is John Wellington Wells,*
> *I'm a dealer in magic and spells,*
> *In blessings and curses*
> *And ever-filled purses,*
> *In prophecies, witches and knells.*

His leading article of commerce—selling even better than penny curses —is his Patent Oxy-Hydrogen Love-at-First-Sight philtre. It comes in four-and-a-half or nine gallon casks, pipes and hogsheads. He allows deductions for cash and to members of the Army and Navy Stores (a sort of cooperative department store in London). The philtre takes effect twelve hours after dosage, first rendering the drinker unconscious, then affecting him so that he falls in love with the first person (of the opposite sex) whom he sees upon awakening. It does *not* affect married people.

Alexis sends Aline to fetch a teapot and arranges to buy enough of the potion to treat the whole village. Mr. Wells prepares to pour out the correct amount, working his power into it with a grand incantation:

> *Sprites of earth and air—*
> *Fiends of flame and fire—*
> *Demon souls,*
> *Come here in shoals,*
> *This dreadful deed inspire!*

And in the shadows of the darkened stage, weird shapes hover and mill about as the spell is cast. When all is done, light returns, and the villagers —unaware of what has been prepared for them—gaily gather to take part in the marriage feast. In each cup of tea there lurks a spell guaranteed to throw every unmarried person into love with someone else within twelve hours. As they carouse and sing, gradually they all sink down until the entire population of the village lies insensible on the ground.

ACT II

Twelve hours later, at midnight, the Sorcerer tiptoes among the prostrate bodies, followed by Alexis and his fiancée, careful not to step on any villager asleep on the ground. It is time now for the potion to have completed its work. The three conspirators step into the shadows as the villagers awaken, one by one. Their first words:

Why, where be oi, and wot be oi adoin'
Asleepin' out just when the dews du rise?

And as each man looks upon each girl, love dawns in each heart. Marriages are immediately proposed and accepted. Among those so oddly smitten is Constance, who had formerly been constant in her love for the vicar; but who now drags herself into view, in tears, leading the old and deaf Notary, the first man she saw when she woke up. Her grief is matched only by her irrepressible adoration of the dry and snuffy old bachelor.

The noble experiment has been entirely successful. Alexis now proposes that he and Aline should take the potion themselves. Not that they are not already in love, but this will make their love durable beyond mere human devotion. The girl is hurt to think that her lover should even consider such a mechanical binder for her emotions, and she refuses to debase it. Alexis, then, cannot believe that she loves him as much as she had promised. They have reached an impasse.

Although everyone had expected that Sir Marmaduke would be potioned into marriage with the Lady Sangazure, when he first made his appearance after treatment it was Mrs. Partlet who swam before his clouded eyes. The dear woman is a bit lower in social station, which causes his son some concern, but;

—any wife of yours is a mother of mine.

All are agreed that though the match would hardly have seemed proper under normal circumstances, the good Mrs. Partlet makes up in soberness what she lacks in beauty.

Lady Sangazure walks alone. No delightful vision of love was there to greet her when her eyes opened. In fact, as she paces about in her melancholy, the first man she sees is the Sorceror John Wellington Wells; a bachelor most appalled at the prospect.

WELLS: *Hate me! I drop my H's,—have through life!*
LADY S: *Love me! I'll drop them too!*
WELLS: *Hate me! I always eat peas with a knife!*
LADY S: *Love me! I'll eat like you!*

In vain he pleads. He claims to be engaged. Ah! That put her off! She is grief-stricken, and the sorcerer feels safe enough to offer her his consolation.

Aline has been thinking about the terrible disagreement, their first, which she has had with Alexis. Alone for a moment she takes the fatal step; impetuously she drinks the potion. But hardly has she gurgled it down when she sees Dr. Daly pensively playing his flageolet. He took the potion also, but every girl had been seen and claimed by another, leaving him forlorn as he walked. When their eyes meet, it is love.

> Oh, joyous boon! Oh, mad delight!
> Oh, sun and moon! Oh, day and night!
> Rejoice, rejoice with me!

Into this passionate scene stumbles the unsuspecting Alexis. But he is too late. Aline and Dr. Daly are so deeply in love that nothing can keep them apart. Alexis calls upon the whole world to witness the perfidy of his former fiancée. Nor is Dr. Daly happy about having caused such an unfortunate rupture in the established order of life. Reluctantly the Sorcerer admits that he knows of an antidote that will erase the effects of the potion: either he or Alexis must—as the formula for the antidote requires—give up his soul to the magic spirit in fair trade for removing the spell. If Alexis should do it, of course, there would be no one to marry Aline once the spell was dispelled. It falls, therefore, to Mr. Wells to make the supreme sacrifice. As he sinks slowly into the flames of the nether world, all the lovers separate and rejoin their former partners. Sir Marmaduke goes to Lady Sangazure, Dr. Daly to Constance, the Notary to Mrs. Partlet, and Alexis to Aline.

> Now to the banquet we press—
> Now for the eggs and the ham—
> Now for the mustard and cress—
> Now for the strawberry jam!

And all the village joins in a general dance as the smoke of the infernal region dissipates.

HISTORICAL NOTE

Carte was thirty-five, Sullivan two years older, and Gilbert forty-one when *The Sorcerer* was first brought out at the Comique. This play was the first production of the new syndicate of gentlemen of means, gathered by Carte for the express object of backing an English comic-opera theater company of which Carte had dreamed for years. The success of *Trial by Jury* had been all the stimulus necessary to put his dream into concrete action. Gilbert and Sullivan were commissioned by this syndicate to write and produce the first comic-opera for the company, with no restrictions as to whom they might hire to play parts, or how they would conduct rehearsals. The original contract stipulated that the authors should receive in advance £210 against a royalty of £6½ per performance, the payment to be equally divided between them. It must have seemed adequate, for the proposal was first put into writing as a note from Sullivan to Carte. But it is worth remembering that these two authors, who undertook their second production after an astounding success with the first, at a fee of about $19.00 per night, were to become fabulously rich in their future collaborations.

The company that was recruited to play *The Sorcerer* became the nucleus of the later permanent D'Oyly Carte Company. Hence, in effect, the types of roles indicated by the story of this opera affected the choice of characters in the writing of subsequent works. Thus, when Rutland Barrington became Dr. Daly, the way was clear for the creation of King Paramount in *Utopia, Limited,* which the same actor played sixteen years later. This establishment of a fairly steady group of actors and actresses has helped to create that general style which we call the Gilbert and Sullivan style. The choice of personnel had as much weight in this regard as did the practical production training each received in the theater, and the individual experience of each of the authors in his profession. All the operas have characters that fit certain sizes of costume and require certain styles of acting. Gilbert used ideas over and over again; he also used people over and over again. When author and composer began to have personal disagreements many years later, the make-up of this company added urgency to the problem.

But to return to *The Sorcerer*: Carte gave Gilbert free rein in choosing the cast and directing rehearsals, knowing that he was an expert at both. It was decided that the policy of hiring actors with fine reputations was not the best for the kind of ensemble the authors wanted to create. Hence they chose people without regard for box-office history. The role of John Wellington Wells was originally intended for Fred Sullivan, who had helped make *Trial by Jury* a comic success. But since that star's death, a new comedian was needed. George Grossmith, who created most of the major baritone comic parts in later operas, was originally a recitalist who toured Y.M.C.A. halls singing sentimental songs. He agreed to play the Sorcerer after some haggling about salary. After becoming famous with the D'Oyly Carte troupe, he returned to the circuit and made an even greater fortune. Rutland Barrington, whose vocal technique was pretty bad by operatic standards, was hired for just that reason and stayed with the company throughout all its premières (except *The Yeomen of the Guard,* which opened while he was out of the company, having his fling at independent theater management).

That Gilbert and Sullivan chose wisely became immediately evident. *The Sorcerer* ran 175 performances, which was fairly good for the time. That they were also right in the long run is to be seen in the fine tradition which they established and which is still carried on by the descendants of that original group.

The Sorcerer is based upon the idea of love potions, a plot possibility which Gilbert used in a short story *An Elixir of Love* and in his first play *Dulcamara,* and which he got originally from Donizetti's *L'Elisir d'Amore.* It is a close relative to the trick of what became known as his "Lozenge Plot," in which people took pills to change themselves into other people. This reliance on silly magic marked some of the author's worst scripts. It was germane to the period.

The Sorcerer was revived in 1884 to replace the faltering *Princess Ida.* It was brought back again in 1898. This latter performance was notable for the fact that Gilbert and Sullivan met to take their last curtain call together after the opening, but did not speak to each other.

H.M.S. Pinafore

OR, THE LASS THAT LOVED A SAILOR

First performed at the Opéra Comique, London, 25 May 1878 TWO ACTS

CAST

THE RIGHT HONOURABLE SIR JOSEPH PORTER, K. C. B., *First Lord of the Admiralty*	Bar
CAPTAIN CORCORAN, *commanding H.M.S.* Pinafore	Bar
TOM TUCKER, *midshipmite (a small chorus girl)*	Silent
RALPH RACKSTRAW, *able seaman*	T
DICK DEADEYE, *able seaman*	B
BILL BOBSTAY, *boatswain's mate*	Bar
BOB BECKET, *carpenter's mate*	B
JOSEPHINE, *the captain's daughter*	S
HEBE, *Sir Joseph's first cousin*	MS
LITTLE BUTTERCUP, MRS. CRIPPS, *a Portsmouth bumboat woman*	C
First Lord's sisters, cousins, aunts, sailors, marines, etc.	Chorus

SETTING

ACT I: The quarter-deck of H.M.S. *Pinafore*, off Portsmouth. Noon.
ACT II: The same. Night.

SONGS AND CHORUSES

ACT I

Chorus: We sail the ocean blue (*Sailors*)
Aria: For I'm called Little Buttercup—dear Little Buttercup (*Buttercup*)
Madrigal: The nightingale sighed for the moon's bright ray (*Ralph, Chorus*)
Song: I am the Captain of the *Pinafore* (*Captain, Chorus*)
Ballad: Sorry her lot who loves too well (*Josephine*)
Barcarole: Over the bright blue sea (*Chorus*)
Song: I am the monarch of the sea (*Sir Joseph, Chorus*)

Song: When I was a lad I served a term (*Sir Joseph, Chorus*)
Glee: A British tar is a soaring soul (*Ralph, Boatswain's Mate, Carpenter's Mate, Chorus*)
Duet: Refrain, audacious tar (*Josephine, Ralph*)

ACT II

Song: Fair moon, to thee I sing (*Captain Corcoran*)
Duet: Things are seldom what they seem (*Buttercup, Captain Corcoran*)
Scene: The hours creep on apace (*Josephine*)
Trio: Never mind the why and wherefore (*Sir Joseph, Captain Corcoran, Josephine*)
Duet: Kind Captain, I've important information (*Dick Deadeye, Captain Corcoran*)
Ensemble: Carefully on tiptoe stealing (*Chorus*)
Octet: Farewell, my own (*Ralph, Josephine, Sir Joseph, Boatswain, Dick Deadeye, Hebe, Buttercup, Chorus*)
Song: A many years ago (*Buttercup*)
Quartet: Oh joy, oh rapture unforeseen (*Josephine, Ralph, Hebe, Dick Deadeye*)

SYNOPSIS

ACT I

Hard at work on the quarter-deck of Her Majesty's Ship *Pinafore*, the gallant crew busy themselves polishing brass and singing:

> *We sail the ocean blue*
> *And our saucy ship's a beauty.*
> *We're sober men and true,*
> *And attentive to our duty.*

The ship is anchored just off Portsmouth; it is high noon as Little Buttercup steps aboard with a basket of tobacco, scissors, ribbons, laces and all the other little things a sailor on the *Pinafore* might buy.

> *I'm called Little Buttercup,—dear Little Buttercup,*
> *Though I could never tell why.*

And indeed, there is some question why. She pauses a moment to ask the Boatswain whether he has ever thought that beneath her round and rosy exterior might lie

> *A canker-worm which is slowly but surely eating its way into one's very heart?*

The Boatswain had not considered it. But Dick Deadeye has had that very thought. Pushing his way through the circle of sailors he comes to tell

Little Buttercup how bitter his own life has been for that reason. His very appearance causes the rest of the sailors to draw back in horror, for he is very ugly and repulsive. His name alone seems sufficient cause for fear and hate. But just as Buttercup begins to speak she notices a new face among the familiar crew. It belongs to a Ralph Rackstraw, a most unlikely type to have joined the British navy. He is an un-educated lad, he tells us later, possessing admirable virtues—a most extraordinary sailor. This young man is hopelessly in love with his Captain's daughter: hopeless because a sailor is not of a class to so much as speak to a member of the family of a captain except in line of duty. Ralph seems to take this a bit hard, to be sure, for he feels that the captain is, after all, no more than a man like himself—but even the thought itself is untenable in these times and aboard such a proper ship as the *Pinafore.*

During the discussion of the fine distinctions that exist between different kinds and different levels, Dick Deadeye has added his voice to the discussion, seeming to speak in favor of just those things the sailors want. But he is such a sinister person that even his agreements are received by the crew as if they were supernatural threats of the most insidious sort. They warn Dick to keep his revolutionary ideas to himself.

The commander of the ship, Captain Corcoran, is highly respected by his men, and respects them in turn so nobly that his entrance becomes an extremely formal, though cordial, ceremony. He wishes his crew a good morning; they gallantly return it. Then he joins with them, democratically and politely, in praise of all:

CAPT: *I am the Captain of the Pinafore*
CREW: *And a right good captain, too!*
CAPT: *You're very, very good, and be it understood*
                I command a right good crew!
CREW: *We're very, very good,*
    And be it understood.
He commands a right good crew.

There is reason for all this solicitous consideration for each other and for its elucidation in song. For this is the one ship in all Her Majesty's Navy aboard which one never hears bad language or abuse.

What, never?
No, never!
What, never?
Hardly ever!

Everyone aboard lives in complete and pleasant harmony and peace, except for one curious fact which the Captain kindly takes the trouble to explain to Little Buttercup. According to the Captain's point of view, the

First Lord of the Admiralty has become more than ordinarily interested in Josephine, the Captain's daughter. Unfortunately, the benighted girl does not seem to realize the importance of what is obviously her duty to her father and her nation. One moment! The pensive beauty approaches even now, singing a sad song to herself.

Sorry her lot who loves too well—

And sorry she is, so in love. Her heart has already been traded for some-one else's. Whose? The Captain is distraught. To a humble sailor on this very ship! The Captain can hardly believe what he hears. Josephine confides in her father, trying to reassure him, saying that although her love for this impossibly lowly tar will forever be true, she will endeavor to conceal it for the rest of her life in respect for the duty she owes her parent. Though she cannot find a trace of love in her heart for the First Lord of the Admiralty, at least she will not make a public advertisement of her difficulty.

The Admiral arrives: Sir Joseph Porter, K. C. B., accompanied by all his sisters and his cousins and his aunts, a crowd that follows him wherever he goes. The great knight pauses as he steps over the rail, to give us a brief summary of his biography.

SIR J: *I am the monarch of the sea,*
             The ruler of the Queen's Navee,
             Whose praise Great Britain loudly chants.
RELATIVES: *And we are his sisters and his cousins and his aunts!*

The Admiral, in a very jovial mood today, warms to this interesting subject, and launches immediately into another song, telling the crew how he began professional life as nothing more than an office-boy in an attorney's firm, required to polish up the handle of the big front door.

I polished up that handle so carefullee
That now I am the ruler of the Queen's Navee.

Such a fine office-boy he had been, as a matter of fact, that he was promoted to the post of Junior Clerk, to Articled Clerk, to Junior Partner in the firm. He grew rich, was elected a member of Parliament, and finally received his royal appointment as First Lord of the Admiralty— without ever having trod a deck. His advice is straightforward and highly practical, good for all times and all ambitions:

Stick close to your desks and never go to sea
And you all may be rulers of the Queen's Navee.

The First Lord pretends to unbelievable gentility. He believes that a navy may best be run not by swearing at the men and shouting, but by avoiding any action or word that might seem improper in polite society. It is because of his general policy that aboard the *H.M.S. Pinafore* there is no unkindness toward the crew, no bad language. It is altogether an admirable code of conduct, one which Captain Corcoran has followed to the letter and in spirit. The Captain assures the Admiral that here no impropriety is even possible. The Admiral puts it to the test, asking the ordinary seaman Ralph Rackstraw, picked at random from among the men, whether his Captain's statement is true or false. The man stands up for his officer, who is, of course, posted very near. Apparently satisfied with conditions aboard this ship, the Admiral retires to the Captain's quarters for a private word on a tender and sentimental subject.

With the great man absent, the crew is free to talk. Ralph Rackstraw, as his shipmates know well, is in love with the Captain's daughter. He would like their vote of confidence at this moment, for he is about to tell the Captain of these feelings: he has been inspired by the Admiral's little speech on the innate nobility of every British tar, which seems to imply that a sailor is as good as an officer in the Admiral's opinion. Agreed? Agreed! They give him their approval and most willingly clear the deck for him to carry out this action alone.

While Ralph shuffles his feet, dilly-dallying a while before making up his mind just how to commence operations, Josephine comes into view. She loves him, but she cannot say so in public. He loves her, but not a word may pass his polite Victorian lips. His speech is most classically eloquent, his words and his syntax fly so high that they seem all but incomprehensible. All he can manage to make clear is:

Josephine!

At first she pretends to be indignant. But suddenly he pours out a torrent of amorous protestations until her delighted ears are ringing with the sound of it.

She rejects him—she must, even though she loves him, because that is the way a modest maiden must receive such uncontrolled outbursts of affection, especially from inferiors.

> *Refrain, audacious tar,*
> *your suit from pressing.*
> *Remember what you are,*
> *and whom addressing!*

And thus their impasse. Ralph rejoins his equals in the crew and tells them how she cast him off. He cannot continue such a life; he decides to end it. The Boatswain, ever helpful, hands him a pistol—as a good friend would when one is in need. Ralph takes aim at his own head. Just as his finger begins to probe for the trigger Josephine runs fearlessly into the crowd of sailors shrieking that she does love him.

Oh joy, oh rapture unforeseen,
For now the sky is all serene.

Only Dick Deadeye, the truly and fully rejected, realizes that what Josephine says to Ralph in the heat of this moment will have very little to do with what her father requires from her in actuality. The chill of this truth falls like cold rain upon everyone. Without debate a decision is made: the lovers will jump ship in the night with the help of their friends. Once ashore they will find a clergyman who will marry them immediately.

This gives Dick Deadeye his moment of revenge for the continuous ostracism he has borne ever since he joined the crew. He shouts to remind them of the rules of society which forbid liaisons between members of such widely separated classes. But nobody listens to him: they are all cheering for the elopement.

ACT II

It is night; Buttercup listens secretly as the Captain sings sadly to the moon, accompanying himself on a guitar. He grieves because everything is at sixes and sevens. His daughter will not accept Sir Joseph Porter; instead she wants a miserable tar. It is a sad, sad state of things.

Buttercup reveals her presence to the lonely man and offers her comfort to him. Actually she is quite taken with the noble officer, who would probably have been equally interested in her had not rank divided them forever. But Buttercup has gypsy blood in her veins; she knows that there is a change coming in the captain's life:

Things are seldom what they seem;
Skim milk masquerades as cream;
Highlows pass as patent leathers;
Jackdaws strut in peacock feathers.

So they do, muses the Captain, although he does not quite catch her drift. While he ponders, moodily, Sir Joseph enters. He demands an explanation for Josephine's apparent lack of interest in the First Lord of the Admiralty. The Captain, his mind in shreds, can supply only the vague possibility that the young girl thinks he is too highly placed for her to encourage. Perhaps if Sir Joseph would say a word or two to her about how love levels all, she might change her mind. A fine suggestion. The Admiral immediately speaks to the reluctant maiden, who is delighted to hear from so official a source that difference in rank is no cause for denying love. The Captain rejoices as he notices her blossoming smile,

{ 27 }

the First Lord again has hope. But it is not Sir Joseph Porter's station in life that the girl is concerned about.

Like the others, Dick Deadeye knows her secret. Although the Captain shrinks as much as the crew from his fearful presence, Dick stays close just long enough to tell him about the merry plan for the daughter to elope with the sailor, with the help of the crew, that very night. The Captain seizes a cat-o'-nine-tails and hides himself in a cloak as the unsuspecting culprits slip out, prepared to go silently and permanently over the side. As they steal across the deck to a chant of caution, the concealed Captain stamps his foot.

> DICK: *It was the cat!*
> CREW: *It was—it was the cat!*
> CAPT: *(Producing the cat-o'-nine-tails)*
> *They're right, it was the cat!*

He reveals himself just before they step up to the rail, and demands to know where his daughter is bound and with whom. Ralph answers. Though humble, base, at one with the dust, still (as the Boatswain sings):

> *He is an Englishman!*
> *For he himself has said it,*
> *And it's greatly to his credit,*
> *That he is an Englishman!*

Such audacity is a rude shock to the Captain of the *Pinafore*, such a shock that he uses an improper word for the very first time in his captaincy. Unfortunately this does not pass unnoticed by the sisters and the cousins and the aunts of the Admiral, who have been near enough to overhear. With their ears seared by his expressiveness, the Captain's downfall is sure. The Admiral has heard too. He will listen to no word of defense; the crime is too monstrous. The Captain is confined to his cabin. With Ralph, who dared to admit that the cause of this catastrophe was his love for Josephine, the Admiral deals with a severity proper for the sailor's station; he has him loaded with chains and cast into the dungeon. There

> *He'll hear no tone*
> *Of the maiden he loves so well!*
> *No telephone*
> *Communicates with his cell!*

Little Buttercup holds the key to the unraveling of all this mess. When Ralph is gone, she requests a hearing from the Admiral and tells him:

> *A many years ago*
> *When I was young and charming,*

*As some of you may know
I practiced baby-farming.*

Which means that she used to take in babies to make a living, to care for them at her home while their parents were on duty in India or otherwise unable to care for them themselves. Once she had two little boys who got mixed up. One was highborn, the other low. When they left her, one became Ralph Rackstraw, able seaman, the other Captain Corcoran of H.M.S. *Pinafore*, reversing their true-born stations. Thus the true captain should be Ralph, and the true sailor Captain Corcoran.

Sir Joseph has both the prisoners brought up—they are already in uniform for their new positions—and announces the change. Now the former Captain's daughter is common. She is far too low for a First Lord of the Admiralty to consider at all, but not too low for her true love, Captain Rackstraw, who marries her while Corcoran weds Buttercup.

HISTORICAL NOTE

What happened to *Pinafore* before, during and after its first run at the Comique in London would make a fine subject for a separate essay on the vagaries of theatrical production in the late nineteenth century. *Pinafore* had one of the greatest successes of all theater in that period, but the fights and political maneuvering that went on around it are a wonder to recall.

Gilbert suggested the plot. This was usual, since he was the author and was expected to have the first organized ideas. But this particular plot is a little more personally his than are some of the others, since it is about the British navy, with which he had had parental connections. He himself was a lover of the sea, so much so that the first thing he did when *Pinafore* provided enough money was to go out and buy a sea-going yacht.

It served the mechanics of his mind to work visually and to have something physical with which he could construct the dramatic movement of his plays. In the case of *Pinafore* the physical structure must have delighted him with its detail and significance. He visited the flagship of Admiral Nelson, the *Victory*, and made sketches of many details of her rigging and deck arrangement. Then he had a model of the deck built to scale, big enough so that he could consider a part of it as his stage, people it in his mind with characters and experiment with different settings and placements of cast. Thus he prepared the script, with exact instructions for the proper naval routine for piping the admiral aboard, with notes about the deployment of the crew during formal ceremonies, and so forth. Later, when the production was ready for final dress rehearsals, he took Sullivan with him to visit the real ship again and to discuss costuming with a tailor who was legitimately employed supplying naval uniforms. Thus, when *Pinafore* first got under way, its magic was enhanced by its almost perfect representation of a real ship with real seamen, making the plot funnier than ever.

Even at this early date in their combined career, sickness entered the picture. Sullivan was already suffering from his kidney ailment and was in pain much of the time while composing the untroubled melodies of *Pinafore*. But this was not yet sufficiently serious to cause, as it did later, interruptions in rehearsals. The score was ready in time for the opening performance, and the cast was well trained.

The opera was instantly successful in that the audience present was instantly pleased. But other events, things the authors could not have predicted or controlled as they did the movements on stage, nearly killed the show. The first performance came on the 25th of May in 1878, late spring. When summer came the temperature rose. The heat grew worse and worse until London was boiling in its most uncomfortable heat wave of many years. Having begun just after the show opened, the heat lasted without a day's relief through June and July. Things got so bad that the audience dwindled almost to the point where expenses exceeded receipts. Six times the board of directors—the little corporation of capitalists that Carte had gathered to produce English comic opera—posted closing notices during the first two months. The cast, however, voluntarily agreed to take a salary cut of one-third until things got better. Still, something had to be done to attract more people.

Sullivan came to the rescue. He was the conductor of the Promenade Concerts at this time, whose programs were usually devoted to the more serious side of music. Breaking precedent, he had the idea that his melodies for *H.M.S. Pinafore* were good enough to be heard out of context. He scheduled them accordingly. The audience that heard them at the Promenade had not realized that such good music was available every night at the Comique. Suiting their actions to Sullivan's hopes, and with the weather beginning to improve ever so slightly, they began to flock to the theater to hear more, thus saving *Pinafore* from a premature closing. By the time fall came, the new Gilbert and Sullivan production had become a gold mine.

But riches led to worse difficulties. The board of directors, the same men who had so frequently felt fear in their pocketbooks and posted closing notices, now decided that they had such a good investment it was a pity to have to pay so much to the authors. They agreed among themselves that since their money had paid for putting the show on stage, the settings must be their own property. One night, during a performance, the stage-door man was brushed aside by a determined herd of plug-uglies sent by the directors to remove the scenery to a different theater where they intended to mount their own production. There was chaos. The audience sat bewildered while stage hands and invaders fought to a finish behind the curtain. Finally, having failed to rip down a single flat, the outsiders were driven out and the rival production was stymied for a short while. But not for long. It soon opened nearby, with scenery of a sort, and a makeshift company of actors. For a while the two rival productions of the same work played practically side by side until the whole schism landed in court, where a decision came down in favor of the authors and D'Oyly Carte. The net result evidently did not hurt the box office—any blast is a boon. The board of directors was paid off and dismissed by Carte and a new company was set up consisting of Carte, Gilbert and Sullivan on equal terms. The production of *Pinafore* continued merrily, running nearly two years.

With the success of *Pinafore*, the question of the money that was being lost in America became tantalizing. Carte had visited the United States and discovered eight separate productions of the work running at one time in New York City, and six in Philadelphia. This prompted Carte to send Gilbert and Sullivan across the ocean on the correct assumption that a production carefully rehearsed with Gilbertian precision, and an orchestra trained under Sullivan's fine hand, would draw more audiences than the pirated versions, simply because of its excitement and beauty. The fact that this worked should be heartening to those who wonder about the low state of the hypnotically advertised, gilded shabbiness of Broadway eighty years later.

Pinafore has been revived many times by the D'Oyly Carte Company, the first occasion being after the closing of *Ruddigore*, when no replacement work was ready. It has played all over the world and shows no sign, even after eighty years, of becoming too dated to continue. Gilbert prepared a children's version of it in December of 1879 and later wrote new words for another children's performance.

Some of the sources for character in the play are worth notice. Little Buttercup was developed originally in a Bab Ballad, "The Bumboat Woman's Story." Captain Corcoran was redrawn from "Captain Reece of the Mantelpiece." Sir Joseph Porter, K. C. B., matched the actual First Lord of the Admiralty, W. H. Smith—who became known as Pinafore Smith—in that Smith was not a navy man at first, but began life as a newsboy. Gilbert *said* there was no intentional resemblance, but it was not the resemblance, precisely. . . .

The Pirates of Penzance

OR, THE SLAVE OF DUTY

First production, Fifth Avenue Theatre, New York,
31 December 1879
First performed at the Opéra Comique, London, 3 April 1880   TWO ACTS

CAST

MAJOR-GENERAL STANLEY	Bar
THE PIRATE KING	B
SAMUEL, *his lieutenant*	Bar
FREDERIC, *the pirate apprentice*	T
SERGEANT OF POLICE	BBar
MABEL, *General Stanley's daughter*	S
EDITH, *General Stanley's daughter*	S
KATE, *General Stanley's daughter*	MS
ISABEL, *General Stanley's daughter*	Spkr
RUTH, *Pirate maid of all work*	C
Pirates, Police, General Stanley's Daughters	Chorus

SETTING

ACT I: A rocky seashore on the coast of Cornwall.
ACT II: A ruined chapel by moonlight.

SONGS AND CHORUSES

ACT I

Chorus: Pour, oh, pour the pirate sherry (*Pirates*)
Song: When Frederic was a little lad (*Ruth*)
Song: Oh better far to live and die (*Pirate King*)
Duet: You told me you were fair as gold! (*Frederic, Ruth*)
Chorus: Climbing over rocky mountain (*Girls*)
Song: Oh, is there not one maiden breast (*Frederic*)
Song: Poor wandering one! (*Mabel*)
Chattering Chorus: How beautifully blue the sky (*Girls*)

{ 32 }

Song: I am the very model of a modern Major-General (*Major-General Stanley, Chorus*)
Solo: These children whom you see (*Major-Gen. Stanley, Pirates*)

ACT II

Chorus: Oh, dry the glistening tear (*Girls*)
Song: When the foeman bares his steel (*Sergeant*)
Trio: When you had left our pirate fold (*Ruth, King, Frederic*)
Duet: Stay, Frederic, stay! (*Mabel, Frederic*)
Duet: Ah, leave me not to pine (*Mabel, Frederic*)
Song: When a felon's not engaged in his employment (*Sergeant, Chorus*)
Chorus: With cat-like tread (*Pirates, Police*)
Ballad: Sighing softly to the river (*General, Chorus*)
Finale: Poor wandering ones! (*Ensemble*)

SYNOPSIS

ACT I

Hidden in a cove beneath a cliff which overhangs the sea, a band of pirates whiles away the time playing cards, drinking, and generally at ease. As Samuel weaves among them, filling their cups, they sing a drinking song in Frederic's honor, for the disconsolate apprentice at long last has completed his schooling, has reached twenty-one and is to be admitted as a fully accredited pirate.

The Pirate King congratulates the young man, but Frederic, while thanking him, announces regretfully that although he appreciates their labors in teaching him their trade, he never wished to become a pirate, and intends to leave the profession. He explains that it was an unfortunate error, a misunderstanding of a word, that had thrown him into this peculiar line of work. He, being a slave of duty, had followed the curriculum to its very end but he never, never enjoyed it. The pirates demand to know the error that caused his misery. Ruth, their maid-of-all-work, has the explanation. When Frederic was a lad he showed an aptitude for things pertaining to the sea. His father instructed Ruth, who was the child's nurse, to go apprentice him to a pilot, from whom the boy could learn an honorable and profitable trade. The poor woman was ever so slightly deaf and was afraid to admit even to herself that she hadn't quite heard the key word. She bound the boy over to some pirates instead, taking a job as their maid-of-all-work so that she could care for him during his formative years.

Not only does Frederic wish to renounce piracy, he is also determined to drive it out of existence because it is a dishonest business. Although he has grown to love each of the members of the band as individuals, taking

{ 33 }

45339

them collectively he intends to exterminate them. Not one of them can blame him for holding such high principles, but they all weep to lose such a fine adherent.

Before he leaves, Frederic offers his friends and former associates a few helpful words of advice on piracy, how to improve their technique even though he has just sworn to destroy them. The pirates have been much too tenderhearted, especially in the matter of orphans. The word has gotten about that, since they themselves are orphans, any victim of piracy who claims also to be without parents will escape not only unmolested but also with all their sympathy. Hence, as a business venture, piracy has begun to fail, for all their victims identify themselves as parentless in youth.

And there is the question of Ruth: Frederic has never seen another woman, let alone a pretty one. He has no way of knowing whether Ruth is as beautiful a creature as she has continually told him, a girl suitable for him to marry. He wishes to reserve judgment until he can actually see more women and have some standard for comparison. Once more, as he makes ready to leave, he pleads with his friends to relinquish their evil profession so that he will not have to exterminate them in cold blood. But their King refuses:

> Oh better far to live and die
> Under the brave black flag I fly,
> Than play a sanctimonious part,
> With a pirate head and a pirate heart.
> Away to the cheating world go you,
> Where pirates all are well-to-do;
> But I'll be true to the song I sing,
> And live and die a Pirate King.

And they leave him to say his personal good-bye to Ruth. Ruth wants to go with him, but he refuses to take her. He discusses again the question of her beauty, saying he must learn more before he can marry her. Just then he hears a sweet sound in the distance, the voices of young girls whom he can see clambering over the rocks. Suddenly the truth becomes evident. Ruth is old, ugly, undesirable. He has been deceived all this time. He renounces her and hides so that he can see the maidens as they approach.

> Climbing over rocky mountain,
> Skipping rivulet and fountain,
> Passing where the willows quiver
> By the ever-rolling river,

And they are all very, very beautiful. He cannot resist. He reveals his presence to them and pleads with them not to be frightened, but to allow him to state his case. Is there one among them, he sings, who feels a philanthropic interest in raising him, untrained in love, unwise in choosing, from the depths in which he lies? Not one. Not one? Yes, one: Mabel. She walks toward him singing:

Poor wandering one!
Though thou hast surely strayed,
Take heart of grace,
Thy steps retrace,
Poor wandering one!

They fall in love immediately and go off together to find a place where they can be alone. This is a little difficult on the open shore of Cornwall, and her sisters are not a little disturbed about the situation. What is proper conduct for them? Should they stay with the girl as chaperones and prevent any meeting of hearts? Or should they leave the girl in the hands of one who, to say the least, *looks* like a pirate. They compromise; they stay near the lovers but occupy themselves chattering loudly about the weather:

How beautifully blue the sky,
The glass is rising very high,
Continue fine I hope it may,
And yet it rained but yesterday.

And in this with simple counterpoint the lovers weave their thoughts. But not for long: the pirates are returning. Frederic urges the girls to leave as quickly as possible while the coast (literally) is still clear. But the sweet chatterers dilly-dally so long making up their minds that they are all captured, each girl by a ferocious pirate. Poor orphans that these brigands are, they are determined to marry and live lives of happy domesticity from now on. This mass entrapment has provided the wives they need.

Mabel shouts down such an idea. There is good reason for the pirates to take care what they do with these girls, for they are daughters and wards in chancery of a Major-General. Lo! at the sounding of his title the Major-General himself enters (amid the patriotic cheers of all present) and relates how perfectly he fits the measure of his office.

I am the very model of a modern Major-General,
I've information vegetable, animal and mineral,
I know the kings of England and I quote the fights historical,
From Marathon to Waterloo, in order categorical; . . .

When he is done, and perceives the situation which stands before his eyes, he takes up the subjects of piracy and marriage. He certainly does not approve of such outlaws as sons-in-law-to-be, nor does any of the pirates want a Major-General for a father-in-law. Suddenly General Stanley has an idea. Assuming a sad expression, and with grief throbbing in his voice, he asks: would they rob a poor orphan boy of these last relatives? So pathetic is his song, so tearful his pleading and so full of hints about their own bereavement that all the pirates are moved by the deepest sympathy, and give in. Frederic, since he has renounced the forbidden profession, will marry Mabel. All the other girls will be bridesmaids, and the pirates remain pirates.

ACT II

Later, by moonlight, the modern Major-General sits alone in a ruined chapel on his newly bought estate. Sadly he contemplates the monstrous lie he told, saying he was an orphan. His daughters, hunting for him in the chilly evening after having missed him inside, gather around and attempt to console him with their beautiful singing. But to no avail. He has insulted his ancestors. Frederic, who is with Mabel and therefore present, points out that those ancestors, being merely the inhabitants of the graves in the chapel, are as newly bought as was the estate. But to the Major-General they are none the less *his* ancestors for all that, and therefore to be considered.

Now thoroughly on the side of Right, Frederic is ready to march against the pirates with an escort of police. He will atone for his years of false apprenticeship by sweeping piracy out of existence, and thus be able to marry Mabel with a pure heart. The police have arrived, as ready as their leader to attack the fearsome brigands. It is a dangerous job, but they have a word to cheer themselves:

> *When a foeman bares his steel (Tarantara!)*
> *We uncomfortable feel,*
> *And we find the wisest thing*
> *Is to slap our chests and sing*
> *Tarantara!*

Mabel joins them:

> *Go, ye heroes, go to glory!*
> *Though ye die in combat gory,*
> *Ye shall live in song and story.*
> *Go to immortality!*
> *Go to death and go to slaughter;*
> *Die, and every Cornish daughter*
> *With her tears your grave shall water.*

This hardly seems encouraging to the stalwart followers of the Right, but the song is thrilling though its words seem ominous. Off go the police to exterminate the pirates, leaving Frederic alone for a last moment.

Seeing him unprotected, Ruth and the pirate King slip out from behind the bushes to appear before him and beg his mercy. Frederic would hear none of it, but mercy, after all, is superior to mere revenge. He listens while they sing of a strange paradox that suddenly became evident to them while they were busily engaged in regretting the loss of their apprentice. According to a most careful reckoning, Frederic was to have served *until his twenty-first birthday* as a pirate. Having been born on the twenty-ninth of February, leap-year day, he has in actual count had only five birthdays and is still, legally, an apprentice in their crew.

Duty reigns above all else. Frederic obeys duty, whatever duty may bid. This paradox, however, splits duty two ways, with half on each side of a dilemma. Piracy is wrong and must be exterminated. But the document of his apprenticeship requires him to be a pirate until he is past eighty. He must abide by that contract.

Again a pirate, he feels it is only right to inform his friends that his new father-in-law, who had escaped their clutches by claiming to be an orphan, was not telling the truth The pirates declare revenge against the Major-General and plan to attack his brand new castle that very night.

The unwilling turncoat, again left by himself, sits despondently, pondering his predicament. Thus does Mabel find him, in despair, when she had expected him to be full of the excitement of preparation for battle against the pirates. He tells of his newly discovered difficulty. Mabel is dismayed. She swears to him that her love will be true even as long as it may take for him to reach his twenty-first quadrennial birthday. Together they sing a most tender and sweet duet after which poor Fred leaps out a nearby window to join—unwillingly—his company.

When Mabel calls the troop of police she tells them of Frederic's defection but holds it up to them as an example of the nobility of his sense of duty. Now, she tells them, they must fight on to death and glory without his inspiring leadership. Reluctantly they realize that they cannot, legally, back out. They sing a little chorus:

SERG: *When a felon's not engaged in his employment—*
ALL: *His employment,*
SERG: *Or maturing his felonious little plans—*
ALL: *Little plans,*
SERG: *His capacity for innocent enjoyment—*
ALL: *'Cent enjoyment,*
SERG: *Is just as great as any honest man's—*
ALL: *Honest man's.*

SERG: *Our feelings we with difficulty smother—*
ALL: *'Culty smother*
SERG: *When constabulary duty's to be done*
ALL: *To be done.*
SERG: *Ah, take one consideration with another—*
ALL: *With another,*
SERG: *A policeman's lot is not a happy one.*

The pirates gather amid the broken columns and make preparations for storming the castle in revenge for having had their sympathy as orphans so insultingly strained by the Major-General. Their stealthy but menacing song frightens the police into hiding as the pirates

with cat-like tread

(as they say, making no sound except for their gloriously loud chorus) come into view, singing to the tune of what we now know as "Hail, Hail, the gang's all here":

Come, friends, who plough the sea,
Truce to navigation,
Take another station;
Let's vary piracy
With a little burglaree!

Suddenly the Major-General is seen approaching, and Frederic hushes his companions. They all hide. Now the tombs hide pirates here and policemen there, as the intended victim, sleepless, wanders about in his dressing gown. He is so tormented by his one act of perfidy that he is full of apprehension. He stops breathing a moment to listen; he thought he had heard a sound.

Ha! Ha!

shout the police and all the pirates from their hiding places. But:

No, all is still,

mutters the intended victim, commencing a delicate barcarole to soothe his own feelings, accompanied by the concealed hosts of warriors.

"What's this?" cry the fair wards in chancery as they find their way into the shadowy chapel, dressed in their peignoirs and carrying candles. They have just located their poor insomniac guardian and are singing softly to him when, with a shout from their King, the pirates leap into view and capture Major-General Stanley.

Seeing Frederic, whom he believes still to be on the side of Right (because the General does not know about the birthday paradox), the prisoner begs for help. But in spite of all protest he is bound. Even Mabel can win no pity from the band of cutthroats, so maddened by revenge. Only the timely action of the troop of Police, who were quite long making up their minds about the situation, seems to offer hope.

But that hope is soon ground into the dust as every policeman is captured. They plead, they would scream that they are orphans, but the pirates are immune to that, thanks to Frederic's warning. At last, the Sergeant realizes that these outlaws must be reminded of higher things. He appeals to their innate nobility as Englishmen to yield in the name of her before whom all else must give way—Victoria, the Queen.

To this the pirates yield. Even pirates have honor; even pirates love their queen. The police, weeping at such a sign of proper loyalty, prepare to lead the brigands away to jail when Ruth intervenes to identify these stalwart souls not as pirates but as noblemen who have gone wrong. No Englishman, of course, could withstand this news without feeling pity. For who would wrong a peer?

> *Peers will be peers, and youth will have its fling!*
> *Resume your ranks and legislative duties,*
> *And take my daughters, all of whom are beauties!*

Then, with a grand chorus of "Poor wandering ones" the former orphaned and unmarried pirates win their wives and renounce their evil profession.

HISTORICAL NOTE

Gilbert and Sullivan were in New York City producing *H.M.S. Pinafore* in an authorized version, trying to win back for themselves some of the ready money that was flowing into the hands of unlicensed impresarios. The Forces of Right won the day, not by legal means but by better craftsmanship, and although they did not exterminate literary piracy, they did make a lot of money. Having achieved their first objective, the two authors went after their second. They had brought with them the preliminary draft of a new opera, *The Pirates of Penzance*, which was to be rehearsed in secrecy and presented in New York rather than in London, so as to forestall piracy completely. The score was completed while Sullivan lived in a hotel on Twentieth Street in Manhattan, and was rehearsed at the Fifth Avenue Theater with guards posted at all the doors to keep out those who were not members of the company. The songs and choruses had been nearly completed in England, and Sullivan had planned only to finish the score on this side of the ocean. But by a last minute slip his sketches were left at home, and he had to rewrite the entire first act from memory. While working he had attack after attack of his painful kidney ailment, which, added to the strain of mounting *Pinafore* and rehearsing *The Pirates,* must have taxed him severely.

In order to insure a legal copyright of the new work at least in their own country, since none was trustworthy in America at that time, it was decided that there must be a token performance in England before the gala opening in New York. Carte arranged that one of the touring troupes would rehearse the work and put on a single performance in some out-of-the-way place. Later, when the authors had returned, it would be possible to have a formal opening in London. This made it necessary for Sullivan to work far ahead of his normal schedule, so that the music could be shipped to England for rehearsals.

The copyright performance took place in Paignton, by the sea in South Devon, on the 30th of December. Costumes were not ready; the actors had to improvise from what they had—mainly bits and pieces from their wardrobes for *Pinafore.* The policemen wore sailor's garb. The music was incomplete, as was the script. There was time for only one rehearsal, thus making it necessary for the singers to carry their music with them on stage. What a performance it must have been, at that seaside resort in the dead of winter! But at least one London critic was present and approved of the opera.

In New York, with Gilbert directing and the first-line company fully rehearsed, things went better, but not without those petty harassments which give American theatrical business—and perhaps that of the Europeans as well—its flavor. Three days before the opening the orchestra went on strike for a higher "scale," basing their claim on the fact that their union rules made a distinction between operetta and "grand" opera, and since the score of *The Pirates of Penzance* had so much music in it, it fell in the higher category and was subject to a higher rate of pay. But for once, just for once, they lost. Sullivan stood up as tall as he could and announced that the management—which anyone in America would have assumed to be quite rich enough for anything—was prepared to import the orchestra of Covent Garden to replace them if the Americans, who were not, it need not be pointed out, as good as Europeans, persisted in their exorbitant demands. The Americans backed down, finished their rehearsals and gave a magnificent performance on opening night.

Portions of *The Pirates* were lifted from other works. The chorus "Climbing over Rocky Mountain" was originally sung by the mortals clambering up the slopes of Mount Olympus in that early failure, *Thespis.* The plot trick of the misunderstanding of the word *pirate* for *pilot* was first used in Gilbert's old play *Our Island Home.*

The score for the New York performance was ready on the 28th of December. The overture had not yet been composed. It was five o'clock on the very morning of the opening when Sullivan and Cellier drew the last bar-lines on that piece. No wonder the performance back in England, with no orchestral score at all, was sketchy! Before they left the United States, Gilbert and Sullivan completed their rout of the literary pirates by training and sending out a quartet of touring companies to every corner of the continent. Finally the opera made its formal debut in London, the following April. It was, of course, a great success and has remained in repertory ever since.

The music of *The Pirates of Penzance* is full of delicious, uncontrived satire of Italian and French operatic styles, just as that of *Iolanthe* satirizes Wagner and his countrymen. One grand scene in particular contains a thrilling and hilarious conversion of the style of Verdi's *Il Trovatore* and *Aïda* to British comedy. It is the solo and chorus in Act II, beginning with "When the foeman bares his steel." Here, against the masculine, rhythmic chorus of "tarantara" from the policemen, Mabel sings "Go, ye heroes, go to glory" with true heroic brilliance.

Patience

OR, BUNTHORNE'S BRIDE

First performed at the Opéra Comique, London, 23 April 1881   TWO ACTS

CAST

COLONEL CALVERLEY, *officer of the Dragoon Guards*	BBar
MAJOR MURGATROYD, *officer of the Dragoon Guards*	Bar
LT. THE DUKE OF DUNSTABLE, *officer of the Dragoon Guards*	T
REGINALD BUNTHORNE, *a fleshly poet*	Bar
ARCHIBALD GROSVENOR, *an idyllic poet*	Bar
MR. BUNTHORNE'S SOLICITOR	
THE LADY ANGELA, *a rapturous maiden*	MS
THE LADY SAPHIR, *a rapturous maiden*	MS
THE LADY ELLA, *a rapturous maiden*	S
THE LADY JANE, *a rapturous maiden*	C
PATIENCE, *a dairy maid*	S
Rapturous Maidens, Officers of the Dragoon Guards	Chorus

SETTING

ACT I: Exterior of Castle Bunthorne.
ACT II: A Glade.

SONGS AND CHORUSES

ACT I

Chorus: Twenty love-sick maidens we (*Rapturous maidens*)
Song: I cannot tell what this love may be (*Patience, maidens*)
Song: If you want a receipt for that popular mystery (*Colonel, Chorus*)
Chorus: In a doleful train (*Chorus*)
Song: When I first put this uniform on (*Colonel, Chorus*)
Recit. and Song: Am I alone, and unobserved? (*Bunthorne*)
Duet: Long years ago—fourteen, maybe (*Patience, Angela*)
Duet: Prithee, pretty maiden—prithee tell me true (*Patience, Grosvenor*)

Finale: Let the merry cymbals sound (*Chorus*)
  Song: True love must single-hearted be (*Patience, Bunthorne*)

ACT II

Song: Silvered is the raven hair (*Jane*)
Chorus: Turn, oh, turn in this direction (*Maidens*)
Song: A magnet hung in a hardware shop (*Grosvenor, Chorus*)
Song: In a doleful train (*Jane*)
Ballad: Love is a plaintive song (*Patience*)
Duet: So go to him and say to him, with compliment ironical (*Bunthorne, Jane*)
Trio: It's clear that medieval art alone retains its zest (*Duke, Colonel, Major*)
Quintet: If Saphir I choose to marry (*Duke, Colonel, Major, Angela, Saphir*)
Duet: When I go out of door (*Bunthorne, Grosvenor*)
Finale: After much debate internal (*Duke, Bunthorne, Ensemble*)

SYNOPSIS

ACT I

Wreathed in aesthetic draperies of sickly color, twenty love-sick maidens approach the drawbridge of Castle Bunthorne, weeping with despair as they sing to the accompaniment of lutes and other quaint instruments that they play themselves. Each of them is hopelessly in love with Reginald Bunthorne, an aesthete among aesthetes.

> *Twenty love-sick maidens we,*
> *Love-sick all against our will.*
> *Twenty years hence we shall be*
> *Twenty love-sick maidens still.*
> *Twenty love-sick maidens we,*
> *And we die for love of thee.*

There is not the slightest chance that any of them will ever find that love returned; thus they, who might otherwise have been deadly rivals, are bound together in common sympathy.

While they languish, unnoticed and uncared for outside the walls of the castle, Lady Jane comes to find them to tell them that Reginald *has* fallen in love, not with one of these forlorn serenaders, but with the village milkmaid, Patience. At that very moment, Patience herself passes by, so utterly innocent of any knowledge of love that she cannot understand why these ladies mope about the drawbridge with such red, red eyes, while she is blithe and gay.

{ 43 }

If love is a thorn, they show no wit
Who foolishly hug and foster it

Nor can she understand why they claim to be so truly happy when they cry so much. Lady Jane offers an explanation:

There is a transcendentality of delirium,—an acute accentuation of supremest ecstasy—which the earthy might easily mistake for indigestion. But it is not indigestion, it is aesthetic transfiguration!

The girls are on the point of leaving when Patience stops them with the news that the 35th Dragoon Guards, to whom they were all engaged only last year, have just arrived in town and are nearby. Chilling tidings. Though they were dull and normal enough twelve months ago to ally themselves with such ordinary men, now, since they have become aesthetic, their tastes have become permanently etherealized. No longer may they consider the vulgar 35th Dragoon Guards when the time for singing a mournful carol to Reginald's unopened door is upon them! They leave to perform that sacred duty as the down-to-earth Guards arrive.

The soldiers of our Queen
Are linked in friendly tether;
Upon the battle scene
They fight the foe together.

To mark the grand occasion of their return to this neighborhood, where all their fiancées live, their Colonel sings a detailed description of what heroism and strength it takes to construct a Heavy Dragoon.

Take all the remarkable people in history,
Rattle them off to a popular tune.
The pluck of Lord Nelson on board of the Victory—
Genius of Bismarck devising a plan—
The humour of Fielding (which sounds contradictory)—
Coolness of Paget about to trepan—

And to all the manly virtues he does not fail to add the:

Grace of an Odalisque on a divan.

A happy lot, this chorus of Dragoon Guards, strong contrast to the Duke, who appears in very low spirits. It is difficult to be a duke, especially to be a rich one. One is subject to:

flattery, adulation, and abject deference, carried to such a pitch that I began, at last, to think that man was born bent at an angle of forty-five degrees!

{ 44 }

The Duke considers himself, and he certainly is, a most commonplace young man. All this attention because of his wealth and position bothers him exceedingly. Only the sight of Reginald Bunthorne, surrounded by twenty love-sick and rapturous maidens, quiets his concern about himself.

Before the wide-eyed, awe-struck gaze of the Officers of Dragoon Guards there passes a strange unearthly procession. It is the poet himself, followed at a respectful distance by the girls who sing softly and play upon their instruments. The poet composes, the girls weep. Not one of them so much as notices the Duke, the Colonel, or any of the others drawn up in ranks.

Although he seems oblivious to everything, Bunthorne tells us behind his hand that he is fully aware that the maidens are there, that they follow him, praying to him, bending their knees. He continues composing. Finally he pauses, and, after a terrible writhing in an agony of creation, he finds the right word, the final word for his poem. He writes it down and is immediately returned to the present world, fully relaxed.

BUNTHORNE: *It was nothing worth mentioning, it occurs three times*
a day.

He bids them all cling passionately to each other and to think of faint lilies while he reads:

OH, HOLLOW! HOLLOW! HOLLOW!
What time the poet hath hymned
The writhing maid, lithe-limbed
Quivering on amaranthine asphodel,
How can he paint her woes,
Knowing, as well he knows,
That all can be set right with calomel?

Having done, the poet wafts his way out. How pure! How precious! The ladies sigh. But the magic moment is shattered by Patience, who thinks it all nonsense. The soldiers do, too, no matter how the ladies try to explain the principles of aesthetics. Nothing pierces the vulgar armor of the military heart as does the suggestion that the Dragoons should wear uniforms of more—how shall we say?—more aesthetic interest:

. . . of a cobwebby grey velvet, with a tender bloom like cold gravy . . .

The men are astounded. Their uniforms have never before been so insulted. They march off in high displeasure.

As soon as the fleshly poet sees that the coast is clear of fawning girls and forbidding soldiers, he steals out by himself to meditate.

Am I alone and unobserved? I am.
Then let me own I'm an aesthetic sham!

{ 45 }

This air severe is but a mere veneer!
This cynic smile is but a wile of guile!
This costume chaste is but good taste misplaced!
Let me confess!

And he confesses that the only reason he puts on

stained-glass attitudes

is that he has a morbid love of admiration. And aesthetic admiration is easy to procure. One must throw transcendental phrases into every conversation, express the complexity of one's mind, be mystic, be *deep.*

And everyone will say,
As you walk your mystic way,
"If this young man expresses himself in terms too deep for me,
Why, what a very singularly deep young man this deep young man
must be!"

. . . . .

Though the Philistines may jostle, you will rank as an apostle in the
high aesthetic band,
If you walk down Piccadilly with a poppy or a lily in your medieval
hand.

His confession is cut short by the entrance of Patience, for whom he immediately resumes his airs. She struggles, poor innocent, to understand these strange mixtures of ideas, his strange syntax, his sudden changes of temperature. They frighten her more than they please. It is only poetry, says he, and perhaps this idea reaches her. But she doesn't like poetry, and tells him so in so many words. That finishes him. Off go the airs and the high-flown nonsense. He admits that he is not satisfied with poetry either, but he loves her, he wants her, he will even cut his overlong hair for her.

Poor Patience. She regrets his love. The only person she ever knew she loved—or was supposed to love—was her great-aunt. Therefore, since Reginald Bunthorne is not even a relative of hers, she cannot love *him.* Broken-hearted, the poet stumbles away.

Lady Angela, to whom Patience addresses her burning new questions about love as soon as possible, tells her that love is the one unselfish emotion. This is interesting news, something a girl can work with. Patience decides forthwith that she will fall in love with somebody—anybody— before nightfall so that she may partake of such a moral feeling. When she was a baby, she recalls, there was another little baby only a little older than she, her playmate, a boy. The two knew they were in love even at so tender an age, a fine love unsullied by adult considerations.

By this time Patience is so impatient that she seizes upon the very first stranger who passes by—Archibald Grosvenor. Together, without the slightest hesitation, they sing:.

> *Prithee, pretty maiden—prithee tell me true,*
> *(Hey, but I'm doleful, willow willow waly)*
> *Have you e'er a lover dangling after you?*
> *Hey willow waly O!*

As they come to the end of their song the poet asks the milkmaid if she does not recognize him. Has she forgotten, in a mere fifteen years, the love of her babyhood? Her little playmate? A bit taller, stouter perhaps, but yet a man, a beautiful man. He is so beautiful—he is the first to admit it—that he is constantly badgered by bewildered females who fall in love with him by the dozens at first sight. He, like Bunthorne, is a poet.

Patience has at last found love.

But there is one problem: her love for him, which has continued unchanged since innocent babyhood, is altogether selfish because it deprives other women of his attentions. Hence it is unworthy and is therefore impossible. But *his* love for *her,* seeing that she is such an ordinary little milkmaid, may be permitted to continue because it deprives nobody of anything anybody could want.

At this moment a heavenly vision appears. It is Reginald Bunthorne, accompanied by his train of rapturous maidens carrying archaic instruments. The fleshly poet announces that since Patience has refused his love, and since he is unwilling to be unfair to any of these secondary female suitors, he will put himself up to be raffled. At this prospect there is an astonished gasp from the assembled Dragoon Guards, who have just marched in to find their former fiancées. But while the soldiers supplicate in vain, the girls line up to buy tickets for the raffle. The numbers are gathered together and shaken. Just as they are about to draw the winner, Patience calls a halt to the proceedings and announces that she will marry Bunthorne after all. Her reason, for she does have a reason, is that she has decided that this would be a truly unselfish act, unalloyed (since she does not love him) with thought of personal gain or selfish joy.

The girls have lost their case now and are about to try, at least to *try,* to recover some part of that duller life they enjoyed before they became aesthetes. Suddenly a new apparition stands before them. It is poetry again, in the form of Archibald Grosvenor, who silently and pensively ambles into sight. Who is he? The maidens pant to know.

> *I am a broken-hearted troubadour,*
> *Whose mind's aesthetic and whose tastes are pure!*

> . . . . .

Aesthetic!
He is aesthetic!

For this they all love him with complete devotion—much to his horror and Bunthorne's fury.

ACT II

A little time has passed. Lady Jane is the only maiden shrewd enough to remain in love with Reginald while all the others have gone over to Grosvenor. Sadly she sits in a forest glade singing, playing her own accompaniment on her violoncello.

> *Silvered is the raven hair,*
> *Spreading is the parting straight,*
> *Mottled the complexion fair,*
> *Halting is the youthful gait,*
> *Hollow is the laughter free,*
> *Spectacled the limpid eye—*
> *Little will be left of me*
> *In the coming by and by!*

The course of aesthetic history repeats itself verbatim, but Grosvenor is now the much-beloved poet who cannot escape the rapturous maidens. He reads the very worst poem imaginable, but his clinging damsels love it. In desperation, to get away from them—it has been a week—he tells them the sad tale of the magnet which spurned objects of lowly iron but conceived a hopeless passion for a silver churn, only to learn that

> *By no endeavor*
> *Can magnet ever*
> *Attract a silver churn!*

It is very effective. The girls straggle away and leave the field to Patience, who loves the love of her childhood as deeply as ever in spite of the logic of its selfishness.

GROSVENOR: *And you love this Bunthorne?*
PATIENCE: *With a heart-whole ecstasy that withers, and scorches, and burns, and stings.* (Sadly) *It is my duty.*

Reginald's entourage has been reduced to only one, Lady Jane, who follows him as dolefully as did the nineteen who now have gone over to Archibald. Bunthorne is disgusted with the "purity" of the love of Patience which permits her to sigh so heartily for Grosvenor. He derides her, claiming she does not know what love is.

PATIENCE: *Yes, I do. There was a happy time when I didn't, but a bitter experience has taught me.*

{ 48 }

Meanwhile the Duke, the Colonel and the Major have got themselves up in aesthetic costumes as nearly like those of the two poets as possible, in a desperate attempt to win back *some* of the girls. Surprisingly enough, when Saphir and Angela see them in their ridiculous positions they come to an agreement that, should Grosvenor not choose either of them, they will not refuse the officers. It will then be only a matter of who chooses whom. There are three officers, but only two girls. This difficult apportionment is deferred.

Bunthorne and Grosvenor have each succeeded in eluding female pursuit for the moment and have sought seclusion. Unfortunately they have each come to the same place and met face to face. The battle is frightening. Bunthorne reduces Grosvenor to tears and pleading by threatening him (not having had a mother) with a nephew's curse. Actually delighted at the prospect, Grosvenor agrees to become a commonplace young man. Bunthorne—a changed man—ceases to be an ill-tempered poet to become, like the former Grosvenor, a happy one—or at least mildly cheerful. Unfortunately this makes Bunthorne perfect, and therefore love for Bunthorne can no longer be an unselfish love. Hence Patience can no longer obey what was formerly her duty. Grosvenor, on the other hand, is now an ordinary young man and therefore imperfect. She can love him without guilty feelings. Thus all ends happily for Grosvenor and Patience, happily for the three officers who have taken Lady Jane to fill the gap between Saphir and Angela. The Duke takes Lady Jane, the Colonel Saphir, leaving Angela to the Major. Only Bunthorne is wife-less. That makes him happy enough, however.

> *Greatly pleased with one another,*
> *To get married we decide,*
> *Each of us will wed the other.*
> *Nobody be Bunthorne's bride!*

HISTORICAL NOTE

Patience is a satire on a flurry of aestheticism that is remembered now as the era of Art Nouveau. Together with that, as represented by Burne-Jones, Oscar Wilde, and Whistler, came a combination of other fads, some of which came to their climaxes a little later—such as the obsession with things oriental, which can be traced in Whistler but which became really important a few years later. It was the fashion in London life as it is in the libretto of *Patience* for those of the aesthetic set to appear to be wafted above and beyond reality. Hence one might carry a drooping lily, or wear a forlorn aspect, or dress in faded yellow drapery.

Costumes for *Patience* were fully described and sketched out by Gilbert himself. He was careful to include details from the actual appearance of more than one leader of the cult, so that, for instance, Bunthorne wore an eyeglass patterned after Whistler's, and a hair style from the same. His velvet coat duplicated that worn by Walter Crane, his knee-breeches were from Oscar Wilde. And it did not stop with dress. Gilbert had always been conscious of styles of movement on stage and was able to bring out the most glaring mannerisms of his models in the gestures and positions taken by his characters. The drooping lily became a hallmark for the poetic profile, taken up with refinement and delicacy by Bunthorne, with stiffness and discomfort by the three Officers of the Dragoons. Bunthorne's description as a "Fleshly Poet" was taken from the title of a pamphlet by Buchanan, published in 1871, which was an attack on the styles and attitudes of Rossetti and Swinburne.

The costuming was done without malice and without anyone's taking offense. When Gilbert was busy working on the plot, Whistler was being sued for libel by John Ruskin. Gilbert took breakfast with Whistler that day in a perfectly friendly atmosphere. Carte, whose business included the management of lecture tours, had Oscar Wilde for a client. He arranged to have Wilde tour the United States and to put on his famous airs *fortissimo* so that, when the opera followed, the audiences were prepared to laugh. This was not *intended* as a ridiculous advertisement, but it had that effect.

It is quite interesting to note that, when Gilbert first worked on the plot of *Patience,* Bunthorne and Grosvenor were not described as poets but as clerics, as much removed from the rough world as are poets, but for a slightly different reason. It was obvious that such a satire might cause a few raised eyebrows that would discomfit the producers. Gilbert decided to change—not the story but the vocations of his stars. The whole subject of aestheticism fitted nicely.

Patience was, and has always remained, a great success. The first performance had eight encores. Business at the Comique grew so well that it became quite evident the theater was not big enough for what it contained. Carte therefore went ahead with his long-cherished plan to build a theater especially for Gilbert and Sullivan. This was the Savoy, seating 1292 people. Inside were twelve hundred electric lights, powered by a steam generator placed outside the building. Not only was this novel in London, but it was a great stride in the history of theater: this was the first time such a building had ever been lit entirely by electricity. The stage was larger, the lighting was brighter; Gilbert had to remount the production of *Patience* for its debut in its new home. After the final curtain of its second opening, Carte went before the audience to demonstrate that they had been in complete safety during the performance, even though in a theater lit by mysterious electricity. To prove it he held up a lighted electric lamp and broke it on stage without causing a fire.

Iolanthe

OR, THE PEER AND THE PERI

First performed at the Savoy Theater, London,
25 November 1882

TWO ACTS

CAST

THE LORD CHANCELLOR	Bar
EARL OF MOUNTARARAT	Bar
EARL TOLLOLLER	T
PRIVATE WILLIS, *of the Grenadier Guards*	B
STREPHON, *an Arcadian shepherd*	Bar
QUEEN OF THE FAIRIES	C
IOLANTHE, *a fairy, Strephon's mother*	MS
CELIA, *a fairy*	S
LEILA, *a fairy*	MS
FLETA, *a fairy*	Spkr
PHYLLIS, *an Arcadian shepherdess and ward in chancery*	S
Dukes, Marquises, Earls, Viscounts, Barons, Fairies	Chorus

SETTING

ACT I: An Arcadian landscape.
ACT II: Palace yard, Westminster.

SONGS AND CHORUSES

ACT I

Chorus: Tripping hither, tripping thither (*Fairies*)
Invocation: Iolanthe! (*Fairy Queen, Fairies*)
Chorus: Welcome to our hearts again (*Fairies*)
Song: Good morrow, good mother! (*Strephon, Chorus*)
Ensemble: Fare thee well, attractive stranger (*Fairies*)
Song: Good morrow, good lover! (*Phyllis, Strephon*)
Duet: None shall part us from each other (*Phyllis, Strephon*)

Chorus: Loudly let the trumpet bray! (*Peers*)
Song: The law is the true embodiment (*Chancellor, Chorus*)
Scene: Of all the young ladies I know (*Tolloller, Mountararat, Phyllis, Chorus*)
Ballad: Spurn not the nobly born (*Tolloller, Chorus*)
Song: When I went to the Bar as a very young man (*Chancellor*)
Finale: When darkly looms the day (*Strephon, Phyllis, Chorus*)
    Ballad: In babyhood (*Strephon*)
    Ballad: For riches and rank I do not long (*Phyllis*)
    Solo: Go away, madam (*Chancellor*)

ACT II

Song: When all night long a chap remains (*Willis*)
Chorus: Strephon's a Member of Parliament! (*Fairies, Peers*)
Song: When Britain really ruled the waves (*Mountararat, Chorus*)
Duet: In vain to us you plead (*Leila, Celia, Fairies*)
Song: Oh, foolish fay (*Queen, Chorus*)
Quartette: Though p'r'aps I may incur your blame (*Tolloller, Phyllis, Willis, Mountararat*)
Song: When you're lying awake with a dismal headache (*Chancellor*)
Trio: If you go in (*Chancellor, Mountararat, Tolloller*)
Duet: If we're weak enough to tarry (*Strephon, Phyllis*)
Ballad: He loves! If in the bygone years (*Iolanthe*)
Finale: Soon as we may (*Phyllis, Ensemble*)

SYNOPSIS

ACT I

In a peaceful glade beside a peaceful river, in a land of simple beauties, the fairies dance and sing without a care. Nobody knows why they do it, but what does that matter? It is for the pleasure of having no purpose. What do fairies live on? Lovers. That's all the nourishment they need.

> *We can ride on lovers' sighs,*
> *Warm ourselves in lovers' eyes,*
> *Bathe ourselves in lovers' tears,*
> *Clothe ourselves in lovers' fears.*

All seems very delicate and perfect. But it isn't, not without their sister Iolanthe. Their revels now are more work than pleasure. Iolanthe was the spark of every happiness. For twenty-five mortal years she has been absent, banished by the Fairy Queen for having married a mortal. By law—that is, fairy law—she should have died for this. But the Queen commuted her sentence to penal servitude for life on condition that she should immedi-

{ 52 }

ately cease all communication with her husband without explanation. The condemned fairy chose to work out her term in the most uncomfortable, chilly, damp place she could find: the bottom of the nearby stream. This is unnerving to the delicate nature of the Queen—the frogs! think of the frogs!

The fairies, one and all, want Iolanthe back. Surely her punishment has been severe enough! The Queen, too, misses her terribly and grants the reprieve that all desire. The fairies call upon Iolanthe to return to the upper world.

> *Iolanthe!*
> *From thy dark exile thou art summoned!*
> *Come to our call—*
> *Come, Iolanthe!*

Like a Rhine Maiden she rises from the placid river. Her dress is tattered and gray, her aspect humble. She is pleasantly surprised to hear the Queen grant her pardon. Her water weeds fall away and she stands glittering with the beauty of the most beautiful of fairies, her diamond coronet returned to her head. She is received once again into the company of the partly blessed.

There is, however, a question in the Queen's mind. Why had Iolanthe chosen to work out her sentence in the bottom of that river? The answer is shockingly simple—to be near her son, born shortly after she left her husband and now twenty-five years old. He is an Arcadian shepherd in love with Phyllis, one of the wards in chancery. Since his father was a mortal, only his top half is fairy. From the waist down he's human.

Strephon, half and half, comes in, playing upon his flageolet and singing

> *For I'm to be married today.*

Not that the Lord Chancellor has agreed to it, but Strephon will not wait any longer. Being half a fairy has caused him certain embarrassments in the human world. His lower half isn't half as useful as his upper. What will his upper half, which shall never grow old, do when his lower half withers? No one has an answer for that.

The Queen believes that this lad is plainly fitted for intellectual work —say, in Parliament. This is an idea worth considering carefully; the fairies leave Strephon to his thoughts.

Phyllis is worried about the Lord Chancellor's negative reaction to the proposed marriage. Neither of the two young lovers can imagine putting it off until she becomes of age two years hence.

> *None shall part us from each other;*
> *One in life and death are we:*

All in all to one another—
I to thee and thou to me!

To discuss the question of a suitable husband for Phyllis, whom each of them loves, the House of Lords assembles in executive session. The meeting opens ceremonially:

Bow, ye lower middle classes!
Bow, ye tradesmen, bow, ye masses!
Blow the trumpets, bang the brasses!
Tantantara! Tzing! Boom!

Then there is an introductory speech by the Lord Chancellor:

The law is the true embodiment
Of everything that's excellent;
It has no kind of fault or flaw;
And I, my Lords, embody the law.

He is forced to admit that he himself is highly susceptible to the charms of the young ladies who are wards of the court—especially those of Phyllis, whom he would like to marry. But, being her guardian, he cannot objectively consider his own suit; whether he can give himself his own consent, or whether he can marry the girl at all without that consent puzzles him. A most painful position! He waives his claim.

The girl has been summoned to appear before the House and now is ushered in.

Oh, rapture, how beautiful!
How gentle—how dutiful!

The Lords Tolloller and Mountararat love her madly. Tolloller sings an explanation that, although she was born at a lower social level, he has enough grammar and spelling for two,

And blood and behavior for twenty!

Phyllis claims to have sufficient grammar for her own purposes and to have been born as everybody was once born. She does not want Lord Tolloller; she does not want a Lord at all. To this the noble gentleman feels compelled to reply with some formality.

Spurn not the nobly born
With love affected,
Nor treat with virtuous scorn
The well-connected.

But nothing will sway the maid. Her heart is already given to a mere shepherd. Indeed, she means to be married this very day. At this unfortunate moment Strephon appears, to put his claim before the Lord Chancellor. The Peer takes the boy aside for a well-deserved tongue-lashing. Strephon attempts to conquer logic with the depth of his emotions, but the Lord is unmoved. He tells Strephon what it means to be called to the Bar, what constitutes legal evidence and truth. Strephon is duly impressed —and depressed. In this sad condition his fairy mother Iolanthe finds him after he has left the august House. She promises him the help of all the fairies against the peers.

Phyllis witnesses the affectionate meeting between her twenty-five-year-old lover and what appears to be an exceedingly pretty girl of only seventeen. The absurd explanation he offers—that the sweet thing is really his mother—brings a perfectly logical reaction from Phyllis, and the Lords who also saw them. Phyllis is deeply hurt. Without hesitation she turns and gives her promise that she will marry either Lord Tolloller or Lord Mountararat—little does she care which. The choice is up to them. Now the fairies intervene, but their appearance only confirms the suspicion of all the Lords that Strephon is dallying with a seventeen-year-old girl while formally paying court to their ward. Finally the Fairy Queen herself speaks on behalf of the boy, but it takes a serious threat to accomplish anything. She tells the gentlemen who she is, and forthwith appoints Strephon a member of Parliament.

> *Every bill and every measure*
> *That may gratify his pleasure,*
> *Though your fury it arouses*
> *Shall be passed by both your Houses.*

The battle lines are drawn. The peers and the fairies make themselves ready for a war to the finish.

ACT II

Before the entrance to Parliament stands Private Willis, on guard, unaware of what is about to happen. He is a contemplative man, made so, perhaps, by his nocturnal employment as a sentry. Parliaments have sat and risen time and again, but the parties seem to last forever.

> *I often think it's comical—Fal, lal, la!*
> *How Nature always does contrive—Fal, lal, la!*
> *That every boy and every gal*
> *That's born into the world alive*
> *Is either a little Liberal*
> *Or else a little Conservative!*
> *Fal, lal, la!*

And he muses, in the peace and quiet of a dimly moonlit London night. But the old order of life has been changed, whether Private Willis likes it or not, for, as peers and fairies now enter to sing,

> *Strephon's a Member of Parliament,*
> *Carries every bill he chooses.*
> *To his measures all assent—*
> *Showing that fairies have their uses.*

One of Strephon's bills, one which must have been most galling, throws the peerage open for the first time in history to competitive examination. The implications of this are almost too horrible to contemplate.

> MOUNTARARAT: *. . . but with a House of Peers composed exclusively*
> *of people of intellect, what's to become of the House*
> *of Commons?*
> LEILA: *I never thought of that!*

The good Earl has put his finger on just one of the many results to be expected when a woman (the Fairy Queen) interferes with politics. He is amazed that a House with such a glorious history can be so rudely converted into something unmentionable.

> *When Britain really ruled the waves—*
> *(In good Queen Bess's time)*
> *The House of Peers made no pretence*
> *To intellectual eminence,*
> *Or scholarship sublime;*
> *Yet Britain won her proudest bays*
> *In good Queen Bess's glorious days!*

The two most forward of the fairies, Leila and Celia, are utterly charmed by the vigor and stateliness of this noble man. Each yearns to have a Peer for herself. When the Fairy Queen hears this, she reminds them that marriage with a mortal is punishable by death. But even as she argues, she becomes so conscious of the attractions of the ever-present Private Willis that she hardly knows which way to turn.

While the fate of fairydom dangles over this new precipice, Phyllis faces her own problem. She is now engaged, against her better judgment, to both Lord Tolloller and Lord Mountararat because of Strephon's seeming duplicity. But all in all, she does not think much of the Peerage *per se.*

The two Lords engaged to Phyllis have to choose between them which one will actually have her. They try; they discuss the possibility of fighting over her; but at last friendship prevails—it would not be right for old friends to despatch one another. But these two are not the only ones in despair. The Lord Chancellor is miserable. He has been having nightmares and must sing them out in every detail. He cannot rid himself of his desire for Phyllis, who is his own ward and therefore unavailable.

At last Strephon leaves the legislative hall, the object of all eyes, the envy of every impotent Lord. He has passed every bill he wanted and is pausing only to think of more. When he sees Phyllis, his manner is restrained; he knows she is engaged to two of his fellow-members. But in the conversation, the girl finally realizes that the seventeen-year-old beauty she saw him with, who he claimed was his mother, really *is* his mother. Being a fairy she has not aged beyond that age which is the most attractive. And her son is half fairy. The poor girl's eyes are thus forced open. They decide—again—to marry immediately before something else gets in the way.

Iolanthe enters, to greet her prospective daughter-in-law, and meets the Lord Chancellor. Their secret is now revealed: he was her mortal husband, Strephon's father. At this moment, the Fairy Queen makes her appearance. By meeting her husband once again, Iolanthe has a second time broken the fairies' law and must be punished, this time with death! But now each fairy is in love with a mortal Peer. Even the Fairy Queen loves Private Willis. What can be done? The Lord Chancellor—an old Equity draftsman—saves the day with the suggestion that the fairy law against marriage with mortals be amended by the alteration of the crucial sentence, so that it will now read that fairies *must* marry mortals. There are no nays; the ayes have it and the law is put into effect. All the Peers are delighted, and in a magical moment wings sprout on their backs as they each take a fairy's hand. Even Private Willis becomes a fairy.

> *Up in the sky*
> *Ever so high,*
> *Pleasures come in endless series;*
> *We will arrange*
> *Happy exchange—*
> *House of Peers for House of Peris!*

HISTORICAL NOTE

One of the best-known stories about the operas of Gilbert and Sullivan concerns this stanza of the Fairy Queen's song in *Iolanthe*:

> *Oh, Captain Shaw!*
> *Type of true love kept under!*
> *Could thy Brigade*
> *With cold cascade*
> *Quench my great love, I wonder!*

And at the opening, the real Captain Shaw was not only present—as he was at many a première—but he happened to be sitting in the center of the front of the house, where the Fairy Queen could see him plainly and stretch out her arms in supplication. His name was Eyre Massey Shaw, and he had become famous and beloved in London for having created a top-flight city-wide fire department.

Iolanthe was the second production to be mounted on the electrically lighted stage of the Savoy, and the very first to be designed to use the new power. When the audience had been carried through all the intricacies of the plot and brought to the magic moment near the end when fairyland was to come into its own, they saw magic little stars gleam from the heads of all the fairies: little lamps mounted in their hair, powered by batteries concealed in their costumes.

This was not, of course, the only trick Gilbert tried. The Peers sprout wings in the same scene: little wire-formed wings spring into place on their backs at the pull of a concealed cord. Gilbert had always delighted in effective machinery and took every opportunity to make use of it in ways which were original and Gilbertian.

Sullivan composed a score for this work filled with allusions to the style of Wagner. *Der Fliegende Holländer* had appeared for the first time in England twelve years previously, and Wagnerism was new. Sullivan had as definite feelings about it as Gilbert did. The writer satirized *Das Rheingold* by having Iolanthe climb out of the depths of a river where she had been spending years of penance. But Sullivan went further. His music parodies Wagner in many places, with allusions to *Die Walküre, Das Rheingold,* and even to "Die Alte Weise," from *Tristan und Isolde* which he parodied in the music for the Fairy Queen. But all the while a canker grew in Sullivan's heart, as he wondered whether he was sacrificing a great art to mediocre theater. *Iolanthe* may not be his best score; certainly it is not his most exciting. But for a musician it is one of his most interesting.

The first hint of the plot, in Gilbert's preliminary thinking, came in the *Bab Ballads,* which first appeared in 1870. In one of them a child born to a mortal and a fairy eventually became a curate in the Church of England. The first version of the opera was set not in Parliament, nor in the church, but in a court of law. Thus did Gilbert work out his ideas in version after version over a fairly long period of time.

Sullivan likewise worked in his own manner. There was no overture ready for the work until three days before it opened. For the New York performance Alfred Cellier had to compose one as best he could, there being none available there. Rehearsals were conducted in secrecy in order to prevent the spies of other theaters from stealing ideas and snatches of the plot. The very title of the new work was kept even from the cast until the final rehearsal. Up to that moment, for every time the word Iolanthe was to be sung, "Come Perola" had been substituted, it having the same arrangement of syllables. There was much scribbling when orders came through to change every "Come Perola" to *Iolanthe*.

Some of the actors went on strike, refusing to obey Gilbert's orders to be clean shaven as Peers of the Realm. But he had his way; mustaches were lopped off (that is, by all but one actor who was himself lopped off the rolls).

Iolanthe is still successful. In certain ways it does not equal *Patience*, which it originally replaced, or *The Mikado* which came later. The trouble between the two creators which had already shown itself in the looseness of some parts of *Patience* became more marked in *Iolanthe* and nearly ruined *Princess Ida*. And yet *Iolanthe* has enough merit to be revived frequently in many parts of the world.

Ten years after the Gilbert and Sullivan opera opened, Piotr Ilyitch Tchaikovsky produced an *Iolanthe*, but on an entirely different subject.

Princess Ida

OR, CASTLE ADAMANT

First produced at the Savoy Theater, London,
5 January 1884

THREE ACTS

CAST

KING HILDEBRAND	BBar
HILARION, *his son*	T
CYRIL, *Hilarion's friend*	T
FLORIAN, *Hilarion's friend*	Bar
KING GAMA	Bar
ARAC, *his son*	BBar
GURON, *Gama's son*	BBar
SCYNTHIUS, *Gama's son*	BBar
PRINCESS IDA, *Gama's daughter*	S
LADY BLANCHE, *professor of abstract science*	C
LADY PSYCHE, *professor of humanities*	S
MELISSA, *Lady Blanche's daughter*	MS
SACHARISSA, *girl graduate*	S
CHLOE, *girl graduate*	Spkr
ADA, *girl graduate*	Spkr
Soldiers, Courtiers, Girl Graduates, *"Daughters of the Plough"*	Chorus

SETTING

ACT I: Pavilion in King Hildebrand's Palace.
ACT II: Gardens of Castle Adamant.
ACT III: Courtyard of Castle Adamant.

SONGS AND CHORUSES

ACT I

Chorus: Search throughout the panorama (*Chorus*)
Song and Chorus: Now hearken to my strict command (*Hildebrand, Chorus*)

{ 60 }

Ballad: Ida was a twelvemonth old (*Hilarion*)
Song: We are warriors three (*Arac, Guron, Scynthius*)
Song: If you give me your attention, I will tell you what I am (*Gama*)
Duet: Perhaps if you address the lady (*Gama, Hildebrand*)
Trio: Expressive glances (*Hilarion, Cyril, Florian*)
Trio: For a month to dwell (*Arac, Guron, Scynthius*)

ACT II

Chorus: Towards the empyrean heights (*Girl Graduates*)
Aria: Oh, goddess wise (*Ida*)
Song: Come, mighty Must! (*Blanche*)
Trio: Gently, gently (*Hilarion, Cyril, Florian*)
Trio: I am a maiden, cold and stately (*Hilarion, Cyril, Florian*)
Quartette: The world is but a broken toy (*Ida, Hilarion, Cyril, Florian*)
Song: A lady fair, of lineage high (*Psyche*)
Quintette: The woman of the wisest wit (*Psyche, Melissa, Hilarion, Cyril, Florian*)
Duet: Now wouldn't you like to rule the roast (*Melissa, Blanche*)
Song: Would you like to know the kind of maid (*Cyril*)
Finale: Oh! joy, our chief is saved (*Ladies*)
   Song: Whom thou hast chained must wear his chain (*Hilarion, Chorus*)
   Solo: Some years ago (*Hildebrand*)
   Trio: We may remark, though nothing can dismay us (*Arac, Guron, Scynthius*)
   Solo: Though I am but a girl (*Ida*)

ACT III

Chorus: Death to the invader! (*Ladies and girls*)
Song: I built upon a rock (*Ida*)
Song: Whene'er I poke sarcastic joke (*Gama*)
Chorus: When anger spreads his wing (*Soldiers*)
Song: This helmet, I suppose (*Arac, Guron, Scynthius*)
Chorus: This is our duty plain towards (*Chorus*)
Finale: With joy abiding (*Ida, Hilarion, Chorus*)

SYNOPSIS

ACT I

All the inhabitants of the castle of King Hildebrand have gathered on its parapets and battlements with telescopes, opera glasses—anything to help search the horizon for signs of the approach of King Gama. Whether it is to be a happy occasion, worthy of great celebration, or one of battle and destruction in which Gama will be sliced and diced depends entirely on whether he brings his daughter with him to be Hilarion's wife. Everyone wonders.

> *Will Prince Hilarion's hopes be sadly blighted?*
> *Who can tell?*

It will mean war, the King proclaims, if King Gama fails to produce the bride by sunset this day. She was betrothed to Hilarion at the tender age of one. As Hildebrand recalls, over the span of twenty years, Gama was extremely ugly, twisted and misshapen. The prospect that his daughter will be good-looking is, therefore, slim.

Suddenly Florian makes out in the distance a speck that might be a horse and rider. It might be Gama. With him, however, rides no slip of a girl but what looks like a steel-coated cavalier of six feet, more or less, with mustachios. Rather than make a snap judgment, preparations are immediately undertaken for both a warm welcome and a chilly imprisonment for the approaching guests. While the horsemen are still far away, Hilarion has time to muse upon the history of this event.

> *Ida was a twelvemonth old,*
> *Twenty years ago!*
> *I was twice her age, I'm told,*
> *Twenty years ago!*
> *Husband twice as old as wife*
> *Argues ill for married life.*
> *Baleful prophecies were rife,*
> *Twenty years ago!*

The first to arrive is not King Gama, but three mustachio'd cavaliers, the three fierce warriors, Gama's sons Arac, Guron and Scynthius, all spoiling, should occasion arise, for a fight. Next comes the King. He is an unhappy man. He feels that he has been misunderstood throughout life and that this is a good time, since he must introduce himself to the throng, to describe himself as he wishes to be known.

> *If you give me your attention I will tell you what I am;*
> *I'm a genuine philanthropist—all other kinds are sham.*
> *Each little fault of temper and each social defect*
> *In my erring fellow-creatures I endeavour to correct.*
> *To all their little weaknesses I open people's eyes;*
> *And little plans to snub the self-sufficient I devise;*
> *I love my fellow creatures—I do all the good I can—*
> *Yet everybody says I'm such a disagreeable man!*
> *And I can't think why!*

Gama, getting now his first glimpse of Hildebrand's castle, does not think much of it, nor of his old friend. Time has dealt badly with him, and even Hilarion, whom Gama last saw as a baby, seems to have changed for the worse. The kings trade a few insults about each other's figures before settling down to serious negotiation.

Why has King Gama not brought his daughter with him? The explanation begins rather lamely. The girl is not here because she is head of a women's university, a forbidding place where live one hundred ultra-intellectual maidens and not one male—not even a rooster. The exclusive population of that fort of learning rises each morning to what sounds like the crow of a cock; but it is really not a cock at all—it is a very accomplished hen. It is because of this extreme isolation, this female determination to remain pure and un-manned that Gama has not brought his daughter to marry Hildebrand's son. Indeed, it would be next to impossible for Hildebrand himself even to approach the lady in her present situation.

A marriage planned and replanned for twenty years cannot, no matter what the complexities, be put off forever. Hildebrand declares Gama his hostage while Hilarion prepares to assault the bastion of femininity.

> *Expressive glances*
> *Shall be our lances,*
> *And pops of Sillery*
> *Our light artillery.*
> *We'll storm their bowers*
> *With scented showers*
> *Of fairest flowers*
> *That we can buy!*

Arac, Guron, and Scynthius accompany their imprisoned king and father into confinement and Hilarion, Cyril, and Florian leave to perform their delicate, dangerous and important mission.

ACT II

Gathered in the garden of Castle Adamant, the girl graduates of the female university ponder questions of deepest philosophy: questions of what to read, what to study. But most interesting of all is the question of man. What is man? What is *a* man? Psyche, the only one who actually knows, provides a damning description of the animal, summing up with:

> *Man is Nature's sole mistake.*

The Lady Blanche interrupts this fascinating study to announce a few routine decisions of the Princess Ida, who rules with unquestioned conviction this seat of one-sided learning. Sacharissa is to be expelled for having brought men inside the castle walls—though they may be chessmen:

> *They're men with whom you give each other mate, and that's enough!*

Chloe is to be punished for having drawn a perambulator in her sketch-book. These preliminaries over, the Princess herself comes down to meet the new students and to instruct them in their conduct within the walls. Woman, who is demonstrably superior to man, must come to grips with the world situation so that she may wrest control from male hands. If they fail, they might as well give up everything—even fashion.

> *Let all your things misfit, and you yourselves*
> *At inconvenient moments come undone!*

Now the time has come for classes. The Princess takes the students away, leaving Blanche, who—not so secretly—yearns to become head of the school. As she ends a heartening, moral soliloquy of ambition, Hilarion climbs over the outside wall, followed by Cyril and Florian. Nearly shredded by the ridge of broken bottles set on top of the brickwork, the men pause to hear their leader list all the ambitions that drive women into such formidable seclusion.

> *They intend to send a wire*
> *To the moon—to the moon;*
> *And they'll set the Thames on fire*
> *Very soon,—very soon.*

The three interlopers stumble upon some collegiate robes. Perfect disguises! They try them on and immediately become indistinguishable from the girl graduates. Hardly have they assumed the proper pose, however, when the Princess herself enters, reading a book. The three men introduce themselves as candidates for the university, and are accepted, provided they promise never to marry men—which they find quite easy to make. The Princess leaves them, satisfied, and Psyche enters. This meeting is not as propitious, however, for Psyche is the disguised Florian's sister. To seize the initiative is often the best way out of a bad situation. Florian tells Psyche who he is, and she recognizes them all, although it is a long time since they all played together as babies. She was always too brilliant and logical for ordinary society. Her qualities show themselves when she explains that she has entered this anti-masculine establishment because she believes

> *That man, sprung from an Ape, is Ape at heart.*

And she sings them the sad history of the Ape who loved a lady of high degree. Since the lady would not have him as an ape, he shaved, cut off his tail, bought dress clothing and made himself into a true specimen of Darwinian Man. But still the lady rejected him, because a Darwinian Man,

> *though well-behaved*
> *At best is only a monkey shaved!*

Melissa has overheard the whole scene. Now she knows that Psyche is speaking with the Forbidden Ones within the walls of the exclusive university. But having never before seen a man, Melissa is thrilled at their beauty. She swears never to betray Psyche's secret.

Re-entering, Lady Blanche is not so easily won over. She hears the five "girls" singing, but two are tenors and one a baritone. This indicates that something may be awry. The bribe of power silences her, however, when Melissa explains that Hilarion has come to claim the Princess Ida as his bride, which will leave the post of headmistress open for Blanche.

Luncheon is served. Its formality provides the Princess with a chance to inquire about the court of Hildebrand from these new students. She wonders about the young Prince, the King's son, whose name she carefully forgets to remember. Hilarion himself, his disguise unpenetrated, tells her all the best things he can think of. But Cyril, drinking the while, is becoming tipsy and a bit loose in the tongue. In vain his companions try to silence him. He becomes louder and louder and reveals more and more with each word until finally he sings a most unmaidenly kissing song which ends with a tremendous punch on the chest from Hilarion.

Their secret is out, their disguises useless. The Princess runs screaming for protection and falls accidentally into the river. Protection—the Daughters of the Plough, who are the working class in this female Utopia—arrives to find a soaking wet Princess already rescued by Hilarion, dressed in woman's clothes. Despite his appeal to love, despite the fact that he saved her from drowning, Ida orders that he be marched off to the dungeon together with his friends.

Hildebrand's army has been gathering at the gates of Castle Adamant. Now they mount their attack and burst in. The King loses not a moment to inform the Princess that she has the choice of marrying Hilarion or seeing her castle destroyed.

> For I'm a peppery potentate
> Who's little inclined his claim to bate,
> To fit the wit of a bit of a chit,
> And that's the long and the short of it!

His threat is reinforced by the exhibition of Arac, Guron, and Scynthius, the warlike brothers of the Princess, in chains ready for slaughter. Defying Hildebrand she has until the next morning to make her decision.

ACT III

The decision is—to fight. The girls mount the battlements of Castle Adamant and prepare for the worst. Not all are willing. Sacharissa, who was appointed surgeon, balks at the prospect of seeing real blood. Ada claims that the girls in the band are too sick today to make an appearance. Psyche, who was supposed to supply gunpowder, is not in favor of war without negotiation. Ida, thus left without gunpowder, without a band to inspire sacrifice, and without a surgeon to bind up the wounded, cannot hope to engage the King's troops. She sits disconsolate.

Under a flag of truce an enemy messenger is admitted. It is Gama, Ida's father. He has been subjected to infinitely subtle torture as Hildebrand's captive. Every attention his little heart desired has been paid to him without question, so that he has had nothing whatever to grumble at and is now nearly crazy with frustration.

It has been proposed that, rather than demean his army in a battle against women, Hildebrand will set Arac, Guron, and Scynthius free to fight Hilarion, Cyril, and Florian. This is an agreeable arrangement. The two teams are brought together and—after the warlike sons of King Gama have removed their armor, which gets in their way more than it protects them—they fight. Gama's side loses. Thus it becomes practically obligatory for Ida, whose brothers need nursing at the moment, to quit her leadership of the women and subordinate herself in marriage to the victor. She would still hesitate, in consideration of the purity of her name in the minds of posterity, but the question of where posterity would come from if her segregationist principles were really put into practice finally decides her future.

> *It were profanity*
> *For poor humanity*
> *To treat as vanity*
> *The sway of Love.*

HISTORICAL NOTE

Gilbert called his *Princess Ida* a "respectful operatic perversion of 'The Princess,'" by Tennyson. But before making it an opera, he had already presented it under Tennyson's title as a play, in 1870. Thus the economical re-use of older material is typified in *Princess Ida,* but it was the last such idea Gilbert had available. *The Mikado, Ruddigore, The Yeomen of the Guard* and the rest were each basically new in plot concept. Only with their last collaboration, *The Grand Duke,* did Gilbert and Sullivan again take up a plot they had used before; it failed.

Princess Ida is the only one of Gilbert and Sullivan's operas that has three acts. All the others, except for the one-act *Trial by Jury,* have two. Gilbert stayed close to his original text as he constructed the libretto, so that his first scene, taking place in Hildebrand's castle, became rather longer (for a mere scene) than it might had he worked directly in his accustomed form. As an independent act, it is short. The rest of the opera is set in Castle Adamant. Naturally, when one considers the practical problem of changing sets during intermissions, it was to Gilbert's advantage to make the scene at Hildebrand's long enough to be an act by itself, and to divide the remainder, which was too long for a single act, into two.

The opera is also unique in its line structure. It is the only libretto written mostly in blank verse. This fact may be attributed, as is the three-act form, to the fact that Gilbert transferred whole sections of his original version directly to the musical stage.

The work very nearly failed. Perhaps the most basic reason for this lay not in its structure, not in the lack of meeting between the minds of Gilbert and Sullivan, but in Gilbert's Victorian bias on the subject of woman's place in society. A lot of ink has been splashed on this peculiarity of the author. He did not get along well with his own mother. His parents were separated and drew so far apart in later life that Gilbert found it utterly impossible to effect even a civil politeness between them. While his father lay near death, his mother could not be forced to be helpful in any way—to say nothing of being sympathetic.

Gilbert undoubtedly looked upon women the way he did partly because of his own mother's attitude. But also he lived at a time when the subject of women's emancipation was an issue in active politics, when any man, intelligent or not, biased or unbiased, could and did speak out vehemently on one side or the other. Gilbert's own views were reactionary in the most obvious sense. To him a good woman was a pretty one, young, who had little activity going on in her brain and who preferred to sit demurely on the alabaster pedestal of his admiration. The very idea that women themselves might not wish to be safely segregated and obscured by a screen of sentimentality sometimes filled Gilbert with wildly imagined horrors. I say sometimes, because he was not a demented man. He has left us a glorious picture, taken from the opposite viewpoint, of the healthy and carefree British girl, in one of the songs in the second act of *Utopia, Limited*. He fought against political emancipation of women in *Princess Ida* even though the end of the battle had already become evident in the real world. He railed against the liberal education of women as if he had something personal to fear from their competition, something unreasoned and unrecognized in his own mind. Hence the intensity of the second and third acts. We are forced, in listening to the libretto, to consider all his arguments because of their importance in the plot, knowing all the while that they are ludicrous and unbelievable in actuality. Our ability, then, to suspend disbelief in order to take part in the reality of this play is weakened by the fact that we cannot accept the ideas the author advocates. Hence the play fails to interest us on that very level—the level of theatrical belief. Other operas may seem quite as implausible on careful analysis, but it takes no analysis at all to disbelieve in the principles in this one, principles which are the main concern of its characters.

Another contributing factor, however, may well have been difficulty in the process of collaboration. Sullivan was sicker during the period of composing *Princess Ida* than he had ever yet been. His kidney trouble gave him such pain, and the pain made him so weak, that there were times when some doubted whether the work would be ready for opening. With the scheduled date only four days away, Sullivan collapsed during a rehearsal. At that moment there were two songs still to be composed. Somehow he got himself going again and finished the score in time. On opening night he was in such pain it took two injections of drugs to keep him on his feet while he conducted. When the curtain came down, he collapsed again. The public was politely informed that the composer was suffering from "a muscular affection of the neck."

But the opera itself was not satisfactory. Both the authors knew it. With the usual post-partum effect of an opening, Sullivan experienced a general revulsion for comic-opera as a whole, and sent Carte a formal notice that he would never again write music for an operetta. What with Gilbert's touchiness and a lot of old-fashioned misunderstanding, this rift widened so much that, when *Princess Ida* finally closed for lack of audiences, there was no new work to replace it. The two partners had not been able to recover their former good feeling for each other and the act of collaboration.

Princess Ida lasted only nine months at the Savoy. For Gilbert and Sullivan this was a disappointment. Other plays did well to last three months, but the two titans were used to counting in years. Revivals have been few. The constellation of things wrong in this opera, while not bad enough to kill it, has served to keep it down.

The Mikado

OR, THE TOWN OF TITIPU

First performed at the Savoy Theater, London, 14 March 1885   TWO ACTS

CAST

THE MIKADO OF JAPAN	BBar
NANKI-POO, *his son, disguised as a wandering minstrel, and in love with Yum-Yum*	T
KO-KO, *Lord High Executioner of Titipu*	Bar
POOH-BAH, *Lord High Everything Else*	BBar
PISH-TUSH, *a noble lord*	Bar
YUM-YUM, *Ward of Ko-Ko*	S
PITTI-SING, *Yum-Yum's sister, ward of Ko-Ko*	MS
PEEP-BO, *Yum-Yum's sister, ward of Ko-Ko*	S or MS
KATISHA, *an elderly lady in love with Nanki-Poo*	C
School-girls, nobles, guards, coolies	Chorus

SETTING

ACT I: Courtyard of Ko-Ko's official residence.
ACT II: Ko-Ko's garden.

SONGS AND CHORUSES

ACT I

Chorus: If you want to know who we are (*Nobles*)
Song and Chorus: A wandering minstrel I— (*Nanki-Poo, Chorus*)
Song: Our great Mikado, virtuous man (*Pish-Tush, Chorus*)
Song: Young man, despair (*Pooh-Bah, Nanki-Poo, Pish-Tush*)
Chorus: Behold the Lord High Executioner (*Chorus*)
Song: As some day it may happen that a victim must be found (*Ko-Ko, Men*)
Chorus: Comes a train of little ladies (*Girls*)
Trio: Three little maids from school are we (*Yum-Yum, Peep-Bo, Pitti-Sing, Girls*)

Quartette and Chorus: So please you, Sir, we much regret (*Yum-Yum, Peep-Bo, Pitti-Sing, Pooh-Bah, Girls*)

Duet: Were you not to Ko-Ko plighted (*Yum-Yum, Nanki-Poo*)

Trio: My brain it teems (*Ko-Ko, Pooh-Bah, Pish-Tush*)

Finale: With aspect stern (*Pooh-Bah, Pish-Tush, Chorus*)
    Solo: As in a month you've got to die (*Pooh-Bah*)
    Song: Oh fool, that fleest (*Katisha*)

ACT II

Chorus: Braid the raven hair (*Pitti-Sing, Girls*)

Song: The sun, whose rays (*Yum-Yum*)

Madrigal: Brightly dawns our wedding day (*Yum-Yum, Pitti-Sing, Nanki-Poo, Pish-Tush*)

Trio: Here's a how-de-do! (*Yum-Yum, Nanki-Poo, Ko-Ko*)

March: Miya sama, miya sama (*Chorus*)

Duet: From every kind of man (*Mikado, Katisha, Chorus*)

Song: A more humane Mikado never (*Mikado, Chorus*)

Trio and Chorus: The criminal cried, as he dropped him down (*Ko-Ko, Pitti-Sing, Pooh-Bah, Chorus*)

Glee: See how the fates their gifts allot (*Mikado, Pitti-Sing, Katisha, Ko-Ko, Pooh-Bah*)

Duet: The flowers that bloom in the spring, Tra la (*Nanki-Poo, Ko-Ko, with Yum-Yum, Pitti-Sing, Pooh-Bah*)

Recit. and Song: Alone, and yet alive! Oh, sepulchre! (*Katisha*)

Song: On a tree by a river a little tom-tit (*Ko-Ko*)

Duet: There is a beauty in the bellow of the blast (*Katisha, Ko-Ko*)

Finale: For he's gone and married Yum-Yum (*Pitti-Sing, Ko-Ko, Yum-Yum, Nanki-Poo, Chorus*)

SYNOPSIS

ACT I

In the elegant garden of the official residence of the Lord High Executioner of Titipu the town's noblemen have gathered, soon to be joined by Pooh-Bah, Lord High Everything Else, and Pish-Tush, a nobleman. They introduce themselves:

> *If you want to know who we are,*
> *We are gentlemen of Japan:*
> *On many a vase and jar—*
> *On many a screen and fan,*
>   *We figure in lively paint:*
>   *Our attitude's queer and quaint—*
>   *Your wrong if you think it ain't, oh!*

This is a purely ceremonial affair. The various lords sit quietly in attitudes of nobility. The sudden appearance of a threadbare minstrel, carrying his Japanese guitar, startles them. He is Nanki-Poo, a handsome young man very much in love with one of the Lord High Executioner's official wards, Yum-Yum. The lords are curious about him; his poverty amidst their splendor and his questions about Yum-Yum demand explanation. The young man is asked to identify himself, which he does.

A wandering minstrel I—
A thing of shreds and patches,
Of ballads, songs and snatches,
And dreamy lullaby!

As stock-in-trade of minstrelsy he can supply sentimental songs, lady-charming songs, patriotic songs, war-songs, sea-chanteys (perfectly British), in fact anything a noble lord might ask. Thus he becomes at once a most popular fellow with the gentle lords of Titipu. As for his business with Yum-Yum, Nanki-Poo explains that he fell in love with her when Ko-Ko was nothing but a cheap tailor. Having heard that Ko-Ko was condemned to death for flirting, which is the only crime punishable in Titipu by death, Nanki-Poo has returned to find her and propose again the marriage that Ko-Ko, when he was free, had opposed.

But the cheap tailor is no longer condemned to death. There was consternation in Titipu when the law against flirting first went into effect. Nobody wished to be beheaded, especially for so natural an act. Hence Ko-Ko was taken out of his death cell and made executioner, on the theory that he could not very well chop off anyone else's head until he had first justified matters by cutting off his own.

Nanki-Poo is impressed with the clarity of the logic of this explanation, given by Pish-Tush. Pooh-Bah completes the tale by explaining that since the noblemen refused to continue their civic service under a Lord High Executioner who came from such a lowly position, they had all resigned in a body. This caused a serious situation to develop in the administration of the town, but fortunately Pooh-Bah humbled himself and took all their jobs upon himself—together with their salaries. Besides being First Lord of the Treasury, Lord Chief Justice, and so forth, Pooh-Bah is also a private retailer of state secrets. A few well-directed hints take effect, and Nanki-Poo finally bribes him—a light enough insult for a man accustomed to hungering for heavier ones—for news of Yum-Yum.

Yum-Yum, that very afternoon, is to marry her protector, the Lord High Executioner, Ko-Ko. Nanki-Poo, who has journeyed a whole month to see her again, has arrived just in time to witness the ceremony. The great man, the groom himself, his huge sword of office slashing the air over his shoulder, makes his formal appearance at last before the assembled lords of Titipu, just after Nanki-Poo leaves. He has come on business; marriage business. He wishes to discuss with Pooh-Bah the arrangements for the celebration of the wedding, a celebration intended to last for one entire week. But first, in order to reinforce his official position with an impressive statement to the gentlemen who have gathered here, the Lord High Executioner describes the way he has arranged things for the maintenance of his official position.

> *As some day it may happen that a victim must be found,*
> *I've got a little list—I've got a little list*
> *Of society offenders who might well be underground,*
> *And who never would be missed—who never would be missed!*

Seeing that he has, indeed, made a sufficient impression upon the noblemen, Ko-Ko dismisses them and speaks about the wedding in private with Pooh-Bah, who advises him:

> *Of course, as First Lord of the Treasury, I could propose a special vote that would cover all expenses, if it were not that as Leader of the Opposition, it would be my duty to resist it, tooth and nail.*

The question boils down to a simple matter of practicality. A person in such a powerful position as Pooh-Bah can be handled politically, but he must be

> *insulted with a very considerable bribe.*

Ko-Ko concedes, and plans are made for the wedding. They go off together in order not to be noticed by the bride and her two companions, who are coming into the garden.

> *Three little maids from school are we,*
> *Pert as a school-girl well can be,*
> *Filled to the brim with girlish glee,*
> *Three little maids from school!*

Ko-Ko cannot bring himself to stay away from such a delicious bride-to-be. And ceremony itself demands that he come to greet her with a kiss. It is quite an ordeal for the girl. When it is at last over, Yum-Yum notices Nanki-Poo standing at one side of the garden. All three girls rush to him, overjoyed, during this sad moment before her marriage to Ko-Ko, to see Yum-Yum's handsome young lover again. Breathlessly they introduce him to Ko-Ko, but in all the confusion the Lord High Executioner has the intruder ushered away so that he may make a ceremony of introducing Pooh-Bah to the girls. After all the formalities have been completed, Nanki-Poo at last finds

Yum-Yum alone. The lovers confess to each other, Yum-Yum telling him that she is utterly miserable about marrying Ko-Ko, and Nanki-Poo telling her that he is slated for marriage with an unattractive lady, Katisha. For he is really not just a second trombone in the Titipu Town Band, but actually the son of the Mikado of Japan and heir to the throne. He is disguised in order to avoid the connubial fate that has been decreed for him. The two lovers move closer to each other, but carefully, for the laws of Titipu are severe about flirting.

> *If it were not for the law, we should now be sitting side by side, like that.* (Sits by her)
>
> . . . . .
>
> *With our arms around each other's waist, like that.* (Embracing her).

They go off and Ko-Ko enters, followed by Pooh-Bah and Pish-Tush. Ko-Ko has received a letter from the Mikado himself stating that the illustrious conqueror is about to pay a visit of state to the town of Titipu. Not only that, but he is also concerned about the lack of executions lately and demands that there be one forthwith. Obviously, as Pooh-Bah is quick to point out, the ex-tailor already sentenced is available to satisfy the Mikado. But Ko-Ko objects. He appoints Pooh-Bah Lord High Substitute, but this flattering honor is respectfully declined.

By the purest and most convenient chance, Ko-Ko passes Nanki-Poo, who has left Yum-Yum in despair and is carrying a rope with which to hang himself rather than see his love sacrificed to Ko-Ko's new social position. Here is a substitute ready made. An agreement is reached in a trice. Nanki-Poo will marry Yum-Yum and keep her for one month, after which he will be beheaded. A capital solution for all the problems. It makes everyone happy: the two lovers may have each other, Ko-Ko may have his marriage later, and Titipu will have an execution to present in honor of the Mikado's visit.

> *This toast with three times three we'll give—*
> *"Long life to you—till then!"*

Everything would have proceeded smoothly had not Katisha come, having discovered where the son of the Mikado hides from her. She intends to claim Nanki-Poo as her own, but her shouting that he is not, as he claims, a second trombone is drowned out by the citizens.

ACT II

Happily having her hair dressed as she sits in the courtyard of the Lord High Executioner's official residence, Yum-Yum listens to a little song and wonders modestly how it came to be that she is so exceedingly beautiful. It must be admitted that she is, for she is a child of Nature. Such a realization cannot be misconstrued as vanity; she sings:

> The sun whose rays
> Are all ablaze
> With ever-living glory,
> Does not deny
> His majesty—
> He scorns to tell a story!

All is unutterably perfect except for the fact that her new husband is scheduled for demolition after one short month. He comes, himself, to prove that a month of bliss is bliss for all eternity. But they are in tears, trying to smile, as they sing a merry, mournful madrigal.

> Brightly dawns our wedding day;
> Joyous hour, we give thee greeting!
> Whither, whither art thou fleeting?

Ko-Ko, passing by, stops a moment to gaze upon this amorous scene. He begs them to kiss in his presence so that he can begin to get used to it: it is torture for him. His tears, however, seem a bit wetter than the situation would warrant. They ask him what may be the matter. He is forced to explain that he has just ascertained that there is a law on the books requiring a beheaded man's wife to be buried alive. To the delicate Yum-Yum, being buried alive seems a bit of a stuffy proposition. The marriage must be called off. Nanki-Poo, therefore, plans to commit suicide immediately as he had originally intended.

Ko-Ko will not allow this. The man is legally doomed to decapitation, and he must be alive for the ceremony. Ko-Ko insists, but Nanki-Poo is just as adamant. They reach an impasse. The Lord High Executioner wins, finally, by a ruse. Sending Nanki-Poo and Yum-Yum away, he has Pooh-Bah, exercising all his offices, draw up a document saying that Nanki-Poo has already been executed according to form. This brilliant notion comes just in time, for the Mikado, with his tremendous entourage, has just entered the gates of Titipu to the words and tune of a Japanese Army march:

> Miya sama, miya sama
> On n'm-ma no mayé ni
> Pira-Pira suru no wa
> Nan gia na
> Toko tonyaré na?

It has been a long time since the Emperor of Japan has honored the little town of Titipu with a visit of state. The Mikado takes the occasion to explain his attitude and to outline his program for the control of crime by making punishment, in all cases, appropriate.

My object all sublime
I shall achieve in time—
To let the punishment fit the crime—
The punishment fit the crime;
And make each prisoner pent
Unwillingly represent
A source of innocent merriment!
Of innocent merriment!

It becomes evident, even to the dullest municipal mind, that the subject of punishment for crime is high on the list of things this Mikado really cares about. To satisfy this as quickly as possible Ko-Ko welcomes the Emperor and hands him a certificate, witnessed by every Lord in office (Pooh-Bah), of the summary execution of a certain criminal. The Mikado desires a more detailed description of the event.

In a state of wild alarm—
The criminal cried, as he dropped him down,
With a frightful, frantic, fearful frown,
I bared my big right arm.

The Emperor is well pleased. But there is another matter that he would like to discuss. His own son, heir to the throne of Japan, and engaged to the lady Katisha, is missing. Does anyone in Titipu know anything about him? His name is Nanki-Poo.

Ko-Ko is flustered. He has just begun to fabricate a statement that may cover their guilty tracks, when Katisha shrieks that she has read the name of the supposed criminal who was beheaded—Nanki-Poo. This is very embarrassing. The Mikado is not a bit angry; after all, the town officials thought they were performing their duty. But of course there is a punishment for every crime. . . . Their execution is scheduled immediately after lunch.

Obviously, Nanki-Poo must be brought back to life. But his bags are all packed. He does not want to change his plans now. And when he hears that Katisha and his father have come in person, he is even more determined not to revive—unless Ko-Ko can get him out of Katisha's mind somehow, perhaps by marrying her himself.

Reluctantly the little ex-tailor shuffles into the presence, in the garden, of the ferocious, but miserably sad Katisha, who weeps alone. Biting his lip he attacks boldly, saying:

Katisha, for years I have loved you with a white-hot passion that is slowly but surely consuming my very vitals!

{ 75 }

Little effect. The deeply wronged lady points out that no one ever died of a broken heart. This is the cue Ko-Ko needs. He sings:

On a tree by a river a little tom-tit
Sang "Willow, titwillow, titwillow."

And the song tells how the little bird refused to say why he sang so sadly, but suddenly flew down into the water and died of his grief. This, surely, is proof enough of the seriousness of blighted love. And indeed it is enough proof for Katisha, who, in tears, agrees to accept the love of little Ko-Ko.

Lunch is done. The Mikado is ready for the afternoon's deadly entertainment. Katisha aproaches the imperial presence to beg mercy for all three culprits: Ko-Ko, Pooh-Bah and Pitti-Sing. After all, Ko-Ko is now her husband in place of Nanki-Poo. The Mikado thinks this over for a moment. As he ponders, Nanki-Poo suddenly makes an appearance with his new wife, Yum-Yum.

Explanations, especially to the outraged Katisha, are definitely in order. Ko-Ko is equal to the task:

When your Majesty says, "Let a thing be done," it's as good as done,—practically, it is done—because your Majesty's will is law. Your Majesty says, "Kill a gentleman," and a gentleman is told off to be killed. Consequently, that gentleman is as good as dead—practically, he is dead—and if he is dead, why not say so?

This unarguable logic, at once flattering to the mind and to the intellect of the Emperor of Japan, satisfies that most important person. The visit of state ends in a gloriously happy finale:

For, he's gone and married Yum-Yum!
Yum-Yum!
Your anger pray bury,
For all will be merry,
I think you had better succumb—
Cumb—cumb!
And join our expressions of glee!

HISTORICAL NOTE

When *Princess Ida* closed in September, 1884, there was no new opera ready to replace it. In fact, there was not even a new opera under active consideration. The two collaborators could not agree on a plot to use. Gilbert had suggested a variation on his favorite idea—the Lozenge Plot. Characters in the play were supposed to be able to transform themselves by swallowing special lozenges. Sullivan, who had already given formal notice that he would write no more comic-opera music, was utterly disgusted at this worn-out proposal.

But a new opera had to be decided upon; there was a legal contract which bound Gilbert and Sullivan to produce a new work whenever the Savoy needed it. Sullivan's declaration was out of order. Wrangling proceeded through the last weeks of *Princess Ida* and into the autumn.

Gilbert, who knew that a complete change of atmosphere would help, suddenly realized that there was a whole world of delight and strangeness right under his nose. In Knightsbridge, which is a wide street running along the south edge of Hyde Park, London, near Buckingham Palace, there was a Japanese Exposition, complete with exhibitions of costumes, pottery, paintings, Geisha girls serving tea and Japanese businessmen. London had gone oriental, Japanese fans whirred here and there, vases of Nippon dominated many a British mantelpiece. London's unreserved adoration for everything from that exotic land struck Gilbert's sense of the absurd.

In his own house there hung a huge ceremonial sword, suitable, let us say, for a beheading. Gradually a plot formed; *The Mikado* began to take dramatic shape in his mind. Sullivan was so delighted to hear that Gilbert had given up lozenges and was not even considering a topsy-turvy sort of world for his new libretto—just a Japanese world, perfectly real—that he agreed immediately to collaborate. The declaration against another comic opera was completely forgotten.

It was too late for *The Mikado* to replace *Princess Ida.* Carte revived *The Sorcerer* and *Trial by Jury* instead, to keep the house full until the new opera would be ready. It took nearly half a year.

Every detail of the actual production, though the script was as British as fish 'n' chips, was authentically Japanese. To give the action style, Gilbert hired two workers from the Exposition to teach the company the proper way to mince its steps, to bow, to nod the head and wield a fan. One of these instructors was an authentic Geisha whose English, because she was required to do nothing at the exposition but sell cups of tea, was limited to "sixpence, please!" Some of the actresses in the production wore authentic, even ancient dresses. Katisha appeared in one that was reputed to be two centuries old. In the opening, George Grossmith, playing Ko-Ko, carried the sword that had been hanging in Gilbert's room. It, too, was the real thing, and old.

One of the famous numbers in the score, the trio of the three little maids from school, was written especially to allow the three shortest stars of the company to work together: they were the Misses Grey, Braham, and Bond. Another famous piece, the Mikado's delineation of his philosophy of punishment, "My object all sublime," had so disappointed Gilbert during rehearsals that he had decided to cut it out. The company pleaded with him, and finally he allowed it to be reinstated. The entrance of the Mikado in the second act, "Miya sama, miya sama," is an authentic Japanese military march, words and all.

Rehearsals for *The Mikado* were more strict than ever, with Gilbert most anxious to have every gesture and every word perfectly distinct. This was so hard on George Grossmith, carrying that huge headsman's sword, that he had a general let-down after the opening and took sedatives to keep himself from fluffing his lines on subsequent nights. Gilbert was also nervous. He left the theater as the curtain rose on the first performance and walked the dismal streets of London alone until time to come back for the curtain call.

The Mikado ran for two years without interruption, a magnificent success. Its record of 672 consecutive performances was unbroken until 1922. Among all the works of Gilbert and Sullivan it won the most popularity not only in England and America, but also in Germany and Scandinavia. It was a favorite of Sullivan's friend, Prince Wilhelm, later the Kaiser of Germany. In New York there might have been the same plethora of pirated versions had not Carte gotten the jump on the Americans by rehearsing a touring company, ostensibly for a circuit of the English hinterland. Suddenly he put them aboard a ship and sent them to New York to begin a run that lasted for 430 nights. Ultimate honor, at least in British social circles, came with a command performance at Balmoral Castle, Scotland, in September of 1891.

The imaginative Gilbert had always loved to experiment with new devices. He had had a telephone mounted backstage at the Savoy so that he could keep in touch with rehearsals even when at home, far from the theater. This practice led to a most important and interesting development. A rehearsal of *Iolanthe* was telephoned to Sullivan's flat, where his guests included Edward, the Prince of Wales. Thus it became the very first opera of any kind to be "broadcast"—in this case by wire—to a distant place. Later, in 1917, *The Mikado* established another precedent, becoming the first opera ever recorded on discs.

In 1907, when the work was famous all over the world, performances were suddenly banned in England during the visit of Prince Fushimi, from Japan. Even short selections of the music were forbidden to be played in army and navy installations. For six weeks Mrs. Carte, now manager of the company, fought and protested. It was pointed out that the Japanese themselves liked the opera and were playing it. But the ban stood. Mrs. Carte went ahead with a production outside London, and invited a prominent Japanese critic, one of the Prince's entourage, to attend. He enjoyed it very much and said so publicly, but the ban was not withdrawn until later. Someone asked if this was to become precedent; would *Hamlet,* for instance, be banned for fear of offending the King of Denmark?

In 1908 Gilbert wrote an up-to-date list of "people who would not be missed," including socialists, suffragettes, et al. Producers, however, generally use the original list. Later he produced a children's version of the same list.

Ruddigore

OR, THE WITCH'S CURSE

First performed at the Savoy Theater, London,
22 January 1887

TWO ACTS

CAST

Mortals

SIR RUTHVEN MURGATROYD, *disguised as Robin Oakapple, a young farmer*	Bar
RICHARD DAUNTLESS, *his foster-brother, a Man-o'-war's man*	T
SIR DESPARD MURGATROYD, *of Ruddigore, a wicked baronet*	BBar
OLD ADAM GOODHEART, *Robin's faithful servant*	B
ROSE MAYBUD, *a village maiden*	S
MAD MARGARET	MS
DAME HANNAH, *Rose's aunt*	C
ZORAH, *professional bridesmaid*	S
RUTH, *professional bridesmaid*	Spkr

Ghosts

SIR RUPERT MURGATROYD, *first baronet*	
SIR JASPER MURGATROYD, *third baronet*	
SIR LIONEL MURGATROYD, *sixth baronet*	
SIR CONRAD MURGATROYD, *twelfth baronet*	
SIR DESMOND MURGATROYD, *sixteenth baronet*	
SIR GILBERT MURGATROYD, *eighteenth baronet*	
SIR MERVYN MURGATROYD, *twentieth baronet*	
SIR RODERIC MURGATROYD, *twenty-first baronet*	BBar
Officers, Ancestors, Professional Bridesmaids, Villagers	Chorus

SETTING

ACT I: The Fishing Village of Rederring, in Cornwall.
ACT II: The Picture Gallery in Ruddigore Castle.
Time: Early in the nineteenth century.

SONGS AND CHORUSES

ACT I

Chorus: Fair is Rose as the bright May-day (*Chorus of Bridesmaids*)
Legend: Sir Rupert Murgatroyd (*Dame Hannah, Chorus*)
Ballad: If somebody there chanced to be (*Rose*)
Duet: I know a youth who loves a little maid (*Robin and Rose*)
Ballad: I shipped, d'ye see, in a Revenue sloop (*Richard*)
Song: My boy, you may take it from me (*Robin*)
Duet: The battle's roar is over (*Richard and Rose*)
Ensemble: In sailing o'er life's ocean wide (*Richard, Robin, Rose*)
Scena: Cheerily carols the lark (*Margaret*)
Ballad: To a garden full of posies (*Margaret*)
Chorus: Welcome, gentry (*Bridesmaids, Bucks and Blades*)
Duet: You understand? (*Sir Despard, Richard*)
Chorus: Hail the bride of seventeen summers (*Bridesmaids, Bucks and Blades*)
Madrigal: When the buds are blossoming (*Rose, Hannah, Chorus*)
Solo: Within this breast there beats a heart (*Richard, Chorus*)
Solo: Farewell! Thou hadst my heart (*Rose*)
Duet: Oh, happy the lily (*Rose, Richard*)

ACT II

Duet: I once was as meek as a new-born lamb (*Robin, Adam*)
Duet: Happily coupled are we (*Richard, Rose, Chorus*)
Ballad: In bygone days I had thy love (*Rose, Ensemble*)
Chorus: Painted emblems of a race (*Family portraits*)
Song: When the night wind howls in the chimney cowls (*Sir Roderic, Chorus*)
Chorus: He yields! He answers to our call! (*Chorus of Ghosts*)
Recit. and Song: Away, Remorse! (*Robin*) (Omitted in modern productions.)
Duet: I once was a very abandoned person (*Despard, Margaret*)
Patter-trio: My eyes are fully open to my awful situation (*Robin, Despard, Margaret*)
Ballad: There grew a little flower (*Hannah, Roderic*)
Finale: Having been a wicked baronet a week (*Robin, Rose, Ensemble*)
(In modern performances a reprise of "Oh, happy the lily" is substituted.)

SYNOPSIS

ACT I

In front of a little cottage in the tiny fishing village of Rederring, in Cornwall, a chorus of bridesmaids has gathered to greet Rose Maybud:

Is anybody going
To marry you today?

This has been going on for several months, the girls dressing themselves in their very prettiest bridesmaids' gowns every morning in the hope that the sweet maiden, so pretty and so willing, will finally be claimed. But today is like every day; though every young man in the village is in love with her the chilly girl frightens each of them into silence with her highly practiced disdain. One might ask why the bridesmaids continue to go through this labor every morning. The answer is simple enough: they are professional bridesmaids, supported in this case by a charitable fund set up for the purpose. They have been at it from ten to four every day for six months, and nothing has happened. Funds are running low; the situation is gradually becoming urgent. They are perhaps the only group of professionals in their line of business in the world, but their working days seem to be numbered; so many bridesmaids waiting so long without a bride!

Hearing no response from the little cottage, the girls turn elsewhere in the hope that some sort of bride can be found. They ask Dame Hannah. Would she be kind to poor working girls and become a bride for the sake of their profession? But Dame Hannah has made a solemn vow never to marry, having been engaged many years ago to the Baronet Sir Roderic Murgatroyd, now deceased. She had left him waiting at the church when she heard that he was an accursed man. His ancestor, Sir Rupert, had been a witch hunter. One of the witches cursed him, saying:

Each Lord of Ruddigore,
Despite his best endeavor,
Shall do one crime, or more,
Once, every day, forever!
This doom he can't defy,
However he may try,
For should he stay
His hand, that day
In torture he shall die!

As for Rose Maybud, who lives in the little cottage, the reason she will not consider marrying any of the available lads of the village is that she treasures a certain book of etiquette above all other possessions. This little volume was all that was left with her (except for "a change of baby-linen") when she, an infant, was deposited at the workhouse door by unknown parents. Whatever the book of etiquette commands, she follows to the letter. No wonder, then, that no man in the village can approach her. There is not one of them who has not committed, and in her presence, some terrible sin, usually one known to be habitual with him. One eats peas with his knife, another bites mouthfuls out of a whole, undivided slice of bread—utterly condemnable according to the book. Only Young Robin Oakapple is blameless, but he is so shy he will not so much as make the attempt to approach her, and, according to etiquette,

> *It's most unladylike to hint—*
> *You may not hint—*
> *You must not hint—*
> *It says you mustn't hint, in print!*

The sweet maiden is in for a bit of a surprise. The bridesmaids have left now, and when Dame Hannah goes, Robin finds the courage to come near for the very first time. He actually speaks to her. Of course he speaks only about the weather, and that in the most general terms. But by the most delicate degrees this conversation develops into a duet:

> *I know a youth who loves a little maid—*
> *(Hey, but his face is a sight for to see!)*
> *Silent is he, for he's modest and afraid—*
> *(Hey, but he's timid as a youth can be!)*

For the moment of the song their meeting of hearts seems very close. But when Rose leaves him Robin despairs. In this state of dejection Old Adam finds him. "Sir Ruthven Murgatroyd" he calls, but Robin hastily shuts that off. He has remained incognito for twenty years, hiding his real identity among the yokels, trying to avoid the witch's curse. Until now this has been successful, for his brother Despard bears the brunt of the curse on the incorrect assumption that Sir Ruthven is dead.

Adam brings news. Robin's foster-brother Richard has arrived safely after a voyage across the sea. He has taken part in a battle with the French off Cape Finistère, and tells about it in a ballad:

> *I shipped, d'ye see, in a Revenue Sloop,*
> *And, off Cape Finistère,*
> *A merchantman we see,*
> *A Frenchman, going free,*
> *So we made for the bold Mounseer.*

Richard has been away ten years. Before he left, while they were boys, the two had sworn that no matter what the circumstances each would be ruled by his heart. For Dick, who has lived by this principle, Robin's difficulty in expressing his love for Rose Maybud is a simple knot to untangle. His heart tells him: go immediately to the young lady and speak with her in favor of his foster-brother. To Robin, the over-shy, the idea that hearty Dick will tackle the job means blessed relief. He leaves everything in Dick's hands.

When the emissary sets eyes upon the lady, the heart that once said "Speak for your brother" is overwhelmed by contrary orders. He wastes not a moment, but woos her for himself and awaits her reply.

Her reply may not be given off-hand. It is necessary first to make a thorough study of the question and its possible ramifications in the book of etiquette. Within its pages is the recipe for the proper handling of a proposal of marriage. She follows it to the letter. Ever so reluctantly, with a tear carefully released from one eye, she accepts him. The book permits one kiss (not to be prolonged). One kiss is exchanged, sealing the engagement that all the boys of the village had given up hoping for.

Robin was not prepared to hear such a report from his ambassador. He demands an explanation forthwith. It is simple enough; Dick follows the dictates of his heart as they both had pledged to do long, long ago. There is no further question about it; Robin accepts the change completely and stoutly defends his foster-brother as Rose Maybud, mentioning for the first time that she has always known that Robin was interested in her, tries to suggest (in spite of the book) that she might be able to change her mind should circumstances (the book) allow. Robin will not hear of it, even though he believes that he is a better catch than Richard. He explains that the heart must rule, and Richard's heart rules for Richard. Much to his surprise, however, Rose Maybud interprets the rule of her own heart and disengages herself from Richard by kissing Robin. One doubts that the book had indicated such a course of action. The happy couple leave the sailor submerged in his grief.

There is another lonely woman in Cornwall. It is Mad Margaret, who weeps a little song of flowers as Rose Maybud happens upon her. To Rose the possessed woman reveals her most searing secret—she intends to do away with one Rose Maybud because she is in love with Sir Despard whom Mad Margaret also loves. Rose tells her the rumor is not true, that she is actually engaged to someone else. This satisfies crazy Meg. Hearing a chorus approaching they slip away.

In come the Bucks and Blades, down from the city for a change of pace. The professional bridesmaids greet them. Enter the Baronet of Ruddigore, Sir Despard Murgatroyd. He is loathed and feared because daily crime has turned him into a terrifying person. He is cursed, as the witch provided so long ago for all his ancestors, but at least he has found a method for somewhat alleviating his condition. He gets up early every morning and gets the day's crime over with as soon as possible. Then he spends the rest of the day in good works: dedicating hospitals, giving to the poor, and so forth, in a desperate attempt to balance his account.

Dick, Robin's foster-brother, has sought out the Baronet because his heart has instructed him not to give up Rose Maybud to anyone, not even his foster-brother, without a fight. He therefore has a plan: he will tell the present Baronet that the supposedly dead elder brother is quite alive; in fact he is not far away. The indicated result is obvious: Dick and Despard will now drive this wedge between the two lovers, telling the bridegroom-elect that his identity is no longer secret and that he must now bear the weight of the incriminating curse.

The marriage ceremony has already begun, with madrigal and dance, with joy and celebration.

> When the buds are blossoming,
> Smiling welcome to the spring,
> Lovers choose a wedding day—
> Life is love in merry May!

This epithalamium ends with a stately gavotte. Until this moment the two celebrants have enjoyed uninterrupted happiness. Now Sir Despard casts joy out the window by pointing out Robin Oakapple and identifying him as Sir Ruthven Murgatroyd, rightful heir to Ruddigore and its horrible curse.

Rose is shocked. Having heard the evidence, she knows she cannot live with a man whose duty is criminal. Pointedly, therefore, she shuns her former fiancé and announces to one and all that she will marry Sir Despard. At this the bridesmaids, professional to the core, take up the nuptial song:

> Hail the bridegroom! Hail the bride!

But Sir Despard, no longer under the interdict of the witch, has become a good person now. He finds it urgent to countermand Rose's announcement, saying that he cannot take her because he is already engaged to Margaret, whom he adores. The bridesmaids surround her;

> Hail the bridegroom! Hail the bride!

And they embrace while Rose and Richard sing; then Rose and Richard embrace while others sing. Joy overflows—except for Robin. Sir Ruthven, newly accursed Baronet of Ruddigore tries to frighten people properly, then leaves with Old Adam.

ACT II

When we see Robin and Old Adam after their first week at Ruddigore, the Baronetcy has wreaked its havoc upon both. Robin is haggard, guilty. Once a weak and shy peasant, he is now Sir Ruthven Murgatroyd, a Bad Bart. It is one of Adam's daily chores to think up crimes for Robin to commit. Today Dick Dauntless has brought Rose Maybud to the castle, for it is necessary for peasants to have the Lord's permission to marry, whoever that Lord may chance to be. Adam recommends that today's crime be accomplished with poison, but Robin will not do it. It seems too heartless. When the couple finally stands before him all he can think of is to threaten prison. But Dick is fully prepared for anything. Over Rose's head he holds the Union Jack, a flag none dare defy. Robin's half-hearted plans are foiled again. He did love her; Rose reminds him of that. If he did, then, she suggests, and if he loves her still, he will grant her anything she asks. Just now her wish is to marry Dick Dauntless. How can the Baronet resist? The wish is granted.

At last Robin goes off to be alone among the portraits of his ancestors in the gallery. He speaks to them. They answer. One by one the paintings come to life and step from their frames, marching solemnly around the room singing of evil and the pleasures of their ghostly holidays at midnight. The most recently deceased, Sir Roderic, speaks for all. They have come to life for a purpose—to remind Robin of the terms of his curse. What crimes has he committed in this first week? Few, few indeed. Monday was a holiday, Tuesday he falsified his income tax—but that is too ordinary to be called a crime! His list of petty misdeeds shows evidence of a desperate inability to be criminal.

The ancestors are dissatisfied with this miserable showing. They suggest he do better, say, carry off a lady to prove he can be really bad if he puts his mind to it. Under subtle and invisible torture he is forced to accede, and the ghosts return to their frames to become painted portraits again. In haste to comply with the new demands, Robin sends Adam to the village to carry off a maiden, any maiden, while Robin paces the floor thinking that crime, like any other trade, must be studied.

As Robin has become wicked, so Despard has become a fine and outwardly formal gentleman. During the week of Robin's futile attempts at dastardliness, Despard and Margaret have been dancing with the joy of love. Once in a while Margaret suffers a slight relapse into madness, but there is a resounding exclamation which always calls her back, the word

Basingstoke! [name of a railway station]

It is the considered opinion of his noble brother that since Robin has actually been the true Baronet of Ruddigore all through Despard's occupancy of the castle, it must be Robin and not Despard who carries the guilt of all the crimes committed during the past ten years. Despard has now become a good man; it is abhorrent to him that his very brother should be so despicable a character. He therefore demands that Robin forsake crime, even though the consequence must be horrible death. Robin takes this under consideration:

My eyes are fully open to my awful situation.
I shall go at once to Roderic and make him an oration.

They sing together. When they are done, Old Adam slips in with the news that the day's crime has now been committed: the kidnapped maiden is already in the castle. It is Dame Hannah. No frail and cringing beauty she, she throws Robin a dagger and offers to do him battle with an ornamental sword snatched off the wall. "Uncle! Save me!" he yells. Sir Roderic steps out of his frame only to recognize "Little Nannikin," his old love. "Roddy-doddy!" Hannah cries. Their meeting is tenderness itself, although he has been dead these ten years while she bewailed him.

Suddenly an idea strikes Robin's mind. The curse stipulates that if he does not commit a crime in any one day, that day will he die. Therefore by *not* committing a crime, any cursed Baronet is committing suicide, which *is* a crime. Hence none of the Bad Barts should have died at all. This faultless logic permits the present, living Baronet to cease his awful career, to love Rose Maybud and to be loved by her. How doth true logic bring happiness to the disturbed!

HISTORICAL NOTE

Eighteen years before *Ruddigore* opened, Sullivan visited a rehearsal of a play in order to hear some music by his friend Frederick Clay. The play had a strange scene in it, one in which portraits came to life and took part in the drama. The play was *Ages Ago,* its author W. S. Gilbert. This was their first meeting. By the time their collaboration reached *Ruddigore,* both men had had vast experience in theater, and were working with Carte, who had provided them with a company and a house in which all the techniques they had learned could be put to the most imaginative uses. For *Ages Ago,* gas made the light and permitted only the most limited changes. For *Ruddigore* there were electricity and the incandescent lamp, which could be turned off and on at will so that, using banks of lights which allowed different numbers of lamps to be lit at different times, it was possible to make the stage gradually darken, even to a black-out. Hence when the ghosts of the Murgatroyds walked again, they came to life in blackness, and danced into the eerie gloom of a bewitched midnight.

Many technical problems had to be solved for this production. During the blackout it was necessary for the conductor to cue the orchestra and yet not have a bright light shining upon him. At first there was an attempt to use phosphorescent material on his baton, but it was difficult to see after a few moments. Finally a special baton was constructed: a glass tube with a fine platinum wire running from end to end, which could be attached to batteries which gave just enough power to make the wire glow a dull red. This worked.

Costumes were elaborate to the point, some might say, of absurdity. But it is well to remember that the detail that means little to us was familiar to the Londoners of 1887. They could recognize the fact that twenty regiments were accurately represented on the stage, all in uniforms of 1810, all correct down to the last button. Not that it would have mattered if there had been alterations or duplications, as far as the story went. It was only the intangible quality of richness in a D'Oyly Carte production that justified such meticulous care.

One week before the play was to open, the score was ready. For Sullivan this may have been some sort of record. There are, after all, many cases of chaotic late rehearsals when new songs were yet to be filled in by the composer. On the 19th of January *The Mikado* closed. The stage was set for *Ruddigore;* the dress rehearsals began in earnest, sometimes lasting until dawn. On the 22nd the new play opened before an audience of the most important people in London.

The authors received a rude shock that night. Somebody booed. By the time the second act was half over the feeling of dissatisfaction was noticeable. The last part dragged. Next morning there were bad reviews mixed with the usual, and less important, good ones. Gilbert and Sullivan put their heads together for a post-mortem. Some of the reviews had criticized certain Old Gilbertianisms, saying that the audience was getting tired of these sway-backed hacks. There were remarks—there had been all along—about the title, which was somewhat offensive to a culture in which *Ruddy* meant *Bloody,* and *Bloody* was a dirty word. No matter how Gilbert tried to remind the world of the true meaning of the word, the offended ones remained offended. Even from France came recriminations about the insult to their navy implied in Dick Dauntless's song "I shipped, d'ye see, in a Revenue sloop." The French objected to being called "Mounseers," and "Parley-voos." Gilbert wrote a letter to a Parisian paper explaining that this was no more intended to be insulting than the French reference to British "goddams," and so forth. All in all, something had to be done.

The title, which had been argued about for weeks, was finally changed from *Ruddygore* to *Ruddigore.* Gilbert had once suggested "Kensington Gore, or, Not so good as the Mikado." Other changes were made here and there, but Dauntless's song remained, and the so-called Old Gilbertianisms were not taken out. The play ran nearly a year before its audience dwindled, and that may be considered a rather successful run.

During the summer of 1886, when Sullivan was beginning his work on the score of *Ruddigore,* his attention was focused more intently on *The Golden Legend,* an oratorio for the October Festival at Leeds. It is ludicrous now to think of the two libretti together, the one stuffed with topsy-turvy nonsense flavored with political and social barbs which still have some edge, the other ultra-purified, and made holy with fine words and elegant, if dull, phrases. Each of the scripts is unbelievable, but the one was intended as such, the other not. When *The Golden Legend* was first heard, it caused a sensation. At last the Composer of the Empire had equalled what had been dreamed for him by all those who urged him on since he first won the Mendelssohn Scholarship. Some may have hoped he would never again sully his soul with the music-hall smoke. But as soon as the oratorio was out of the way, Gilbert and Carte reminded Sullivan of his contract, and he resumed work on *Ruddigore*. The flush of apotheosis must have still affected him, however. Gilbert later remarked that the music of the ghost scene was more fitting for a serious work than for a comic-opera, and that it threw the lightness of the first act out of balance. This was very close to the criticism Gilbert had made of the first Sullivan work he ever reviewed, back in the time when he made his living writing a column for *Fun*. The quarrel about the imbalance of their collaboration began to become serious during the composition of *Ruddigore,* and was not resolved. In fact, it continued through the work on *Yeomen of the Guard* and was only temporarily smoothed over at the time of *Gondoliers* in 1889.

The D'Oyly Carte Company also suffered a few minor disturbances during the run of *Ruddigore*. But the only trouble worthy of mention here was at once bad and good. Within a week of the opening, George Grossmith was hospitalized and operated upon for peritonitis. Henry Lytton replaced him, and went on to become one of the most famous of all the Company. Another member, Durward Lely, had inadvertently mentioned during a rehearsal that a sailor's hornpipe might be appropriate. Pretty soon he found himself taking lessons from a ballet master and performing the violent dance. Gilbert, of course, was always open to suggestion.

All in all, Sullivan did not feel satisfied with his part in the work. To him it seemed to be less an opera than a play with a few songs here and there. Gilbert, on the other hand, thought that the music overshadowed his words. Their dissatisfaction with the work added to the discomfort of the already long-drawn-out personal quarrel.

Ruddigore is one of the more expensive operas of the series, with complicated costumes (designed in detail by the author of the play), and fairly elaborate stage mechanisms. This prevented any revivals until 1920, when it met with great success.

The Yeomen of the Guard

OR, THE MERRYMAN AND HIS MAID

First performed at the Savoy Theater, London, 3 October 1888   TWO ACTS

CAST

SIR RICHARD CHOLMONDELEY, *Lieutenant of the Tower*	Bar
COLONEL FAIRFAX, *under sentence of death*	T
SERGEANT MERYLL, *of the Yeomen of the Guard*	BBar
LEONARD MERYLL, *his son*	T
JACK POINT, *a strolling jester*	Bar
WILFRED SHADBOLT, *Head Jailer and Assistant Tormentor*	B
THE HEADSMAN	Mute
FIRST YEOMAN	T
SECOND YEOMAN	Bar
FIRST CITIZEN	Spkr
SECOND CITIZEN	Spkr
ELSIE MAYNARD, *a strolling singer*	S
PHOEBE MERYLL, *Sergeant Meryll's daughter*	MS
DAME CARRUTHERS, *housekeeper to the Tower*	C
KATE, *her niece*	S
Yeomen of the Guard, Gentlemen, Citizens	Chorus

SETTING

Scene: The Green of the Tower of London.
Time: The sixteenth century.

SONGS AND CHORUSES

ACT I

Song: When maiden loves, she sits and sighs (*Phoebe*)
Chorus: Tower Warders, Under orders (*People and Yeomen*)
Song: When our gallant Norman foes (*Dame Carruthers and Yeomen*)
Trio: Alas! I waver to and fro! (*Phoebe, Leonard, Meryll*)

Ballad: Is life a boon? (*Fairfax*)
Duet: I have a song to sing, O! (*Elsie, Jack Point*)
Trio: How say you, maiden, will you wed (*Elsie, Point, Lieutenant*)
Recit. and song: I've jibe and joke (*Point*)
Recit. and song: 'Tis done! I am a bride! Oh, little ring (*Elsie*)
Song: Were I thy bride (*Phoebe*)
Finale:

> *Chorus:* Oh, Sergeant Meryll, is it true— (*Yeomen*)
> *Chorus:* Leonard Meryll! Leonard Meryll! (*Yeomen*)
> *Couplets:* Didst thou not, oh, Leonard Meryll! (*1st and 2nd Yeomen*)
> *Trio:* To thy fraternal care (*Wilfred, Fairfax, Phoebe*)
> *Solo:* Oh, Mercy, thou whose smile has shone (*Elsie, Chorus*)
> *Trio:* As escort for the prisoner (*Fairfax and two Yeomen*)
> *Solo:* Oh, woe, is *you?* Your anguish sink! (*Point*)
> *Ensemble:* All frenzied with despair I rave, (*Lieutenant and Chorus*)

ACT II

Chorus: Night has spread her pall once more (*Chorus*)
Solo: Warders are ye? (*Dame Carruthers*)
Song: Oh! a private buffoon is a light-hearted loon, (*Point*)
Duet: Hereupon we're both agreed, (*Point, Wilfred*)
Ballad: Free from his fetters grim— (*Fairfax*)
Quartet: Strange adventure! Maiden wedded (*Fairfax, Sergeant Meryll, Dame Carruthers, Kate*)
Duet and Chorus: Like a ghost his vigil keeping— (*Wilfred, Point, Chorus*)
Trio: A man who would woo a fair maid (*Elsie, Phoebe, Fairfax*)
Quartet: When a wooer goes a-wooing (*Elsie, Phoebe, Fairfax, Point*)
Duet: Rapture, rapture when love's votary (*Dame Carruthers, Sergeant Meryll*)
Finale

> *Elegiacs:* Comes the pretty young bride, a-blushing, timidly shrinking— (*Chorus of women*)
> *Ensemble:* Oh, day of terror! Day of tears! (*Ensemble*)
> *Solo:* Oh, thoughtless crew! (*Point*)

SYNOPSIS

ACT I

On Tower Green, alone at her spinning, surrounded by the walks and turrets, the hulking battlements that make up the Tower of London, sits Phoebe, singing sadly to herself as she broods over the coming execution of the young and handsome Colonel Fairfax. This poor unfortunate, about to add his blood to the dried-up stains of centuries in that prison, is condemned, according to Wilfred Shadbolt, for having had dealings with the Devil. Wilfred is considerably put out because Phoebe is so concerned about Fairfax. He is, indeed, jealous, for he has been in love with Phoebe for a long time and has had no success. They go off separately.

A crowd of people enter with the colorfully dressed Yeomen of the Guard, sing a chorus, then disperse. The Yeomen talk with Dame Carruthers. There was a fire in the Beauchamp Tower last night, and the housekeeper has her hands full today because of it. One of its inmates was Colonel Fairfax. Since today is to be his last, it is the responsibility of Dame Carruthers to prepare his final cell for him. She is a life-long resident of the place, born in the old Norman Keep (The White Tower) in the center of the green, and she has grown gray in service within these walls. She is proud of the history that surrounds her:

When our gallant Norman foes
Made our merry land their own,
   And the Saxons from the Conquerer were flying,
At his bidding it arose,
In its panoply of stone,
   A sentinel unliving and undying.

Phoebe is left by herself. Her father, Sergeant Meryll, enters and tells her that her brother Leonard, a national hero at the moment because of his extreme bravery in battle, has been appointed as Yeoman of the Guard and will arrive today. It is just barely possible he'll have with him a royal reprieve for Colonel Fairfax, for whom Sergeant Meryll, whose life the gentleman had twice saved, has high regard.

But Leonard brings no reprieve. He is as sad as his father because of it—but no reprieve was granted. Since no one saw Leonard come, and since he, too, would do anything to save Colonel Fairfax, Sergeant Meryll works out a plan by which the prisoner may escape. Leonard will lend Fairfax his uniform and then stay out of sight, letting Fairfax take his place until he can slip away in safety. It is a dangerous scheme; to get him out, Phoebe must get the keys to the Colonel's new cell from Wilfred Shadbolt,

And shall we reckon risks we run
To save the life of such an one?
   Unworthy thought!

At this moment the condemned man appears on his way from the Beauchamp Tower to his solitary death cell in Cold Harbour Tower, guarded. He is brave; he faces death this time with an appreciation of the fact that it will come at an appointed time and place, efficiently. He would rather have it that way than not to know when to expect it.

> *Is life a thorn?*
> *Then count it not a whit!*
> *Man is well done with it.*

Phoebe weeps. Her father takes her away. Colonel Fairfax has but one request to make of the lieutenant: his cousin, one of the Secretaries of State, has had him charged with sorcery in order that he, the cousin, may inherit the Colonel's estate (he dying unmarried). The condemned man asks that someone, anyone, be persuaded to marry him. She will be a widow tomorrow, with one hundred crowns to spend. This would thwart the cousin properly. The Lieutenant, who holds such a treacherous brother in contempt, is willing to let the marriage take place even though the request is most extraordinary.

At this moment, Jack Point and Elsie Maynard, entertainers, the one a fool and the other a singer, are driven into the Tower grounds by a crowd of rowdy Londoners who scream to be shown some fun or they will throw both into the filthy river. Their demand, after some argument, is fulfilled with:

> POINT: *I have a song to sing, O!*
> ELSIE: *Sing me your song, O!*
> POINT: *It is sung to the moon*
> *By a love-lorn loon,*
> *Who fled from the mocking throng, O!*
> *It's a song of a merryman, moping mum,*
> *Whose soul was sad, and whose glance was glum,*
> *Who sipped no sup, and who craved no crumb,*
> *As he sighed for the love of a ladye.*
> *Heighdy! Heighdy!*
> *Misery me, lackadaydee!*

Music to soothe any mob. But the turmoil recommences shortly after the song's spell has worn off. It takes the sight of the Lieutenant and his armed guard to save Jack Point and Elsie from further attack.

Elsie, not married, is a perfect candidate for the bride of the condemned Colonel Fairfax. There is a hundred crowns in it for her if she agrees. But Jack wishes to be sure, before he gives *his* consent, that the proposed husband will surely make her a widow within the hour. The girl, too, thinks it over, then allows her eyes to be blindfolded and herself conveyed to the death cell in Cold Harbour Tower.

What is to be done with Jack Point? The Lieutenant decides he would like a jester in his own household, and opens preliminary discussions toward a contract with Jack. He tests him with hypothetical situations to which Jack supplies ready jests, none of which seem satisfying to the Lieutenant, who is preoccupied with the duties of his position. Just as they leave, Wilfred escorts the still blindfolded Elsie, now a bride, out of Cold Harbour. In half an hour she is to become a widow.

> *O weary wives*
> *Who widowhood would win,*
> *Rejoice that ye have time*
> *To weary in.*

Wilfred was not permitted to see the ceremony; the keyhole had been deliberately stopped up. He would very much like to know just what went on in there. While he thinks about it, Phoebe comes to speak with him about the prisoner. Poor Wilfred is so jealous of her love for the Colonel that he does not notice her stealing the very key to the cell from his belt and handing it to Sergeant Meryll under cover of conversation. While the Sergeant is busy, Phoebe keeps the jailer occupied with a song:

> *Were I thy bride,*
> *Then all the world beside*
> *Were not too wide*
> *To hold my wealth of love—*
> *Were I thy bride.*

And while she sings, the Sergeant slips the key back into her hand and she refastens it on Wilfred's belt without his once suspecting. The song ends:

> *But then, of course, you see,*
> *I'm not thy bride!*

As soon as Wilfred leaves, Sergeant Meryll brings out Colonel Fairfax, shaven and dressed as a Beefeater. There is just time to remind him that his new name is Leonard Meryll before the rest of the Yeomen come in. One and all are thrilled to have heroic "Leonard Meryll" in their company. They sing his praises in full chorus.

When they are done, the disguised man is nearly undone by not knowing who Phoebe is supposed to be. But Phoebe rushes into his arms to claim him loudly as her long-absent hero brother. Fairfax has not been told about Phoebe, but fortunately no one notices his look of bewilderment. Wilfred commends his girl to "her brother's" care, and preparations are started for the immediate execution of Colonel Fairfax. The false Leonard Meryll and two other guards are dispatched to bring in the prisoner. It is the disguised one who has the pleasure of shouting:

> *He is not there!*

There is not a trace to show how the prisoner escaped. The Lieutenant has Wilfred arrested on the spot, but Wilfred is not the only one sorely surprised: Elsie Maynard is now married to a man who is *not* dead, and Jack Point has lost his sweetheart.

ACT II

Two days pass. It is night, and there is no trace yet of Colonel Fairfax. Dame Carruthers is utterly disgusted with the Tower Warders. Every nook and cranny of the Tower has been searched, but no prisoner has been found out of his cell. The guards are in despair. So is Wilfred. So is Jack Point, but for more important reasons. For diversion, Wilfred suggests to Jack that he would like to become a professional wit. Jack tells him some of the details of the life of a jester, then agrees to teach Wilfred the art of being a fool in exchange for a bit of false testimony by which Jack's sweetheart will be free again. Wilfred is to say he shot the prisoner as he jumped into the river in the act of escaping—a story that can be told without the necessity of physical evidence to support it. Thus Elsie will become, in the eyes of the law, a widow, eligible to marry Jack. With a shake of hands the deal is concluded.

For his part, the living Fairfax is perplexed to be free in one sense, but still a prisoner in another—he is married to a woman he has never actually seen. While he speaks to Sergeant Meryll, Dame Carruthers (thinking Fairfax is Leonard Meryll) comes to warn him that she believes Elsie Maynard is attracted to him. He is not to allow an attachment to develop, because, the Dame knows, although she knows little else about it, the girl is married to the escaped prisoner. This identification of the bride is not unpleasing to the disguised Fairfax. At the first opportunity he woos the maiden, in the name of Leonard, to see how she reacts. He pleads with her to marry him. This she would, willingly, but for the fact that she is already married. He begs her to come away with him anyway, but the good girl will not hear of such a scandalous project. At this moment they hear a shot from the river's edge. It brings the whole cadre of the Guard to the green.

Wilfred runs in, with Jack Point close behind. It was he, Wilfred claims, who fired the shot. And in a detailed and heavily dramatic narrative, punctuated by Jack's editorial remarks, Wilfred describes how he caught the escapee somewhere within the walls, fought with him and lost him into the water where he, who could not swim, could not follow. Snatching a gun from a conveniently posted sentry he shot the man through the head as the current carried him away. Now Wilfred, who had recently been ready for the axe, is a hero.

Jack Point is happy now that Elsie is a widow. He describes the face of the dead man in such terms that the living Fairfax swears under his breath to repay the fool for such insults. When Jack prepares once more to offer marriage to Elsie, the false Leonard Meryll interrupts to criticize the way he woos. Thereupon, with the fool's acquiescence, the disguised prisoner proceeds, as if it were an academic situation, to kiss the girl. Needless to say, neither Phoebe nor the jester is amused.

> *When a jester*
> *Is outwitted,*
> *Feelings fester.*
> *Heart is lead!*

Phoebe is so broken-hearted that her solitary weeping interests Wilfred very much. When he hears that it is caused by the affair with Elsie Maynard, Wilfred is deeply shocked. How could the girl be so jealous of her own brother? It must not be her brother. It must be Fairfax!

Phoebe is alarmed. She points out that Wilfred has just made public claim that he shot Fairfax. That quiets him for the moment. But to save the Colonel permanently she agrees to marry Wilfred, although she considers him a brute.

> WILFRED: *My beloved!* (*Embracing her*)
> PHOEBE: (*Aside*) *Ugh!*

The real Leonard Meryll runs in, out of breath. He has great news. A reprieve for Colonel Fairfax has been delivered to the Lieutenant. It was purposely held up by the conniving Secretary of State, but Fairfax is now a free man! Phoebe smothers the messenger with kisses (much to Wilfred's amazement).

But the eavesdropping Dame Carruthers hears the news; now she understands the part Sergeant Meryll, whom she yearns for, must have played in the conspiracy. To buy her silence as his daughter did Wilfred's, the poor guard sacrifices himself to her in marriage.

> *Doleful, doleful!*
> *When humanity*
> *With its soul full*
> *Of satanity,*
> *Courting privity,*
> *Down declivity*
> *Seeks captivity!*
> *Doleful, doleful!*

And thus three bridegrooms take three brides. But Fairfax and Elsie have already had their ceremony. At first she misunderstands, thinking the Leonard Meryll she loves is someone other than the Fairfax who faces her. But when she finally looks directly into that face, the joy of recognition replaces her sorrow.

Only Jack Point is unhappy. Jack Point has lost his sweetheart:

Heighdy, heighdy!
Misery me, lackadaydee!
He sipped no sup, and he craved no crumb,
As he sighed for the love of a ladye!

As the beautiful song ends, the fool falls insensible at the feet of the girl he lost through chance.

HISTORICAL NOTE

Gilbert himself said that the idea for an opera on the general subject of the Guards at the Tower of London—the Beefeaters—came to him one day as he stood in a railway station gazing at a poster which advertised furnishings, with a large picture of the Tower. The author was under pressure from Sullivan and Carte to invent a plot that would *not* depend upon magic lozenges or evil potions to make its characters interesting, and that would not be set in the same old topsy-turvy world that had been worn to a nubbin by so many previous libretti. By December of 1887 he had an outline ready for discussion. No axe-grinding was involved, no butt for ridicule could be seen in it. There was humor, but without ulterior motive. Essentially it was a simple story of a prisoner, with characters perhaps more realistic than most of the stereotypes that had been developed in the company.

It was the year of Queen Victoria's jubilee, and an opera on so historical a subject was certainly appropriate. Some of the details of *The Yeomen* can be traced to other sources, although the play itself, unlike most of its predecessors, was not originally worked out in a ballad or any other form. The marriage scene, with the prisoner prevented from knowing the identity of the bride, or what she looked like, figured in the opera *Maritana*, which was popular in Gilbert's time. The famous song "I have a song to sing, O!" was written around Gilbert's recollection of an older English folksong, known in slightly different form in the backwoods of Tennessee and Kentucky. Sullivan, having Gilbert's words before him and realizing that the author must have had a particular tune in mind, asked his collaborator to hum a bit of it. Hardly had Gilbert begun to tune up than Sullivan stopped him, saying he had it. He was so stimulated by the first note or two that he was able to rush home and compose one of the most beautiful pieces of music in the whole tradition of Gilbert and Sullivan operas.

Gilbert did everything he could to please Sullivan and to avoid a recurrence of their old personal differences. For lyric after lyric he supplied alternate versions, so that the composer could have a choice of word-rhythms to work with. As was usual with him, he immersed himself in the physical atmosphere he wanted to re-create on stage, spending many a drizzly day rambling about the grounds within the walls of the complex Tower of London, thinking of past times and past styles of speech, dress and gesture. He read much from the period, the sixteenth century, to help him with the feeling of the language. All this work was well justified by the smooth jointing and natural style of the resultant play.

But Sullivan was not entirely mollified by his friend's efforts to be serviceable. While he worked, on vacation in Monte Carlo, he heard that Cellier's *Dorothy*, at the Gaiety (bigger than the Savoy) had reached its 500th performance. In terror at that cloud on the horizon, he wired Gilbert that something drastic must be done. As a matter of fact, *Dorothy* did even better, closing finally after 931 nights. But compared with the steady success of the team of Gilbert and Sullivan, it would seem that this was nothing much to worry about.

The Yeomen of the Guard stands apart from all the other works of the pair in its seriousness and the reality of its characters. Though he usually reproduced stereotyped caricatures of people, Gilbert became much more involved in the personalities in *The Yeomen*. Phoebe and Elsie are more interesting and human than their counterparts in *Patience, The Pirates of Penzance* and *The Sorcerer*. Even Shadbolt and Sergeant Meryll have some reality inside the uniforms. But Jack Point fairly kidnapped his creator, becoming not only a very real character, but one who demands such sympathy from the audience that his personal tragedy—the loss of his fiancée to another—very nearly turns the intended comedy into a sad play. Actors have tried to play him in various modes, sometimes as a clown, sometimes as a tragic character. But the play as a whole will not be forced either way. Jack Point is an uneasiness in the structure, a symbol of meaning not fully explained by his actions.

The night *The Yeomen of the Guard* opened—it was a Wednesday instead of the usual Saturday—the professional Gilbert behaved like a nervous expectant father. He popped up here and there backstage with an unsettling word or two for any actor he could buttonhole. Nobody can be at ease on an opening night, but the author's worries unnerved everyone. This is the only one of the operas that opens with a solitary person on stage. Jessie Bond, trying to compose herself for that moment, finally had to urge Gilbert to leave before the overture—which was already in progress—ended and the curtain would rise to reveal him. "Please go, Mr. Gilbert, please go!" she begged, trying to remember how she had constructed her characterization. Gilbert left, stumbled out of the theater and walked over to Drury Lane to sit in the darkness at somebody else's play until his own had been presented. When he returned he found that *The Yeomen of the Guard* had already proven itself, with nine resounding encores.

{ 98 }

The Gondoliers

OR, THE KING OF BARATARIA

First performed at the Savoy Theater, London,
7 December 1889

TWO ACTS

CAST

THE DUKE OF PLAZA-TORO, *a grandee of Spain*	Bar
LUIZ, *his attendant*	T
DON ALHAMBRA DEL BOLERO, *the Grand Inquisitor*	B
MARCO PALMIERI, *Venetian gondolier, Giuseppe's brother*	T
GIUSEPPE PALMIERI, *Venetian gondolier, Marco's brother*	Bar
ANTONIO, *gondolier*	Bar
FRANCESCO, *gondolier*	T
GIORGIO, *gondolier*	B
ANNIBALE, *gondolier*	Spkr
THE DUCHESS OF PLAZA-TORO	C
CASILDA, *her daughter*	S
GIANETTA, *contadina*	S
TESSA, *contadina*	MS
FIAMETTA, *contadina*	S
VITTORIA, *contadina*	MS
GIULIA, *contadina*	S
INEZ, *former foster-mother of the king*	C
Gondoliers, Contadine, Men-at-arms, Heralds, Pages	Chorus

SETTING

ACT I: The piazzetta, Venice, about 1750.
ACT II: Pavilion in the Palace of Barataria, three months later.

SONGS AND CHORUSES

ACT I

Chorus: List and learn, ye dainty roses (*Chorus of Contadine*)
Song: For the merriest fellows are we, tra la (*Antonio, Chorus*)

Duet: Buon' giorno, signorine! (*Marco, Giuseppe, Girls*)
Duet: We're called *gondolieri* (*Marco, Giuseppe*)
Song: Thank you, gallant *gondolieri!* (*Gianetta, Tessa, Chorus*)
Ensemble: From the sunny Spanish shore (*Duke, Duchess, Casilda, Luiz*)
Song: In enterprise of martial kind (*Duke*)
Recit. and duet: O rapture, when alone together (*Casilda, Luiz*)
Duet: There was a time— (*Casilda, Luiz*)
Song: I stole the Prince, and brought him here (*Don Alhambra, Ensemble*)
Quintet: Try we life-long, we can never (*Duke, Duchess, Casilda, Luiz, Grand Inquisitor*)
Song: When a merry maiden marries (*Tessa, Chorus*)
Finale

> *Song:* Kind sir, you cannot have the heart (*Gianetta*)
> *Quartet:* Then one of us will be a Queen (*Marco, Giuseppe, Gianetta, Tessa*)
> *Duet:* For every one who feels inclined (*Marco, Giuseppe, Chorus*)
> *Duet:* Now, Marco dear (*Gianetta, Tessa*)
> *Chorus:* Then away we go to an island fair (*Chorus*)

ACT II

Chorus: Of happiness the very pith (*Marco, Giuseppe, Chorus*)
Song: Rising early in the morning (*Giuseppe, Chorus*)
Song: Take a pair of sparkling eyes (*Marco*)
Chorus and Dance: Dance a cachucha, fandango, bolero (*Chorus*)
Song: There lived a King, as I've been told (*Don Alhambra, Marco, Giuseppe*)
Quartet: In a contemplative fashion (*Marco, Giuseppe, Gianetta, Tessa*)
Chorus: With ducal pomp and ducal pride (*Duke, Duchess, Men*)
Song: On the day when I was wedded (*Duchess*)
Duet: Small titles and orders (*Duke, Duchess*)
Gavotte: I am a courtier grave and serious (*Duke, Duchess, Casilda, Marco, Giuseppe*)
Quintet: Here is a case unprecedented! (*Marco, Giuseppe, Casilda, Gianetta, Tessa*)
Finale

> *Recit.:* Now let the loyal lieges gather round— (*Don Alhambra, Ensemble*)

SYNOPSIS

ACT I

Just outside the palace of the Duke of Venice, on the piazzetta which leads to the water's edge where gondolas tie-up, the *contadine* (country girls) busy themselves tying bouquets of roses white and roses red. Sadness grips each tender heart. There are two gondoliers more handsome and desirable than all the others—but only two; whereas there are twenty-four lovesick maidens pining to become brides! The other, less adorable, gondoliers stroll in, one by one, to plead with them for a fair share of the girls' attention. But with their hearts full of longing for the unattainable, these substitutes are below consideration. Marco and Giuseppe Palmieri must first choose their brides; then and only then will the remaining twenty-two heartbroken girls be able to look at other men. As Vittoria puts it so neatly;

In the meantime we tacitly ignore you.

The two heroes have arrived in their gondola and step ashore only to be mobbed by adoring females who drown them in sighs and bury them in mountains of flowers. In order to be fair and princely, considering that most of the girls are pretty enough and *all* are lovesick, Marco and Giuseppe formally announce a method by which they will each be able to choose a bride, then and there, in such manner that the choice shall be entirely impartial and controlled solely by chance. Each permits himself to be blindfolded, with Vittoria and Fiametta making sure that the blindfolds are thoroughly effective. Then, in a game of blindman's buff, the brides are chosen: Gianetta for Marco, Tessa for Giuseppe. Now all the others are free of longing; every girl may find her substitute groom and go off with him.

There is a flourish of brass. Fresh from Spain, bedraggled by an arduous voyage, the Duke of Plaza-Toro arrives with his Duchess, his daughter Casilda and his attendant (his "private drum") Luiz, each of whom is determined never to set foot on deck again if ever they get back to Spain alive. The Duke is somewhat disappointed not to be met by a large military guard of honor and to see no brass band firing the crowd with its music. In fact, there is no crowd. According to Luiz no such demonstration could be arranged without paying the performers in advance, and this was, deplorably, out of the question.

The Duke sends his lackey to ring the bell and inform the Grand Inquisitor of his safe arrival. In privacy for the moment, with the menial gone, he takes the opportunity to divulge a family secret, kept even from his daughter for all these twenty years. It is that she was married by proxy, while still a baby, to the infant son of the "immeasurably wealthy king of Barataria."

Casilda is shocked and dismayed. Of course, she had no choice in the matter, and she considers that her father has taken an unpardonable liberty. But he explains that the King, her father-in-law, had been censured by the Grand Inquisitor for having become a convert to Wesleyan

Methodism, a forbidden sect. Later he died in a local insurrection. His baby son was stolen away, however, and resides now, a grown man, somewhere in Venice. This is the reason for the Duke's uncomfortable journey across the sea: to bring his daughter, the rightful Queen of Barataria, to her husband—wherever in Venice the young man may be found.

Incidentally, the Duke is penniless at the moment, but he has at least taken the preliminary steps necessary to ameliorate this condition by incorporating himself as a public, limited company, and appointing an influential board of directors. He suppresses his daughter's objections to such ignominy by explaining to her that he does not follow fashions, but leads them, as he did in days gone by when he was in the military.

> In enterprise of martial kind,
> When there was any fighting,
> He led his regiment from behind—
> He found it less exciting.
> But when away his regiment ran,
> His place was at the fore, O—
>   That celebrated,
>   Cultivated,
>   Underrated
>   Nobleman,
> The Duke of Plaza-Toro!

He leaves, taking the Duchess with him into the palace. The moment they are gone, Casilda, who is deeply in love with Luiz, rushes into his arms. Tearfully she tells him of her proxy marriage. Luiz has heard the story of the King's son; his own mother had been the nurse entrusted with the young prince's care at the time when he was abducted. But Casilda's fate is legally sealed. All the lovers can do is recollect their mutual affection and reinforce their memories with kisses. Sadly they sing:

> There was a time—
> A time forever gone—ah, woe is me!
> It was no crime
> To love but thee alone—ah, woe is me!
> One heart, one life, one soul,
> One aim, one goal—
> Each in the other's thrall,
> Each all in all, ah, woe is me!

In comes the Duke with his Duchess and the Grand Inquisitor Don Alhambra del Bolero. Introductions finished, the Duchess immediately (and in the best tradition of Victorian ladies) raises the important question: where is the young prince, Casilda's husband? For a moment, all too brief, the girl hopes that the prince may be permanently among the missing. But Don Alhambra crushes her with a song explaining everything:

> *I stole the Prince, and brought him here,*
> *And left him gaily prattling*
> *With a highly respectable gondolier,*
> *Who promised the Royal babe to rear,*
> *And teach him the trade of a timoneer*
> *With his own beloved bratling.*

Both the babies were healthy, each grew up to be a strong young man, so much alike that the old gondolier, who saw things through a never-lifted haze of alcohol, at last could not remember which was his own son and which the Prince of Barataria. In other words, either Marco or Giuseppe is the real prince, but Don Alhambra does not know which. But in any case there is hope, for the nurse who cared for the prince before Don Alhambra stole him away will be able to identify him for certain. She is Luiz's mother, and Luiz is sent to find her.

A crowd of girls and gondoliers dances in, bubbling with joy over the double wedding of Tessa with Giuseppe and Gianetta with Marco. But the black-robed solemnity of Don Alhambra interrupts their revelry. Thinking him to be nothing but an undertaker (a bad omen for newly-marrieds, but something to be dealt with and gotten rid of as quickly as possible), Giuseppe proudly tells him that they are all just married, they are all ardent republicans, two are sons of a famous revolutionary leader, and that since they detest rank and station (particularly kings and clerics) he should take his rank and station it elsewhere. When Don Alhambra informs them that he knows that one of them is the rightful King of Barataria, they are taken aback. Grudgingly they must now admit that not all kings are wholly objectionable. Each would strive to be a good king. Since only one such office is available, Don Alhambra brings the matter to a practical decision by suggesting that the two candidates join arms, so to speak, and rule together as King of Barataria until Luiz's mother can be found and a proper identification concluded.

There is, however, one small detail. Don Alhambra can hardly find words to express it without giving away his other secret. The kings may not take their wives with them—at least not yet. He will not say why, but women are not admitted, at this stage of events, to the palace.

The Don leaves, removing his ornamental black shadow from the previously joyful scene. For the last time together the girls and gondoliers celebrate in a grand finale before setting off for the new, all-male kingdom. Gianetta and Tessa are left—with all the other gondoliers' wives—to wonder why this strange prohibition has been established against them.

ACT II

In the pavilion of the Palace of Barataria, three months later, the two who are King, seated on identical thrones of state, with all their old friends, the former gondoliers, dressed in various uniforms and robes of office before them, rejoice in their perfect unanimity, and in the happiness and wealth of their shared realm. Royal affairs are run on strictly republican lines. All affairs of state are handled by experts. The King(s) take it upon themselves to do all the remaining little jobs that need doing about the palace, such as polishing the Regalia and the Coronation Plate—the things a King is called upon to do in these constitutional times. The only sadness amidst their bliss is that they miss their brand new, three-months distant, wives.

Back home in Venice the time has hung heavily also over the girls—all twenty-four girls. They have decided that they can stand it no longer. Borrowing a ship, they have crossed the sea against the strict orders of the Grand Inquisitor, and are now bursting into the palace to find their husbands. Everyone—at least, everyone who is still young—is happy again. Still, Luiz's mother had not yet arrived to identify the real King. This prevents the couples from being completely happy; for after all, one of the brides is about to become a Queen, but nobody knows which one. But in the simple joy of being together again and in Barataria, they all dance a Cachucha.

Scandalized at the promiscuous mixing of lowly servants with haughty royalty, Don Alhambra calls a halt to the frivolity and lectures the crest-fallen Kings on their impossible plebeianism. That done, he gets down to business. The Duke and Duchess of Plaza-Toro, recently incorporated, together with their beautiful daughter Casilda, have at last arrived in Barataria. This is the time for Don Alhambra to announce that the one who is the rightful ruler (but who knows which?) is also, by proxy, the husband of that incomparable lady. His Highness appears to be, therefore, unintentionally a bigamist; but this can be straightened out. The news causes no end of concern to Tessa and Gianetta, neither of whom has a chance now of becoming Queen. Don Alhambra, having delivered his message, goes off to speak with Luiz's mother, who is already in the palace torture chamber—strictly routine of the day—awaiting the interview.

The Duke, the Duchess, and the little girl who is Queen enter the palace of Barataria with stately pomp and in richest magnificence. The Duke sends lackeys to announce his safe arrival. Altogether, this great moment fully makes up for the miserable way he was greeted in Venice. When they have a moment alone, Casilda asks her parents just how she may be expected to love a husband she was not able to choose for herself? Her mother replies that the passage of time can work wonders with one's feelings in that respect. She herself, after all, had once found it impossible to love the Duke. She had tried to be demure, but this accomplished nothing but an increase in his imperiousness. Later she discovered that by keeping up a threatening appearance, by domineering, she could tame him with ease. She then came to love him, and has kept him in abject subjection ever since. But Casilda complains that she simply cannot love this husband under *any* circumstances. She hopes only that he will withdraw his claim to her when he hears of the shady nature of the family he is marrying into. This the Duke protests. He has made quite a sum of money since his legal incorporation, by selling titles and unimportant orders to rich people of the lower classes, giving testimonials for patent medicines and the like. He sees nothing at all improper in this fast-growing business.

At this moment the two royal gondoliers enter to receive the visiting Duke and Duchess and to meet the girl one of them is said to be married to. This meeting turns out to be quite flat, for Casilda cannot work up any spark of her usual vivacity when she considers how deeply she loves Luiz, and how unhappy she is at the prospect of marrying one of these Venetians. Still, no one knows which gondolier is the real King. Nothing at all can go forward until that identification has been determined. There is little to do but wait.

The Duke seizes the moment to complain of the niggardliness of his reception in Barataria, the lack of a proper number of saluting guns and of bands of musicians. Marco and Giuseppe reply that theirs is a republican kingdom where all are on an equal footing; hence such salutes are impossible and out of place. To this the Duke retorts that their present position demands at least a certain etiquette, even though they harbor these revolutionary ideas. In an elaborate gavotte he endeavors to instruct these bumpkins in the gentle art of noble manners.

When Giuseppe and Marco at last have a moment alone with Casilda, they express their very great sorrow for the fact that they are each already married.

> *O moralists all,*
> *How can you call*
> *Marriage a state of unitee,*
> *When excellent husbands are bisected,*
> *And wives divisible into three?*

At last the truth is discovered. Don Alhambra enters the royal presence to announce that Luiz's mother is ready to declare which young man is the true King of Barataria. The wracked old woman is brought in and everyone urges her to speak. In a brief recital of the history of the case, she reveals that when traitors came to her house so long ago to steal the little prince, she substituted her own little boy and kept the royal child in his place. That royal prince is Luiz; it is he who is the real king of Barataria and husband to Casilda.

With great rejoicing Luiz and Casilda, who were in love anyway, take office as King and Queen. After the coronation, the gondoliers, each with his beloved, are happy at last.

HISTORICAL NOTE

The Gondoliers came into being in the midst of an upheaval that gradually split the partnership between Gilbert and Sullivan. In a sense the very format of the opera represents a symbol of reconciliation. Gilbert intentionally chose a story with two central characters who shared equal importance and whose chief preoccupation was to render everyone equal and secure. At one stroke this became a satire on British class divisions and the stirrings of democratic (or socialistic) ideals, and an embodiment of a personal hope that Gilbert the librettist and Sullivan the composer might work in harmony as equal masters of a double art rather than with one subordinate to the other. And there was a third effect, directly involved with the make-up of the company of actors. Grossmith had left the Company, hoping to make more money at his old trade as a club entertainer. Some of the remaining members were beginning to think that their longevity entitled them to special treatment. Gilbert, who knew that the precision and style of D'Oyly Carte productions was created and could be maintained only by full cooperation among all concerned, constructed the plot of *The Gondoliers* in such manner that there is no one star. On every level of the cast there are at least two actors of equal importance. Thus subtly—or not so subtly—he brought the Company back together for one last success in its old style.

The world of this story was not created from the whole cloth in Gilbert's imagination. Venice had become a top tourist attraction for the English, partly because of the works of John Ruskin and his discussion of the emotional importance of seeing great paintings in their proper locations, partly because Thomas Cook & Son offered an excellent package tour which could be adjusted to fit practically any pocketbook. Besides, Gilbert had previously made note of a political fact that interested him extremely: the account of the creation of the republic of Venice and how the city became, in the fifteenth century, a hotbed of equalitarianism, at least in making state policy. This appealed to his sense of the ludicrous, for Venice never really became, in our accepted meaning, a democracy, but still had its Duke who ruled absolutely (though elected). Gilbert thought it a fine setting for a spoof on rulers who try to appear common. The idea of the kidnapped baby was, of course, autobiographical. Gilbert himself had been kidnapped at the age of two while his family was visiting Naples. He used the event as a plot idea for both *Gondoliers* and *H.M.S. Pinafore*. Even the name of the kingdom of Barataria came from a specific source: Cervantes' novel *Don Quixote,* where it represents the "island" kingdom of Sancho Panza. With these details to orient him, Gilbert spent five months writing the play. As work progressed, the whole business of a republican kingdom became so entertaining that the authors went so far as to compose a national anthem for it, but this was erased before opening night.

Sullivan, who was in considerable pain from his kidney disease, kept his musical comedy technique whetted and prevented the personal depression of feeling that he was bastardizing his art by working simultaneously on both *The Gondoliers* and his grand opera *Ivanhoe*. For a while he was able to take up the one or the other as the mood moved him, always composing at his best. In *Gondoliers* he indulged in the pleasures of pure music more than in most of the previous works. The opera opens with a long choral piece; the first line of spoken dialogue is delayed about eighteen minutes from the beginning. Gilbert provided this opportunity, even writing the text of the chorus in simple Italian, so that his friend would have less need to complain of being secondary in the composition. There are dances from Italy, Spain, a barcarola for Venice and a gavotte to represent France. By the time Sullivan was ready to compose the finale, Gilbert begged him to set the proper pace and rhythm before he would write the words. He did not compose words to fit music, as in the case of the "doggerel" of *Utopia, Limited,* but allowed Sullivan to choose the structure—a cachucha—before he fitted the words. Five days before the opening, Sullivan sat down and composed its overture. That same day a title was chosen, and the last brilliant jewel of their collaboration went into its final polishing.

From *Gondoliers* onward, the partnership was heavily beset with internal troubles. Each of the authors suffered from illness, making it harder and harder for either of them to be considerate of the other's peculiarities. One of the triggers that set off their worst explosion was the expense account for the production of *Gondoliers*. Production expenses were supposed to be shared equally by all the partners—Gilbert, Sullivan, and Carte. Expenses that were strictly for the building itself, such as fuel, janitorial service, and taxes, were Carte's affair. When Gilbert saw the accounting for *Gondoliers* he objected to everything on it. The total was near £4500, with £460 for a gondola, a sailing boat, columns, chairs, and a fountain; £100 for one of Miss Brandram's dresses. But the item which he found particularly objectionable was one for £500 for carpets for the lobby of the theater. Gilbert considered this outrageously high, and not the responsibility of the producing company. Each of the partners was irritable to begin with, and this quarrel, added to the rift caused by the composer's feeling of inferiority, brought the two famous men to an impasse. This time it was Gilbert who sent formal notice to Carte stating that he would supply no more libretti for the company and that their rights to his previous works would cease after Christmas of that year. The argument ended in open court, where Gilbert filed suit against both Sullivan and Carte, holding up distribution of the profits for *The Gondoliers* and making a nasty public scandal of their personal antipathies. It was Mrs. Carte whose firmness at last smoothed out their differences and brought the men together again.

There was another legal entanglement at the time that caused a very small annoyance, in comparison with the carpet matter. One Mr. Octavius Cohen, of South Carolina, claimed to have sent Sullivan a script for a comic opera which contained the basic ideas of the plot of *The Gondoliers*. He threatened to sue the partners for plagiarism, but he never did.

In 1891 Queen Victoria commanded a performance of the work at Windsor Castle, where it was mounted on a specially built stage in the Waterloo Gallery. The old monarch, symbol of her era, enjoyed the satire on royalty very much and is said to have followed the libretto in such detail that she noticed each time the actors inserted "gags" *ad libitum*. She demanded an explanation of these liberties. Since neither Gilbert nor Sullivan was present, it fell to Carte to please her with the knowledge that these "gags" were only permitted up to a point, and that the other type of gag, used to keep prisoners quiet, was not necessary with such fine actors.

When *The Gondoliers* first opened in London the publisher Cassell was ready with 70,000 copies of various arrangements of its music for sale in stores, so trustworthy was the reputation of the two Savoyards in their last successful collaboration. Twice again they tried, with *Utopia, Limited* and *The Grand Duke,* but the old fire had been damped down with age and acrimony. *Gondoliers* remains their last success.

Utopia, Limited

OR, THE FLOWERS OF PROGRESS

First performed at the Savoy Theater, London, 7 October 1893 TWO ACTS

CAST

KING PARAMOUNT THE FIRST, *King of Utopia*	BBar
SCAPHIO, *Judge of the Utopian Supreme Court*	Bar
PHANTIS, *Judge of the Utopian Supreme Court*	BBar
TARARA, *Public Exploder*	T
CALYNX, *Utopian Vice-Chamberlain*	Spkr

Imported Flowers of Progress

LORD DRAMALEIGH, *a British Lord Chamberlain*	Bar
CAPTAIN FITZBATTLEAXE, *of the First Life Guards*	T
CAPTAIN SIR EDWARD CORCORAN, K.C.B., *of the Royal Navy*	B
SIR BAILEY BARRE, *Q.C., M.P.*	Bar
MR. BLUSHINGTON, *of the county council*	Bar
MR. GOLDBURY, *a company promoter, afterwards Comptroller of the Utopian Household*	Bar

THE PRINCESS ZARA, *eldest daughter of King Paramount*	S
THE PRINCESS NEKAYA, *her younger sister*	S
THE PRINCESS KALYBA, *another younger sister*	S or MS
THE LADY SOPHY, *their English gouvernante*	C
SALATA, *Utopian maiden*	Spkr
MELENE, *Utopian maiden*	Spkr
PHYLLA, *Utopian maiden*	S
Maidens, Guards, Citizens of Utopia	Chorus

SETTING

ACT I: A Utopian Palm Grove.
ACT II: Throne Room in King Paramount's Palace.

SONGS AND CHORUSES

SYNOPSIS

ACT I

In the distance the glistening sea lends ultimate perfection to the gardens of King Paramount's palace. Here, in a grove of palms, lazily lounging in the lap of bliss, a sweet concert of maidens sings of what it means to live in Utopia.

In lazy languor—motionless,
We lie and dream of nothingness.

In such a tranquil and blessed abode, no interruption by ill news could be allowed. Hence, when Calynx enters, it is good news he brings. His Majesty's intelligent daughter, the Princess Zara, having spent the past five years studying the ways by which that distant Empire, England, reached its present state of power and glory, is now about to return home and anglicize Utopia. What can anyone hope to gain, in this land that is already perfect? Why, English institutions! English tastes, and English fashions. Surely these are desirable! Already the English language has replaced the Utopian. When the Princess arrives the groundwork will have been laid.

In Utopia the second highest office, answerable only to the Supreme Court, is that of Public Exploder. Tarara is the present incumbent. Today he is in a towering rage. It is his duty to blow up whatever is intolerable in the state, including the King himself, should the two wise men who guard the nation's morals determine that the King must go. Tarara has managed to get his hands on a forbidden journal of palace scandals, the *Palace Peeper*, in which he has just discovered that the King himself has committed all kinds of horrible immoralities. For some reason the wise men have not given an order for regicide; hence Tarara is extremely put out.

These two supreme governors, the wise men, are Scaphio and Phantis.

O they never make a blunder,
And no wonder,
For they're triumphs of infallibility.

Scaphio is 66 and has never yet loved. Phantis is 55, but he cannot escape the plague of constant yearning for love. He loves, at this moment, no one less than the Princess Zara. Knowing that together, because of the unanswerable power they both hold over their king, a power that can achieve miraculous results in the form of dynamite triggered by the Public Exploder, Phantis begs Scaphio to help him in this matter of his heart. Scaphio agrees, quite whole-heartedly, that together they should use

{ *111* }

their unquestionable influence to effect a marriage for Phantis. They consult in private about their project.

The two youngest daughters of the King have recently been put into the hands of a highly experienced English governess, Lady Sophy, in order that they may become examples for all the kingdom of what the perfect Utopian girl should be, trained on British principles. The girls, Nekaya and Kalyba, having now completed their course of instruction, are to be exhibited to the public every day from ten till four. Today is their first presentation. With eyes cast down in that aspect of modesty which they have practiced for hours and hours, the girls sing.

> *Although of native maids the cream,*
> *We're brought up on the English scheme—*
>
> . . . . .
>
> *For English girls are good as gold,*
> *Extremely modest (so we're told),*
> *Demurely coy—divinely cold—*
> *And we are that—and more.*

Lady Sophy, in the best tradition as a lecturer, carries a pointer in her hand as she is introduced to the people by the King himself, who admires her without reserve. This morning's demonstration is to be on the subject of the proper handling of courtship. Lady Sophy delineates the problem as the two girls act out her words:

> *Bold-faced ranger*
> *(Perfect stranger)*
> *Meets two well-behaved young ladies.*
> *He's attractive,*
> *Young and active—*
> *Each a little bit afraid is.*
>
> . . . . .
>
> *Though they speak to him politely,*
> *Please observe they're sneering slightly,*
> *Just to show he's acting vainly.*
>
> . . . . .
>
> *English girls of well-bred notions*
> *Shun all unrehearsed emotions.*
> *English girls of highest class*
> *Practice them before the glass.*

And when the demonstration ends, Lady Sophy curtly announces that it will be repeated in ten minutes at the town market-place, toward which the citizens of Utopia move, leaving the King.

This King is a man of excellent disposition, full of enjoyment of the humorous side of life. It is *he* who has been writing those devastating denunciations of the King's supposed immorality, stories which have so tortured the Public Exploder. Those little reports are not all, however. There is also a comic-opera written to satirize His Majesty, a most personal and biting satire which the King finds a bit difficult to enjoy, although he wrote it himself. All has been composed and published at the order of the two justices of the Utopian Supreme Court, Scaphio and Phantis. Pity the poor monarch who cannot help chuckling and laughing at the sharp jokes his judges force him to invent against himself! Today especially he is concerned, because his daughter is coming home after five long years. He certainly does not want *her* accidentally to come across a copy of the paper and to read the scandals—much less to see the opera!

But the secret is getting out. Lady Sophy has just read some of the accusations. She cannot understand how it can be that such defamatory statements are allowed to be circulated in the realm of an absolute monarch—nay, within his very castle! Hardly can she conceive a proper punishment for the writer, should that criminal ever be discovered. Neither can the king:

—I am in constant communication with the Mikado of Japan, who is a leading authority on such points.

Lady Sophy cannot tolerate a king who will not so much as contradict scandal about himself, nor hunt out the propagator and have him violently executed. In high dudgeon she declares that she will thereafter never consent to the love which His Majesty has obviously offered.

At last the Princess arrives, richly escorted by the magnificent First Life Guards and accompanied by that British warrior of great renown, Captain Fitzbattleaxe. One might guess that she is quite drawn to the Captain. This is not lost on Scaphio and Phantis, who have witnessed the military ceremony of her arrival from a hidden vantage point. Scaphio, who had promised faithfully to aid Phantis in his approach to the girl, has become so overwhelmed by the sight of her that he is beside himself with love, incoherent with adoration. When the Princess, accompanied now only by the Captain, comes upon them quite by accident, Scaphio immediately informs her:

We love you—this man and I—madly, passionately!

British reared and British born, the Captain knows precisely what this situation demands of him. The two wise men, he insists, are to settle between themselves which one is to blow out the other's brains. Meanwhile the girl shall remain in the custody of the British officer, whose honor is not to be discussed.

When sages try to part
Two loving hearts in fusion,
Their wisdom's a delusion
And learning serves them not.

The Princess Zara, much to her father's chagrin, has somehow managed to see a well-worn copy of the *Palace Peeper*. It is the same copy that the Public Exploder had lent to Lady Sophy. The girl upbraids her father and demands an explanation of the scandalous, ungrammatical stories that she has found inside, and of the opera that is reviewed in it. The King finally breaks down and admits that he is only nominally a despot in Utopia. He is actually under the heavy thumb of Scaphio and Phantis.

Princess Zara has a remedy for that situation. She has brought with her six representatives of the principal causes that made Great Britain great: six Flowers of Progress. She introduces them: Captain Fitzbattle-axe of the military, Sir Bailey Barre who can prove that anything is anything else, Lord Dramaleigh and the county councillor, Mr. Blushington, who constitute a sort of public purity-watching team, Mr. Goldbury who promotes, and Captain Sir Edward Corcoran of Her Majesty's Ship the *Pinafore*, the symbol of England's greatness on the seas. Together these six can turn Utopia into a thriving, successful empire instead of a quiet, perfect little kingdom. The King is delighted. Not so the wise men and the Public Exploder. They foresee a need for regicide by dynamite if things go too far.

ACT II

Captain Fitzbattleaxe, poor fellow, was once a tenor. Now that he is in love with Princess Zara, however, his normally silken voice is beginning to show signs of too much strain from the fervor of his serenading.

You can't do chromatics
With proper emphatics
When anguish your bosom is wringing!

The good Princess is very tolerant; the higher qualities of the heart are much more important to her than the high tessitura of his voice. But enough of these light topics! The Princess is pleased with all that the six imported Flowers of Progress have effected in the kingdom since they arrived. They have remodeled the army, the navy, and all the other departments of government along British lines. Of course, having no Parliament to slow them up has been a great help. Mr. Goldbury, the promoter, has already converted every private citizen into a stock company along capitalist lines. In short, Utopia is more perfect than ever, if a bit more complicated. The Princess leaves to prepare her first reception in the

{ *114* }

English style as the six importees arrange themselves on chairs in a line across the stage as in a minstrel show. The King is now to open his first cabinet meeting. He reports on the state of the realm:

KING: *Society has quite forsaken all her wicked courses,*
Which empties our police courts, and abolishes divorces.
CHORUS: *Divorce is nearly obsolete in England.*

And everything is changed. A horde of Lords and Ladies now swirls into the palace to attend the Princess's first reception. Each nobleman has his ceremonial title, and each is magnificently arrayed in his uniform. The King takes his stand before the throne as the ladies line up. Each guest presents her card to the Groom in Waiting, who passes it to the Lord in Waiting, who passes it to the Vice Chamberlain, who passes it to the Lord Chamberlain, who reads it to the King. Thus the best British tradition is faithfully reproduced in this distant island. Naturally, since formality is everything in England, nothing else happens. When the last lady has handed up her card and been announced, the reception ends. Everybody leaves except Scaphio and Phantis, who are seething with anger.

SCAPHIO: *With fury deep we burn—*
PHANTIS: *We do—*
SCAPHIO: *We fume with smothered rage—*
PHANTIS: *We do—*
SCAPHIO: *These Englishmen who rule supreme,*
Their undertaking they redeem
By stifling every harmless scheme
In which we both engage.

They are determined to regain the absolute power they held before. They demand that the King do something to restore the revenue they once received from their monopolies in various businesses, all of which have been erased by the economic arrangements of the new government. The King, secure at last, refuses them, and they are more furious than ever as their power ebbs. Tarara is their refuge and their strength. The two wise men retreat with their Public Exploder into a whispered conference. After a good deal of argument, *sotto voce,* they arrive at a capital plan—but they keep it to themselves.

While they are away working on their destructive idea, Mr. Goldbury and Lord Dramaleigh converse with the ultra-demure princesses Nekaya and Kalyba. Put off by their extreme aloofness, Mr. Goldbury endeavors to explain that a real English girl is not quite as retiring as Lady Sophy has taught these two to be:

She'll waltz away like a teetotum,
And never go home till daylight's dawning.

Lawn-tennis may share her favours fair—
Her eyes a-dance and her cheeks a-glowing—
Down comes her hair, but what does she care?
It's all her own and it's worth the showing!

. . . . .

Oh, sweet surprise—oh, dear delight,
To find it undisputed quite,
All musty, fusty rules despite,
That Art is wrong and Nature right!

If Lady Sophy has been somewhat overzealous in her training it is no accident. She is a woman of her word. At fifteen she had promised herself she would marry no one but an absolutely perfect, absolutely angelic king. Such a promise requires a steadfastness beyond the ordinary. No doubt it is natural that she wants the girls to be as firm as she is.

The King, King Paramount, was listening as the dear lady mused by herself on this subject. He heard between the lines that she would really be glad to accept *him* if it were not for the scandals she has been reading in the *Palace Peeper*. Coming out of hiding, the King confesses everything, and she understands at last why he reacted so oddly in their earlier discussion. They dance together in rapturous agreement.

The two little Princesses see this remarkable coming together. They have Lord Dramaleigh and Mr. Goldbury with them, and it takes only a hint to weave all four into the dance, as well as the Princess Zara and Captain Fitzbattleaxe. Pretty soon all the couples are involved in a happy tarantella.

Utopia is now so rich, so powerful, so perfect, that life has come very nearly to a standstill. There are no wars to keep the military busy, no diseases to keep doctors alive, the laws have been remodeled, crime is extinguished, the state is in a terrible state.

One thing is missing: government by party, the foundation of England's greatness. Utopia, formerly a Monarchy, Limited, becomes a Limited Monarchy by edict of the King. Scaphio and Phantis are jailed as dangerous menaces to the public, and the once perfect state is now perfectly perfect and more invincible than ever.

HISTORICAL NOTE

Perhaps the only reason that *Utopia, Limited* had such a limited stage life until quite recently is that it requires a cast of stars. It has been remarked that the opera needs "at least five" top-flight comedians—not so easy to gather together in a musical production. The original presentation at the Savoy was expensive, also. The bill came to about £7200 at the time of opening, perhaps the highest of all although a higher figure for

Ruddigore has been reported by some. Certainly the plot of *Utopia, Limited* hangs together less shakily than do some of the others. The satire is too good to be compared to such personal axe-grindings as that of *Princess Ida*. But *Utopia* ran for only 245 performances at its initial production, and was not revived professionally until 1956. At that time the American Savoyards presented the opera so successfully that it was kept as part of their permanent repertoire and is now played as frequently as any of the other operas with the exception of *The Mikado, The Pirates of Penzance,* and *H.M.S. Pinafore.*

After *The Gondoliers,* the ability of the two authors to get together and create was increasingly weakened by their advancing ages, debilitating diseases, and souring muses. Gilbert, for one, had tried working with other composers until he was thoroughly disgusted and craved a return to the smooth old days when he could trust to Sullivan's mastery not only of music but of the technique of matching score to words and of having it ready on time—if even at the last minute. Friends had been at work for a long while trying to arrange some method for bringing the two to an arbitrated truce in their *Gondoliers* quarrel. But at last Sullivan hushed these intermediaries and brushed the past aside by proposing that Gilbert drop in at his place for a good smoke. A new opera was agreed upon; slowly the collaboration again ground into motion. But long delays ensued. Gilbert's notorious touchiness made every letter in their detailed correspondence a matter of the most delicate diplomacy, at once lengthy and ponderously involved with emotional interpretations. Sullivan had a hard time getting started on the music.

The composer went to Monte Carlo for his health. In January Gilbert visited him there to read him the script, and then returned to London. More letters, more argument about how the financial arrangements were to be made with Carte—Gilbert did not wish to risk another loss like that he claimed to have suffered in the expenses of *The Gondoliers.* Sullivan objected to the treatment of Lady Sophy in the second act; he was tired of Gilbert's shabby treatment of older women in the scripts. Finally Gilbert told Sullivan to go ahead and compose a finale; he would write words to fit the music. This was done, and in the author's own words as he handed his work over to Sullivan: "It is mere doggerel—but words written to music are sure to be that. You may chop this about just as you please." The resulting finale, inevitably unsatisfactory, was performed only four times. A new one was substituted, which Sullivan had set to Gilbert's words in their usual manner.

In rehearsals, Gilbert directed as usual, but he had to use crutches to get about because of his gout.

Some of the ideas in *Utopia, Limited* were prefigured elsewhere. The notion of legally incorporating private individuals as if they were factories or limited companies was used in *The Gondoliers*, in which the Duke of Plaza-Toro established himself as such to acquire capital to live on. The throne-room scene in the second act was modeled directly on the standard royal receptions held in Queen Victoria's drawing room. The arrangement of the cabinet in a single row of chairs across the stage was taken from the classic seating of Christy's Minstrels, a company then playing in the St. James Theater, London.

The critics were generally pleased with the results, and gave the work good reviews. Among them was George Bernard Shaw who, however, complimented Carte more than either of the authors, for his revolutionary effect upon the operations of British theater. The public was glad to see a new Gilbert and Sullivan work after so long a lapse. The applause at the end was such that Sullivan strode across the stage to shake Gilbert's hand in a demonstration of what he hoped would be a new era of good feeling and good production. But after only seven months the opera was shelved.

One of the stars in *Utopia, Limited* was Nancy McIntosh, whom Gilbert had heard at a party. At his suggestion, Sullivan auditioned her and approved of her being cast as the Princess Zara. This girl, born in the United States, later became the Gilberts' adopted daughter and lived with them at Grim's Dyke.

The Grand Duke

OR, THE STATUTORY DUEL

First performed at the Savoy Theater, London, 7 March 1896   TWO ACTS

CAST

RUDOLPH, *Grand Duke of Pfennig-Halbpfennig*	Bar
ERNEST DUMMKOPF, *a theatrical manager*	T
LUDWIG, *his leading comedian*	Bar
DR. TANNHÄUSER, *a notary*	T
THE PRINCE OF MONTE CARLO	Bar
VISCOUNT MENTONE	Spkr
BEN HASHBAZ, *a costumier*	Bar
HERALD	Bar
THE PRINCESS OF MONTE CARLO, *betrothed to Rudolph*	S
THE BARONESS VON KRAKENFELDT, *betrothed to Rudolph*	C
JULIA JELLICOE, *an English comédienne*	S
LISA, *a soubrette*	S
OLGA, *member of Dummkopf's company*	S
GRETCHEN, *member of Dummkopf's company*	MS
BERTHA, *member of Dummkopf's company*	MS
ELSA, *member of Dummkopf's company*	MS
MARTHA, *member of Dummkopf's company*	Spkr
Chamberlains, Nobles, Actors, Actresses	Chorus

SETTING

ACT I: In the Public Square of Speisesaal, about 1750.
ACT II: Hall in the Grand Ducal Palace.

SONGS AND CHORUSES

ACT I

Chorus: Won't it be a pretty wedding? (*Actors and actresses*)
Song: By the mystic regulation (*Ludwig, Chorus*)
Song: Were I a king in very truth (*Ernest, Chorus*)

Ballad: How would I play this part (*Julia*)
Chorus: My goodness me! what shall we do? Why, what a dreadful situation! (*Chorus*)
Song: Ten minutes since I met a chap (*Ludwig, Chorus*)
Song: About a century since (*Notary, Chorus*)
Quintet: Strange the views some people hold! (*Ludwig, Lisa, Ernest, Julia, Notary*)
Chorus: The good Grand Duke of Pfennig-Halbpfennig (*Chamberlains*)
Song: A pattern to professors of monarchical autonomy (*Rudolph*)
Duet: As o'er our penny roll we sing (*Baroness, Rudolph*)
Song: When you find you're a broken-down critter (*Rudolph*)
Finale: Come hither, all you people (*Rudolph, Ludwig, Chorus*)
    Duet: Big bombs, small bombs, great guns and little ones! (*Rudolph, Ludwig*)
    Song: Oh, a monarch who boasts intellectual graces (*Ludwig, Chorus*)
    Song: Ah, pity me, my comrades true (*Julia*)
    Duet: Oh, listen to me, dear (*Lisa, Julia*)
    Song: The die is cast (*Lisa*)

ACT II

Chorus: As before you we defile (*Chorus*)
Song: At the outset I may mention it's my sovereign intention (*Ludwig, Chorus*)
Song: Take care of him—he's much too good to live (*Lisa, Ludwig*)
Duet: Now, Julia, come (*Ludwig, Julia*)
Chorus: Your Highness, there's a party at the door (*Chorus*)
Scena: With fury indescribable I burn! (*Baroness, Ludwig, Chorus*)
Song: Now away to the wedding we go (*Baroness, Chorus*)
Song: Broken every promise plighted (*Julia*)
Duet: If the light of love's lingering ember (*Ernest, Julia*)
Chorus: Now bridegroom and bride let us toast (*Chorus*)
Song: I once gave an evening party (*Baroness, Chorus*)
Solo: The Prince of Monte Carlo (*Herald*)
Duet: We're rigged out in magnificent array (*Prince, Princess, Costumier, Nobles*)
Chorus: Away to the wedding we'll go (*Chorus*)
Finale: Happy couples, lightly treading (*Chorus*)

SYNOPSIS

ACT I

There is a theatrical troupe in the Grand Duchy of Pfennig-Halbpfennig, managed by one Ernest Dummkopf, in which there are two

{ 120 }

Scene from *H.M.S. Pinafore*, Century Theatre, New York City, 1926.
The cast included Fay Templeton, Marguerite Namara, William Danforth, and
John E. Hazard. (*All photos courtesy of the Museum of the City of New York.*)

James Watts and Vivian Hart in *Patience,* Masque Theatre, New York City, 1927.

Lillian Russell as Aline in *The Sorcere*

Henry E. Dixey
as the Lord Chancellor
in *Iolanthe*.

Lillian Russell as Patience.

Sallie Reber in *Iolanthe*.   Marie Jansen in *Iolanthe*.

Thomas Whiffen as Sir Joseph Porter
in *H.M.S. Pinafore*.

Digby Bell in *Patience*.

Scene from *Iolanthe*, Park Theatre, New York City, 1920. From left:
(3) Craig Campbell, (4) Gladys Caldwell, (5) Sarah Edwards, (6) Herbert
Waterous, (7) Cora Tracy, (8) William Danforth, (12) Ralph Brainard.

De Wolf Hopper and
Alice Brady (right)
in *The Mikado*,
48th Street Theatre,
New York City, 1915.

Lillian Parsloe and
Harry Davenport
in the children's
H.M.S. Pinafore.

Four members of the
Gilbert & Sullivan Opera
Company with De Wolf Hopper
(center) as Jack Point in
The Yeomen of the Guard,
48th Street Theatre,
New York City, 1915.

De Wolf Hopper as
Ko-Ko in *The Mikado*.

Fred Billington as
Pooh-Bah and
George Thorne as Ko-Ko
in *The Mikado*.

Cartoon of Gilbert and Sullivan, 1888.

members about to be married. The bride, Lisa, wears a not-too-well-fitting dress; her hair is—well—hardly well done. The groom, Ludwig, is no prize either—at least he does not think so himself. But they are in love; it is sure to be a pretty wedding. There is only one really important difficulty; they lack a parson. All the clergy have been summoned to the Grand Ducal palace to work out the details of Duke Rudolph's forthcoming marriage to the Baroness von Krakenfeldt. Thus there is no one who can, officially, perform the ceremony for Ludwig and Lisa until 6:00 p.m., which will be almost too late to allow them time to get ready for their evening performance in *Troilus and Cressida,* which begins at 7:00. Because of this unforeseen difficulty—and for other reasons as well—the two young lovers nurse a fiery hate for the highly placed Duke. For many weeks, lately, a group of conspirators has been planning an insurrection that will unseat this unpopular ruler and substitute Ernest Dummkopf, the manager of the theatrical troupe. Then every member of the company will have an official position at court and all will be happy. There is no question that the manager has the qualifications necessary for the administration of the Grand Duchy:

> *Oh, the man who can rule a theatrical crew,*
> *Each member a genius (and some of them two),*
> *And manage to humour them, little and great,*
> *Can govern this tuppenny state!*

One detail of the transfer of power to Dummkopf will be the proper assignment of positions in the court. Each actor or actress will have to be provided with a title and a job fitted to his, or her, degree of importance in the profession. Hence Julia Jellicoe, who plays the leading lady in all productions, will perforce have to be Grand Duchess, whether she likes it or not. Actually, it is not the role that displeases her but the fact that she will be playing opposite Dummkopf himself, who will be the Duke and therefore her husband. Julia is unutterably beautiful; Dummkopf loves her breathlessly even though she holds him in contempt. It is beyond the manager's wildest dreams that she, whom he has followed like a whipped dog for so long, should suddenly fall, as it were, lovingly into his arms without the slightest effort. Will she really do it? Will she play the part as if it were true? Why, of course! Mere professional perfection would indicate that she would.

JULIA: *My good sir, throughout my career I have made it a rule never to allow private feeling to interfere with my professional duties. You may be quite sure that (however distasteful the part may be) if I undertake it, I shall consider myself professionally bound to throw myself into it with all the ardour at my command.*

Unfortunately, all these detailed plans and fervid hopes are slashed to ribbons when the troupe learns that Ludwig, in his excitement about the imminent overthrow of the government, mistook a ducal detective for a fellow-conspirator and revealed the whole plot. The situation is desperate. If the Duke hears this, as he surely will, the whole troupe will be arrested and the conspiracy will be nipped in the bud. But the notary has an idea. If the Duke can be convinced that the conspiracy has been quelled by his loyal subjects, the thespians, he then will not suspect them of continuing to plan his overthrow. This can be arranged by making use of an ancient law which is still on the books, but which is due to become null and void tomorrow. The law was originally intended to prohibit bloodshed caused by duels. In place of duels the law stipulates that combatants now may decide questions of honor by the simple drawing of cards. He who draws the highest card wins; he who loses is declared legally dead, and all his properties and responsibilities devolve on the winner. Since the law has only one day to run, the loser of today need remain legally dead only twenty-four hours. After that he can come to life again if he wishes. By this means, the notary believes, suspicion can be diverted. If, for instance, Ludwig and Ernest were to hold a statutory duel on the point that the one had discovered the other plotting against the Duke, and if the winner were to appear before the Duke and inform him that the loser is (legally) dead and his conspiracy dead with him, then the Duke will be thrown off the scent and the conspiracy may continue. There is even an added factor of safety; the Duke will certainly not prosecute the "dead" man after he returns to life tomorrow, for a man may die only once, after all. It seems a capital notion. Cards are drawn; Ludwig wins by drawing an ace.

The target of all this machination, Duke Rudolph, is a puny little man, hidden under a mountain of medals and decorations. He is best known in his Duchy for extreme niggardliness. He has decreed himself a magnificent wedding celebration, but one arranged in such a way that the householders and citizens of the duchy will have to create their own demonstrations of festivity at their own expense. The Duke says this will help keep taxes down.

The Ducal bride, however, has discovered a snag. Proceedings come to a shuddering halt as she announces—and in public—that the Duke cannot become her husband until he solves the problem of his betrothal in infancy to the Princess of Monte Carlo. The Duke considers this an unnecessarily magnified affair. The Princess was supposed to marry him before she became of age. Since that deadline is to be reached tomorrow, it is only necessary to schedule the ceremony with the Baroness von Krakenfeldt for a later hour. It is somewhat interesting that the Duke did not marry the Princess but will accept a Baroness in her place. The reason is simple: the Princess is from a very, very poor family, a bad investment.

Thus one difficulty after another is overcome. Plans for the wedding continue to be worked out, and the Duke actually believes that all will proceed on schedule. But then he hears the terrible news, from his detective, that a conspiracy against him has just been discovered. The Duke is faint with nausea at the possibility of losing his office when Ludwig comes to him, ready to denounce the legally dead Ernest Dummkopf as leader of the plot. Seeing the miserable state the Duke is in, Ludwig withholds his information for a moment and thinks it over. Suddenly he has a new idea. He tells the Duke about the law of statutory duels and proposes that in order to avoid being deposed, the Duke should draw cards from a stacked deck with himself, Ludwig. Ludwig will win, take the Duke's place and be deposed in his stead. Then, when the law becomes null and void tomorrow, the Duke may return to power unfettered and unfrightened.

The Duke agrees, and a verbal fight is staged for the benefit of the bystanders. Insults are hurled freely until the one challenges the other to a statutory duel. Ludwig, as before, draws the ace and claims victory. The Duke goes off by himself, legally dead as a doornail, speeded by the derision of the crowd of his former subjects. It is Duke Ludwig, now, in Pfennig-Halbpfennig. Julia is required to be Ludwig's wife, not Ernest's, and Lisa is left forlorn.

ACT II

The new court style of dress is that of ancient Athens. Together with this should go a complete study and practice of Greek manners, classic dances, Attic gesture. But some of the dances would be too licentious to pass theatrical censorship, which actors and actresses take very much to heart. The problem of just how Julia is to play her part as duchess is under discussion already. Ludwig, knowing Julia's temperament, wants her to attempt to play it submissively and modestly, always wringing her hands in silent, unobtrusive grief as he, playing the Duke, abandons himself to pleasure. Julia, however, thinks that a different sort of characterization, as a virago, would be better suited to her professional reputation. While these details are being ironed out, the Baroness von Krakenfeldt comes in. She has heard about the statutory duel, and its result. She has also heard that Ludwig, being Duke, has had the act extended for a hundred years, so that the legally dead Rudolph will not be permitted to come to life again in that time. This fills the Baroness with joy. For, by the law, Ludwig has won not only the Dukedom but also all its responsibilities, including that of being engaged to her.

The extension of the act, unfortunately, has had other effects. Dummkopf heard about it and is, to say the least, shocked and dismayed. He cannot, being dead, win even that delicious Julia who has been thrust aside by the Baroness.

Into this terrible situation marches the Prince of Monte Carlo. He is no longer a poor man. While puttering about in his palace with nothing to do but avoid creditors, he invented the game of roulette, with which he discovered that he could make money. He has now paid off all his debts and become rich, just in time to bring his daughter—before she becomes of age—to marry the Duke to whom she was betrothed so many years ago. This is an unprecedented situation. There are now no less than four women each claiming to be the one and only legal fiancée of whoever is duke.

The notary again saves the day. He has discovered that the statute regarding duels, upon which Ludwig's present exalted position and insoluble predicament are based, expressly decreed that in drawing cards, the ace shall be considered as lowest of the deck. Hence everything that has happened has been illegal. That is that. Ludwig is again merely the bridegroom of Lisa, and Rudolph gets the Princess of Monte Carlo who has turned out to be not so poor a bargain after all.

HISTORICAL NOTE

Gilbert and Sullivan began their collaboration with a play about players who exchanged places with the Gods of Olympus for a year and turned the world topsy-turvy. That play, *Thespis,* was a failure. At the end of twenty-five years the same partnership failed again with a play on a very similar basic plot. The only really important difference was that the final plot of *The Grand Duke* was hung upon a contrivance that most playwrights would be too embarrassed to use: the drawing of cards to determine the victor and loser of a duel. It is not that the other, successful, operas had plots containing much more action; but rather that in *The Grand Duke,* what little action there is in the basic idea of the play is reduced to near stagnation by such devices. What could have been a life and death duel, if I may make an extreme example of a small one, has been reduced to a fake where the loser suffers only a change of label. Certainly it is funny that the rest of the characters treat the loser as if he were a ghost just because he is, by a legal fiction, dead. But nothing is made of this besides the joke, nothing reaches the audience except secondhand by the words of the joke. But this is even too much of an analysis for the thin fabric of the plot.

Thespis ran, it is said, not more than sixty-four performances—nine weeks. *The Grand Duke* lasted for twenty weeks. Gilbert, as early as 1894, had said this would be his last comic-opera. Perhaps he found it difficult to think creatively after having made up his mind he was near the end. His plot, compared with the earlier failure, was a bad one. Nevertheless, work began without the bickering and gloom that had shadowed *Utopia, Limited; The Gondoliers;* and *The Yeomen of the Guard.* It may have seemed for a while that this last work would be a fine valedictory for both men. But the plot itself doomed it. Nothing less than the obliteration of the story by beautiful music would have brought about a different result.

New people had entered the company from time to time, and some of the old ones were gone. Thus this opera was cast in a very different mold. A foreign actress, Ilka von Palmay, was imported to play Julia, on the theory that her accent would supply the separation of languages that was needed between the citizens of Pfennig-Halbpfennig and Julia Jellicoe from England. She did well enough and stayed to play Elsie Maynard after *The Grand Duke* had closed.

There never was another Gilbert and Sullivan opera. Four years later the composer died. Gilbert lived on, writing a few plays from time to time. But it was *The Mikado, Patience, The Yeomen of the Guard, The Pirates of Penzance,* and the others that paid the bills. *The Grand Duke* had nothing to contribute.

WILLIAM SCHWENCK GILBERT

In the gallery of the mind of that towering man Gilbert there was, as it were, a comfortable library, furnished in overstuffed Victorianism, full of newspaper clippings, classical European history, dark paintings in gilded frames, and recollections of conversations that covered everything from the political uprisings of sixteenth-century Venice to details of British naval discipline. This storeroom had a better than average supply of legal information which was constantly augmented by diligent study and alert observation of the progress of science and politics. This was the mind of a perfectly healthy, intelligent, slightly skeptical citizen of nineteenth-century London. It might have put itself to any of a number of practical uses, from the law to politics, but because of the peculiar temperament to which it paid obedience, it devoted itself to the musical theater.

William Schwenck Gilbert was born into a comfortable level of society, where servants were part of the establishment and travel on the continent was accepted as normal recreation. But the family was discomfited by internal dissonances. His mother came from Scotland, the daughter of a doctor. His father was a surgeon in the navy. For some reason, man and wife saw each other more as enemies caught in a forced truce rather than as companions in a pleasant world. It has been said that the ordinary nonchalance of easy affection never existed between these parents; a husband and wife who could, as these did later in life, be so cold to each other that the one would not offer assistance to the other in his final illness, could never have felt the warmth of love. Probably that is true. But for some reason—perhaps the compulsion of society in an overly romantic age—they did marry and did produce a child.

Gilbert was born on the eighteenth of November in 1836. At that time there was no rubber for raincoats to keep out the drizzle of London's late fall, no gas lighting in the streets. The first horse-cars had appeared here and there, but stage-coaches still carried most of the inter-urban traffic. Water, where the city provided it, or where groups of citizens joined to establish a common supply, was carried not in iron pipes, but in carefully hollowed-out logs. Gilbert, who was to become one of the first playwrights to see his work by electric light, was twenty-three years old and had a dull job in the government before the first successful electric lamp was invented, and it was another twenty years before Edison patented the incandescent lamp that made lighting practical. London had just enjoyed its first performance of *L'Elisir d'Amore*, by the Italian composer Donizetti, when Gilbert came into the world; when he was thirty he took up the same subject in his own play, *Dulcamara*, and in 1877 again with *The Sorcerer*. The year after his birth, Victoria ascended the throne of England. It was Gilbert—with Sullivan—who created for the Victorian age its most brilliant self-portrait.

One of the earliest important events of his life, one which demands attention because it supplied one of the basic references for the library of his mind, happened when he was a baby just learning to walk, still in the care of a nurse. His parents were visiting Naples and had left the infant in the hands of a governess for a walk in the famous Italian sun. Two enterprising Neapolitans managed to convince the girl that they had been sent by the baby's father to pick him up and deliver him at home. He could not have been in actual danger, for the love Italians bear for babies is well known. But it cost his father twenty-five good English pounds to get him back. Like everything else that could be interpreted whimsically in his absurd world, Gilbert put this little detail into his plays. In two of the most famous comic-operas, a baby later destined for great position is lost or kidnapped while in the care of a dunder-headed nurse: once in *Gondoliers*, once in *H.M.S. Pinafore*. Identity, and its distortion during childhood, is involved in many of his plots. But it seems to be not so much a problem in his daily psychic life as it is an engaging means of setting up a dramatic situation. Gilbert had his social difficulties—his emotionally estranged mother certainly contributed to his inability to make a serious emotional contact with most women—but he seems otherwise to have kept himself under control, even to have made money out of his peculiarities. He was a thoughtful man and a frugal playwright who used every item of his experience in the most efficient manner in his work.

As we look back, we see that he never was far out of contact with the absurd side of daily life, which became so much the basis of his plays and which was a taste he inherited from his father. But although Poe had been publishing his most famous and most lugubrious tales by the time Gilbert knew how to read, he did not slip into that sluice of morbidity. Perhaps another sort of work influenced him more directly: Edward Lear's *Book of Nonsense* which came out when Gilbert was ten. We know that Dickens was such a favorite that he was almost always involved in one of his books throughout life.

In 1854 Britain became involved in war in the Crimea. That October the battle of Balaklava took place—that famous battle during which the British

Light Brigade was ordered to charge and was wiped out. Gilbert was eighteen at the time and considered volunteering to rush into uniform to save his country, but he was not ready yet for serious war. Perhaps he read also of a most intriguing bit of American action that occurred just then: Commodore Perry negotiated a treaty with the hidden nation of Japan, opening up trade with that strange country whose emperor was called The Mikado. It took thirty years for the trade to grow to such proportions that business men could afford to have a Japanese exhibition in London. By then all England was enthralled by oriental teas, beautiful silks, tightly upswept hairdo's—everything from Nippon. The exposition suggested a subject for opera to the mature man, but the treaty probably interested the young student more as a curiosity.

Arthur Sullivan, six years younger than Gilbert, brought up as a working-class boy who played in the streets while Gilbert went about in a carriage in the company of his father, had his first song published in 1855. At that time Gilbert was a gadfly student at King's College in the University of London, more interested in reading Shakespeare and arguing about it—somewhat like Steven Dedalus in Joyce's *Ulysses*—than in the drudgery of his curriculum. He did well enough as far as grades counted, but he had a reputation for counting more on his quick mind than on hard work. The boy from the working class, still in knee-pants, became a bit of a celebrity in musical circles; official hands were often stretched to pat his head in congratulation. But the college student was an upper-middle-class nobody except to his classmates.

The very next year, Sullivan was elected as first recipient of the Mendelssohn Scholarship, a national honor. Jenny Lind had given a concert to help raise the money that would send this little boy from Lambeth to Germany to study with the great masters. At that time Gilbert, out of college and therefore out of the small world in which his height made him noticeable, faded into the almost final limbo of the civil service. He took a position as clerk in the Education Department of the Privy Council. How he must have been bored! His job was to write legibly, all day long, the dull figures and trite words of bureaucracy. But he did have a certain amount of fun observing, and recording in little sketches, the stupidities and obliquities of official procedure. Sometimes he signed them "Bab," because they were playful, and he had been called "Bab" when he was a child.

While in college he had written a little, making himself just well enough known so that when a translation for a foreign song was needed on a concert program the job fell to Gilbert. It was his first appearance in print, and he was proud enough to make a point of going to hear the concert—sung by the famous Madame Parepa—so that he could watch people as they read *his* words. Years later the singer married Carl Rosa, an opera

{ 128 }

conductor, who was interested in establishing an English opera company. One of the little works they commissioned was a one-act comedy entitled *Trial by Jury* by W. S. Gilbert. But Madame Parepa died before her husband could write the music. It was Arthur Sullivan who finally composed the score.

The little song translation stimulated the young author to make every attempt to get his poems and other writings into the public eye. By the age of twenty-four he had written fifteen stage works, of which not one was produced. It was a long time before the steady flow of rejection notes was diverted by an acceptance.

In 1860 he inherited a little money. Being convinced that life was to be lived while one is alive enough to enjoy it, he quit his dull office job to study law and three years later set himself up as a barrister with a little office among colleagues and a set of the right clothes for court appearances. He was hardly the energetic case-chaser whom one would expect to make a success of law. He had very few cases and spoke, even in them, to little effect. He once endured the supreme embarrassment of having one of his own clients throw a shoe at him in court because of the miserable defense he offered her. While not speaking, he spent his court-time drawing caricatures and sketches of court-room activity, filling his notebooks with hundreds of little pictures, mostly humorous, in place of diligent annotations of law.

Earlier, but only after a long period of artistic fumbling with the two halves of his art, the routine of creation brought words and sketching together in a single piece—a column of prose and a small illustration which he submitted to a new magazine, *Fun*. It changed the direction of his life. Within a few days he had signed a contract to write a regular column, with illustrations, for each issue of the periodical. He was now twenty-five years old; this was the beginning of the *Bab Ballads*. Sullivan, too, had just gotten his first artistic job—he was six years younger—playing the organ in church. The two who had yet to meet or even to hear of each other had commenced professional life.

At first, indeed the very day the contract with *Fun* was offered to him, Gilbert could not imagine where he would find enough material for another humorous article. But the ballads came out with perfect regularity and produced laughter all over London. Gradually he experimented with and refined certain techniques and ideas which would later be known as Gilbertianisms. Some of the details of later operatic plots were first worked out in the *Bab Ballads*. Many of his little drawings illustrating verses in *Fun* have been used to enliven the pages of published librettos of the later works. Among the plot ideas invented at this time was one in which a child was born to a mortal and a fairy. This became the nucleus of the plot of *Iolanthe*.

It was five years before the poetical journalist turned at last to the stage with a play that was producible. He took up a subject that had always interested him—love potions. With Donizetti's opera *L'Elisir d'Amore* as a source, Gilbert wrote *Dulcamara, or the Little Duck and the Great Quack.* It was produced at the St. James Theater in 1866 by Tom Robertson. Robertson was an excellent and practical director in the theater. His manner of conducting rehearsals and of staging the play, and the way he moved actors about on the boards were revolutionary in an age when actors did as they pleased and pampered their vanities before considering the meaning or the total effect of the play. During rehearsals of his first work, Gilbert learned the foundation of that technique which was to revive the precision of stage movement for which his productions were to become famous. Having learned his writing by turning out a weekly column of poetry or prose, he learned theatrics from the very best teacher available in England at the very best moment of his career, with his first play. Looking back from our point of view, we see that not a moment of his life was wasted; everything led him toward the perfection of a brilliant series of comic-operas. But from his point of view as he sat in the empty house listening to Robertson work with an actor over an uncomfortable line, it must have seemed as if it all were a waste. He must have wondered what this all might lead to. Nothing else of that period in British theater has survived to give us a criterion. There was not much in the way of a definite style or trend for the young man to measure himself against. *Dulcamara* led to *La Vivandière*, which led to *The Merry Zingara.* He was mastering a technique for stage comedy, but only a technique.

Let us not forget that this ladder to fame was made of flimsy lumber. Gilbert was producing something very close to doggerel, with long sections of—to us—unbearable sentimentality. The great composer Mendelssohn created his masterpiece, the music for *A Midsummer Night's Dream,* when he was young. He was never again quite able to regain that height of brilliance. With Gilbert it was the other way around, he began with bad works, using them to develop a mastery. His plays were only slightly above the level of what London saw every evening—a very low level indeed. But from this beginning he perfected a technique and then improved his material so that his mature works were masterfully made.

Later in life, the author expressed his feeling about the art of the playwright (he hated that label; it smacked of low craft, like that of the wheelwright or the shipwright) in disparaging terms. It "does not call for the highest order of intellect—it demands shrewdness of observation, a nimble brain, a faculty for expressing oneself concisely, a sense of balance both in the construction of plots and in the construction of sentences." In other words, he was not excited by the form itself; he did not, as did the Greeks for instance, consider the drama to be on a level with religion. Unfortunately for Gilbert, who was in a position to become a really great creator for the English stage, he was unable to look deeper into his art, beyond this superficial consideration of its artificiality.

In 1867, when he was thirty-one, Gilbert married Lucy Turner. She was the daughter of an officer in the army in India. She stayed with him through life, and was the one woman for whom he felt a continuous affection in all her ages. She was sweet seventeen when they married, an age when a girl was a most exquisite work of the art of nature in Gilbert's rose-tinted eyes. But she became eighteen, then nineteen, and older and older without his once dropping the chivalrous shield that protected that image. This is really quite remarkable, for Gilbert made two reputations in his life, the one as a writer of humorous libretti, the other as a severe and even a nasty critic of older women. We have seen a hint of how his mother's chilliness in the family may have contributed to it. Who knows how bad—or how seriously interesting—this trait might have become if Lucy Turner had not found the secret of keeping him in a state of romantic enchantment for the rest of his life. They never had children of their own, but their deep affection for the young must certainly have helped them keep their extraordinary balance as life lengthened. With his marriage, the author's way of life established itself on a pleasant and stable basis. He had a well-developed understanding of the mechanics and economics of living, so that whatever he produced on stage or on paper was turned to increasing security and finally wealth. From this time on, what changed in his life was only detail, variation on a constant theme. Undoubtedly, considering his ability to burst into petulance, his difficulties with Sullivan, Carte, and the whole world, it was the forcefully maintained peace and quiet of the home Lucy Turner built so surreptitiously around him that kept Gilbert sane and successful.

Oddly enough, Gilbert reviewed a work of Sullivan's that same year. It was a performance of the composer's very first and very tiniest comic-opera, Cox and Box, at the Adelphi Theater, quite an appropriate moment for the one to become conscious of the other. They did not meet, however. There was no reason yet to think that each might not go his own way: Sullivan to become oratorio composer to the Empire, Gilbert to remain a journalist writing a series of somewhat polished, humorous, but unimportant extravagances for the music hall. The reviewer thought that the composer had not fully understood what was needed for such a libretto as Cox and Box, that the music he had composed was unfortunately too good for the play, resulting in a mismatching of intent and effect which hurt the total production. When the two collaborators parted many years later, after the most successful career in English theatrical history since the Restoration, it was the same sort of difficulty that came between them. Sullivan thought his music was too much subordinated to Gilbert's writing and direction; he felt he was not getting the attention in comic-opera that his melodic style deserved. But that was at the end; we are concerned here with the beginning.

Gradually Gilbert became primarily associated with theater. In 1869 he was at work directing rehearsals of his play *Ages Ago*, with incidental music by a man named Frederick Clay who was a friend of young Sullivan's. Clay wanted Sullivan to hear his composition, and had invited the now famous composer to pay a visit to the theater during rehearsals. Thus Gilbert and Sullivan met for the first time, appropriately in a theater, and coincidentally during rehearsal of a play which contained a scene in which portraits came to life as they were later to do again in *Ruddigore*. The meeting, however, was only a meeting. Gilbert spent the next year writing and producing four more plays while Sullivan composed for the festival at Birmingham. It was in 1871 when they first tried collaboration. The play was *Thespis*. Of its music, all but two pieces have been completely lost; only the libretto survives. It was put together on short notice, rehearsed under difficult circumstances, and ran not more than sixty-four nights before closing forever. When it was over, Gilbert went back to his other composers and Sullivan continued on his royal road to Knighthood. To all intents and purposes that was that. Nothing remarkable in the history of theater had yet happened.

Gilbert wrote *The Wicked World, Charity, On Bail, Topsy-Turvydom, Tom Cobb*, and seven more plays before Sullivan was again wooed into the picture. The young Richard D'Oyly Carte, who worked as a manager in a small musical-comedy theater in Soho, was pleased one day to receive Mr. William Gilbert, who had dropped by unexpectedly, while Carte was worrying about how to fill the other half of a double bill that would include Offenbach's *La Périchole*. He needed something really different, something that would attract an audience which may have had enough of French comedies by this time, and was perhaps hardly aware of the existence of Carte's theater. Something English, he thought, for he had a long-established desire to help bring back the English theater that had been dead—with the exception of one work, *The Beggar's Opera*—since shortly after Cromwell ascended to a more tranquil abode.

Gilbert, as it turned out, had a script already written that might literally fill the bill. It had been published as a ballad in the magazine, then expanded into a humorous cantata for Madame Parepa-Rosa to use on tour with her husband's opera company. But the great prima-donna had recently died, leaving the piece unused. Carte knew that Rosa would have been good enough as a composer, but Sullivan had a bigger name. He suggested Sullivan. Gilbert agreed to present the idea, which he did by reading the script aloud to Sullivan one miserable day in March. Thus

Trial by Jury was born. It worked. It brought such audiences that all three men felt the urge to go on to better things in triple collaboration.

Gilbert provided one of his favorite plot ideas for the next: it was *The Sorcerer,* which appeared in 1877. Carte had leased a theater for his proposed new era of English comic-opera, and Gilbert began training the acting company that was to become the first really good repertory organization in the English-speaking nineteenth-century world. It was Gilbert's job to direct rehearsals, to create what is now known as "the production" of the play. He always discussed details with Sullivan, but Gilbert was a highly trained theatrician, and by default ran the whole show. This eventually contributed to the break-up many years later.

Gilbert's method of working was developed to such a point that he was able to plan everything except the music itself while still drafting his dialogue. In later years, when the Savoy Theater was in operation, he had an exact model of its stage built, with every part of the permanent structure in place. On this he could construct an experimental set for any scene he wished, starting perhaps with a sketch from his notebook and gradually working it out into three dimensions. For each member of the acting company he had a little wooden block—three inches high for a man, two-and-a-half for a woman. Each block was painted with stripes whose scheme indicated which voice the person whom it represented had. With these blocks he could work out the placement of every actor in every scene, so that he could come to the very first rehearsal with an exact outline of what was physically to take place. Thus, though in other theaters and under other directors the actors might argue about their placements to the point where a director would abdicate his responsibility and let them move by whim, at the Savoy (when it was finally built) Gilbert had such a firm and well worked-out idea of the blocking that he could answer any argument with irrefutable authority. The brilliance of his productions showed it.

Gilbert's method, in actual rehearsal, was based upon a prototype of the production script which the professional stage director uses today. Gilbert would cut the pages of his script apart—he always worked from a printed script, since typewriters were not so reliable then as they are now—and paste the pages into a large notebook, always leaving the left hand side blank. Into this book he would pencil his changes of stage directions, perhaps illustrating with sketches. The book then became a permanent record of the first, and authoritative, production of each of the operas. This technique had much to do with establishing the reputation for precision and excellent blocking that the D'Oyly Carte Company has enjoyed ever since. But a man who could work that way with a finished script would, by nature, be a man who would also design that script to make the best possible use of stage movement. He became, therefore, a better dramatist with every production he directed.

While we are concerned with rehearsal technique, there is another aspect of Gilbert and Sullivan style that is famous and very important to the theater in general. It is the excellent prosody and crystal-clear diction of the D'Oyly Carte productions. This is maintained by two active principles, the one composed into the work and the other drummed into actors' heads during rehearsal. That we can understand the words at all, even in amateur productions, is attributable to the fact that Gilbert had had practice from the beginning in making his words fit together in such manner that their meanings were never obliterated by involved syntax. Sullivan, likewise, had composed for choruses for so long that his sense of the way to sing words had become real mastery. This is one of the qualities for which each of the collaborators can be compared to the greatest theatrical creators of history. It is built into the structure of the lines themselves, and is crystallized by the musical setting. The only improvement—at least in technique—that could have been wished would consist of integrating the two men into one, making them like Sophocles, who composed his words and his music as one. But then, neither Gilbert nor Sullivan worked on such a level.

The other principle is diction. Ah, diction! The singer's vitamin D. Gilbert would not hesitate to stop any performer in the middle of the most beautiful passage of song if he could not hear and understand distinctly not only the syllable, but the word, not only the word, but the sentence. Choruses are commonly reminded about this note by note in rehearsals, but solo singers are frequently so thoroughly trained to produce the most beautiful vocal tones that they automatically reduce the harshness of consonants as much as possible and try to ease every vowel into a laryngeal shape that will permit the smoothest tone for any particular pitch. Gilbert exercised real authority in rehearsal, as we have seen. He would not permit his words to be so obscured. But at the same time he wrote with such smooth internal syntax that he helped provide the singers with fine sounds to sing. Sullivan's marvelous technique, then, could make beauty easy. Hence productions of the operas, when rehearsed to such standards as are still held by the D'Oyly Carte Company, have a clarity and an immediate communicativeness within fine music that can be equaled by practically no other operas in English. In this they are supreme.

H.M.S. Pinafore is a perfect example. It was such a success it made its authors famous as a team on both sides of the ocean. Carte had gathered a company of respectable people who had backed the opening of the Opéra Comique—a theater in London—in its productions of the earlier works. But when *Pinafore* began to win its tremendous victories in London, in the country at large, and (in pirated versions) in America, the board of directors tried to open a rival production themselves, with which they hoped to make more money without having to pay Gilbert, Sullivan and Carte. There was, of course, a court battle. The directors lost, and a new company was formed consisting of the three principals only. This became their permanent arrangement.

When they began their association, in the days before *The Sorcerer*, Gilbert and Sullivan received only six guineas a night, which would today be twenty dollars or so. By the time *Pinafore* had gotten well out to the sea of touring companies, Gilbert had made enough from it, from royalties from printed librettos, and from his other plays, to buy a sea-going yacht. After all, the man who built the *Pinafore* was a sea-faring man. When the money was available, its use was clearly indicated. But he was also a lover of a certain group of earth-bound sports. Tennis was his favorite. With his height he must have been able to serve an unreturnable ball very often. He would frequently play a set before breakfast, thereby keeping himself in excellent physical shape. Every detail of the routine of his life reveals a healthy man, comfortably housed, peaceably married, active, alert and productive. He was over six feet tall, with bristling side-burns and piercing eyes. His very presence, outside the quiet of home, dominated everyone.

But he had no children. This certainly affected his well-being. About the time *Pinafore* was cruising along on its own power, he took on as protégée Marion Terry, a young actress, the sister of Ellen Terry. He helped her find her way into what became a good career.

In 1879, while *Pinafore* continued well enough to make it unnecessary yet to work up a replacement, Gilbert accompanied Sullivan to New York to produce an authorized version of the opera in that city. The pirated versions had been doing well, but the copyright law of the United States was so muddled that Gilbert and Sullivan could not get any money from them or even exercise artistic control. But Gilbert's direction of a hand-picked Carte troupe and Sullivan's training of the orchestra were so much more exciting as theater than the unauthorized productions that the authorized version did very well indeed, even without legal protection.

While they were in New York, they worked on and finished the script and score of *The Pirates of Penzance*. In this case, in order to beat the American pirates at their own game, they produced the opera in New York City after rehearsals held in such secrecy that no spy could discover the name or plot of the work ahead of the opening. The same calendar day there was a perfunctory one-night performance of the same opera at an English seaside resort (it was in December!); this insured a valid copyright in the empire. Of course, the work was successful everywhere.

Pinafore sailed magnificently along in the provinces, and *The Pirates* pondered their problems at the Comique while, in April of 1881, a new opera, *Patience,* was made ready for its debut. Gilbert had begun the work as a satire on some of the functionaries of the church, but as the plot developed in his notebooks, through adjustment after adjustment, he substituted the cult of aestheticism that was then sweeping London. The world of art and literature at that time was sprinkled with the faint scent of decaying lilies. The curve of beauty was taken to be a falling spiral, a curve of weakness. Color was best if it seemed pale beside the harsh brilliance of the uncomfortably real world. The same sort of insistent neurosis has infected the history of culture since Nero and before, and has continued to return with each age of progress as imitators always follow makers. Its recurrence gives us perhaps some faith in the steadiness of the human mind, even in its reactions. But to every reaction there is eventually an opposite. To Oscar Wilde and Burne-Jones there was, at least, Gilbert.

The author himself designed the costumes for the show, taking particular care to make use of the most noticeable ornaments and symbols of the age as they were used by certain figureheads in self-decoration. He was undoubtedly, being an illustrator, well acquainted with Burne-Jones and so-called *L'Art Nouveau.* The very make-up for Reginald Bunthorne in the opera exhibited this. Bunthorne wore Whistler's hair style, and items from the wardrobes of both Walter Crane and Wilde. Gilbert directed the actor to use many of Wilde's mannerisms in performance. Thus he combined the attributes of several in order not to offend any one of them. And thus completely did he *design* his production, to the very style of gesture, far beyond merely writing the words. Had he lived in the following century, he might have brought forth a new tradition of drama, using film, in which he could exercise his unique talents to the fullest with absolute control. But Gilbert was Gilbert; he lived when he lived.

The Company was doing so well that Carte built it a new theater, The Savoy, into which *Patience* moved on the 10th of October. This new building had electric lights, of which Gilbert made dramatic use as soon as possible. *Iolanthe* crawled out of her private Rhine the following year into a sparkling supernatural world wherein each fairy wore a battery-powered lamp in her hair, so that the stage danced to little stars.

Gilbert had a telephone installed also, one instrument at home, another backstage so that he could be in close touch with the theater at all times. Over such a system, a rehearsal of *Iolanthe* was transmitted to Sullivan's flat, where his guest the Prince of Wales could hear it, with his receiver clapped to his ear, thus making *Iolanthe* the very first opera ever to be transmitted to a remote place.

But at the time of which we were speaking, Gilbert was forty-six, still able to enjoy such scientific toys, but also mindful of the comforts he wanted at home. He was a rich man now, with a large house built especially to suit him, and an income more than twice that of the Prime Minister of England. His collaborator, Sullivan, was, on the contrary, made penniless by a stock failure the night *Iolanthe* opened. Gilbert knew how to manage his investments conservatively so that his wealth consistently increased, while his friend took little care, and became rich only because Carte always had more money to hand over to him from his share of the receipts. It was not only that Sullivan gambled; he could not manage money the way Gilbert did.

During 1883 the composer began to suffer feelings of inferiority while the librettist, never one to let an argument tiptoe by without challenge, blunderingly made the situation worse and worse. Little signs of friction began to develop with hints of unhappiness from Sullivan which Gilbert's brusque bark did nothing to soothe. That year, however, Sullivan was knighted. Gilbert was not. This tended to nudge the composer farther away from comic-opera, to make him even less satisfied with the fact that he was spending most of his best effort making brilliant accompaniments for ridiculous words. Not that there were bitter exchanges—yet. But the next opera, *Princess Ida*, did not keep the pace the previous works had set.

In *Princess Ida* Gilbert attacked an enemy that had been with him since so early a time that he could not have recognized her objectively. He thought of her as the personification of that political bugaboo, Women's Emancipation. But the labor with which he mounted his attack betrays the depth of his obsession. The script lacks the freshness that underlined his other works. The smaller numbers were good enough, and the piece did last for a little time on the stage, but the roots were badly gnarled. Gilbert's inability to cope with the philosophical problem of woman's place in the world made the general decline of relations between the collaborators suddenly visible to the public, forcing Gilbert to re-assess his outlook and his art. He was well aware that something had to be done about the artistic situation itself, although he had no inkling of the personal myopia that brought it to a head. His first suggested remedy was startlingly stupid.

Gilbert had an inordinate love for a certain plot idea—the Lozenge Plot. In it every character has the power to become something else merely by taking a pill. This plot had been suggested and rejected many times in the past without ill results. But now Gilbert dusted it off again, when the team was really in difficult inter-personal trouble, a surprising thing to do when it seemed to contain all the very worst attributes of the kind of comic-opera the two collaborators had replaced with their own. Perhaps he actually could have made something funny of it, but it is hard even to imagine how. At this time in their re-assessment, the very mention of the Lozenge Plot was enough to push them farther apart than ever.

At last, in desperation, Gilbert did stumble across a new idea, entirely new: Japanese. The Japanese government had set up an exposition in town, and Londoners had gone wildly oriental because of it. As Bunthornism had seemed ridiculous to Gilbert, so did this fad. In the spring of 1885, *The Mikado* appeared on the stage of the Savoy, one of the most brilliant plays Gilbert ever wrote, completely new and completely wedded to its music.

But the partnership was a bit less steady than it had been. The re-assessment had to be made all over again. When *The Mikado* finally reached a temporary halt in its long first run, Gilbert again proposed the pill business and was again flatly turned down. But this time he rebounded more quickly. In the early part of 1887, out came *Ruddigore,* an old-fashioned melodrama. It is full of image-work, such as the introduction of dances within songs, dances which are supposed to communicate ideas from character to character. In *Ruddigore,* thrifty Gilbert re-used the trick of having portraits come to life, as he had in *Ages Ago,* ages before.

It became part of the process of collaboration for Gilbert to pass around his box of Lozenges every time a new plot was called for. When *Ruddigore* closed he tried it again, and again had it tossed back. Desperate for an idea, one day he saw a railway poster advertising a furniture company with a picture of the Tower of London, that bloody prison begun in the time of William the Conqueror and used for executions for many centuries. From this image came his most serious play, *The Yeomen of the Guard,* in which there is a peculiar mixture of comedy with real tragedy that leaves one feeling quite discomfited and unsure. Jack Point, a jester, a character with whom one is made to feel a great deal of sympathy, loses his love to another and falls dead at her feet at the end of the play while everyone else—including the girl—is dancing for joy. Gilbert was a jester also; perhaps Jack carried some hint of Gilbert's view of Gilbert to that death scene.

The partnership broke completely after *Yeomen.* At last they could find no way to work together harmoniously. Sullivan felt terribly subordinated by Gilbert; Gilbert had already complained that an opera librettist is always swamped by the composer. It was 1889 before Gilbert could find a plot that would in every way provide Sullivan with the chance and the recognition he wanted. The opera was *The Gondoliers.* The script allows a long musical introduction and an elaborate opening chorus for a total of nearly eighteen minutes before the first word of dialogue is spoken. There are dances from every corner of Europe; the plot deals with two men who share a throne, and Sullivan and Gilbert should share theirs. It was the last time their collaboration succeeded.

The following year they fell out again because Gilbert refused to accept Carte's accounting of the finances of the company. This came up primarily because of the expense of replacing carpets in the front of the theater, which was not, to Gilbert's legally trained mind, an expense the production company should bear, but purely the affair of the owner of the building—Carte. Gilbert argued and demanded, and finally filed a suit against both Carte and Sullivan, holding up the division of the proceeds from *The Gondoliers*. Though each of his friends in turn tried to mollify him one way or another, and each thought he had succeeded, Gilbert rebounded each time with a more stringent demand. Having started the process in his mind, the mechanics of legal procedure built up a momentum that none of the friends could stop. At last there had to be a general accounting, to see if Carte and Sullivan were conspiring to defraud their old friend. This accounting showed that Gilbert had received, from the royalties of eight operas in eleven years, and not including money he may have received from other sources, £90,000! In those days that was quite a sum; even today it would be worth more than a quarter of a million dollars.

At the climax—or would you say the nadir?—of their quarrel in the courts, Gilbert declared in writing, on the 5th of May, 1890, that he would write no more for the Savoy Company, and that his previous works were to be withdrawn on the following Christmas. Then, to top it off, he demanded a complete and detailed accounting of every aspect of the company's operations since the first agreement was signed.

The quarrel became so legally involved that it could not but hurt Sullivan deeply. Sullivan did everything he could to win his friendship back, but Gilbert was so blinded by the facts of the case that he could not see what was really going on. Finally, although Sullivan had practically begged him to accept a pair of tickets for the opening of his grand opera *Ivanhoe*, Gilbert refused to go unless Sullivan formally retracted the statements he had sworn to in an affidavit that Carte had written against Gilbert. Sullivan denied that he agreed with the substance of that affidavit, but he could not withdraw it. Gilbert did not attend the opening. He won the financial case, but the collaboration was shaken almost to the ground. Only after thirty performances did Gilbert finally stop by to see Sullivan's opera. His approval was cordial, but meaningless.

Now his life took on the appearance of comfortable retirement. He was fifty-five when he bought a house on 110 acres of beautiful countryside near London. Here he had a tennis court built, leveled a lawn for croquet, and dug a little lake to swim in. Here at Grim's Dyke he became a gentleman of leisure, tending a few fruit trees and observing the social habits of animals. When the fixtures from the set of *Yeomen* were put up for auction, Gilbert bought the headsman's axe and block to keep in his home. He began to become an old man.

Gout came upon him while he was working on *Utopia, Limited*. As before he met Sullivan, Gilbert was turning out play after play for various lesser theaters and with other composers. But *Utopia* was for the Savoy and Arthur Sullivan. It was produced in 1893. The very choice of the subject implies an old man, one who had been reading the parliamentary column of the London *Times* for scores of years and not lost his humor.

Three years passed before another Gilbert and Sullivan work was presented. It was *The Grand Duke*, which failed miserably. The partnership was at an end.

Gilbert acted for a while as magistrate in his home district—he had begun independent life as a barrister. Frequently he dissented and became the goad of other judges in the court. But generally he won a reputation as a benign old fellow, full of good feeling. Once he played The Learned Judge in a benefit performance of *Trial by Jury* at Drury Lane. That was in 1898, when he had achieved sixty-two years. That year he and Sullivan met for the last time, taking a bow at a revival of *The Sorcerer*. They did not speak to each other.

He traveled. In Egypt he was trapped in an overturned carriage in a railway accident, but was not hurt. By the time he had returned to England, Sullivan was dead. Gilbert bought an automobile, then another, a third and a fourth in which he rode about the countryside scaring the peaceful cows. There were two chauffeurs in the house. He enjoyed the company of animals, of children, pigeons, cranes. He contemplated works by Rubens and del Sarto which he owned and kept in his library. He took up photography.

In July of 1907 he was knighted at last, after his work had all but come to an end. In many plays he had wryly complained about the lack of official recognition. Now it came, too late to be of much use.

He pulled out his dried-up old Lozenge Plot again, this time for another composer. It appeared as *Fallen Fairies*. It was terrible. Then came *The Hooligan*, a serious play, also not so good.

One bright day, the 29th of May, 1911, he leaped into his swimming lake to help a lady who was in some difficulty. The exertion was too much; he floated dead in the water.

THE LARGER WORKS OF W. S. GILBERT

1861	The Bab Ballads (*begun*)		Harlequin, Cock-Robin and
1866	Dulcamara		Jenny Wren (*pantomime*)
1867	Le Vivandière	1868	Robert le Diable
	True to the Corps	1869	Ages Ago
1868	The Merry Zingara		No Cards

1870 Our Island Home
The Princess (*later* Princess Ida)
The Palace of Truth
1871 Great Expectations
Pygmalion and Galatea
Randall's Thumb
Thespis
A Sensation Novel
1872 Happy Arcadia
1873 The Wicked World (the Lozenge Plot)
The Wedding March
The Happy Land (*parody on* The Wicked World)
1874 Charity
Sweethearts
Topsy-Turvydom
Ought We to Visit Her?
1875 Broken Hearts
Tom Cobb
Trial by Jury
Eyes and No Eyes
1876 Dan'l Druce, Blacksmith
Princess Toto
1877 The Sorcerer
On Bail
Engaged
1878 The Forty Thieves

H.M.S. Pinafore
The Ne'er Do Weel (*originally* The Vagabond)
1879 The Pirates of Penzance
Gretchen
1880 The Martyr of Antioch (*libretto for an oratorio by Sullivan*)
1881 Patience
Foggerty's Fairy
1882 Iolanthe
1884 Princess Ida
Comedy and Tragedy
1885 The Mikado
1887 Ruddigore
1888 The Yeomen of the Guard
Brantighame Hall
The Brigands
1889 The Gondoliers
1891 Rosencrantz and Guildenstern
1892 The Mountebanks
Haste to the Wedding
1893 Utopia, Limited
His Excellency
1896 The Grand Duke
1897 The Fortune Hunter
1904 The Fairy's Dilemma
1909 The Fallen Fairies (the Lozenge Plot)
1911 The Hooligan

ARTHUR SEYMOUR SULLIVAN

Across the river from the houses of Parliament, and a few blocks upstream, in Lambeth, Arthur Sullivan was born on the thirteenth of May, 1842. His father was a theater musician, a clarinet player, and later bandmaster in the Royal Military College. Theirs was an Irish home in a working-class cockney district, pleasant and full of the warmth of a good-natured family with a healthy approach to living.

His father wanted both Arthur and his older brother Frederick to know music, and perhaps to make some use of it in the world. He did not try to drive Arthur into business and took care that the boy was not discouraged from playing a piano that sat in the front parlor as much as its owner —who had rooms in the building—would permit. He even allowed his son to play in rehearsals of his military band when he was old enough to be trusted in such serious company. Arthur was eight years old when he composed his first anthem, to the words of the 137th Psalm, "By the waters of Babylon."

The world of English music at that time was completely dominated by the oratorios of Felix Mendelssohn, who died when Sullivan was five. In 1842, Liszt was thirty-two, Rossini fifty, Beethoven and Schubert had both been dead nearly fifteen years. Not one of them was British. The last English composer of any continuing importance was Thomas Arne, who died sixty-four years before Sullivan was born. In my mind Arne is associated with the times of the Whigs and the Tories. I seem to see him conducting his works for an audience of members of Parliament who had spent a day arguing whether to let the American Colonies have a voice in tax debates. The era of Sullivan seems to be of an entirely different time, unrelated to Arne's. The practice and creation of English music seems to have come to a complete standstill so that Sullivan's work had to begin from scratch.

Balfe's *Bohemian Girl,* an opera with a few sentimental tunes overwhelmed by an impossible libretto, came out in 1843. But surely by the time Sullivan became old enough to sit in a theater seat, it was not Balfe who occupied the center of the stage, but Verdi, with Donizetti standing by. *L'Elisir d'Amore* received its first ovation in London in 1836, and impressed English musicians with its extremely florid lines, its coloratura writing, not only in the soprano but in every part. Even that work has practically passed from our memory now.

One song of the time remains with us, even if only because we sometimes love to wrap ourselves in the heavy velvet of sentimentality. It is *Home, Sweet Home.* H. R. Bishop (1786-1855), a prolific English composer, established legal claim to this melody after it had attracted attention in *Clari, or The Maid of Milan* (1823), an opera based on a play by John Howard Payne, since he had published it earlier without Payne's lyrics as a "Sicilian folk melody." Perhaps this one remaining song can best serve us as a sample of the taste of the time when Arthur Sullivan began to listen.

Much of the music he heard as a boy must have reached him through the medium of an instrument the like of which the world has not seen for nearly a century—the battle piano: the "prepared" piano of the romantic period. May public taste preserve us from it, and its cheap descendants, forever! It was common in those days for composers to render scenes of battles, complete with mechanical sound effects, operated by bellows or pedals or whatnot attached to the piano. Thus one would hear the rhythms of marching feet, colored by heroic major triads, as the armies marched onto the field in preparation; then the rattle of drums would send shivers down one's spine as the signal to begin firing was given. Drums would give way to musketry which would soon be drowned in the sound of heavy cannon, all coming from the belly of that overloaded keyboard instrument. It must have given many a parlor-genius his opportunity to dazzle his wife and three small children. The idea infested the music of even the best composers. Beethoven sometimes played around with such programmatic effects; Schubert turned one of the tricks into a fine accompaniment for his *Erlkönig*, with its hastening steps. We may thank Arthur Sullivan for having been intelligent enough to win a scholarship that got him out of London and into the hands of classic-minded German teachers early enough to prevent assimilation of much of the terrible racket that was going on in every properly equipped home.

Outside the home, the main source of music for a lower-middle class family like the Sullivans was the music-hall. What went on in the smoky air of those cavernous traps could not have been very stimulating to a musical ear. It is well known that the instrumentalists of London at the time where a badly trained lot, with sloppy technique and no particular reason to improve. Only when a touring company visited from the continent would one have been lucky enough to hear music well played. But such visits were not always supported by low ticket prices, and could not have been as frequently attended by the lower classes as were the music-halls. Sullivan must have heard Donizetti and Verdi much the way many of us have usually heard Sullivan: played by second rate professionals or earnest amateurs, but without the precision and eloquence of a really fine ensemble.

There was, however, another source of music available to the family, and it did provide a solid tradition, well preserved; it was the church. When Arthur was one month short of twelve years old, his father managed to get him a position as chorister in the Chapel Royal, where he would receive excellent choral training and have opportunities to advance himself. This had an immediate effect, not only because of the fine instruction he received, but because he was placed in a very conspicuous light, as a member of a very small, select group of young boys with sweet voices. Fifteen months after he entered, the Novello company published a song, *O Israel*. It was Arthur Sullivan's first appearance in print.

There was a general feeling among English music lovers that the death of Mendelssohn had made the low condition of musical culture in their country most evident. Acting upon a proposal from the musicians in Leipzig, where a music school was endeavoring to set up some sort of living monument to the master, a group of English gentry established a Mendelssohn Scholarship which would pay the expense of sending some young student to that city for a complete course of study. Contributions were gratefully accepted from all the fine families, but one of the biggest boosts came when Jenny Lind gave a special concert, the proceeds of which were donated to the cause. There was an open competition which seventeen students entered. Arthur Sullivan, youngest of the lot, won the prize. He went to Leipzig—after completing his work with the Chapel Royal—and studied with some of the best teachers in all Europe, some of whom numbered such masters as Mendelssohn, Beethoven, Schubert, and others among their own teachers or friends. There he himself met Spohr, Liszt, and von Bülow.

By the time he returned to England, in 1861, he had become a master of the arts of orchestration, counterpoint, and fugue, better trained than anyone his own age in his own country, and probably better than most of his elders. Fortunately the training took root in excellent soil. Arthur Sullivan's musical technique ranks among the very best of his century.

He needed to put himself to use. As soon as he had fully settled down at home, he took a job as organist of St. Michael's Church. Beethoven had also been a church organist, so had Bach. The practical necessity of playing every week and of supplying, or at least arranging, music for church services makes any composer aware of the difficulties and the possibilities of choral music, of what happens when voices and instruments mix, of the fact that beauty in such music comes about by different means than does the beauty of, say, music of the piano. One can hear the result all through the famous works he produced later, but Arthur Sullivan would have snorted at the ridiculous suggestion that playing the organ in church would be a practical step toward comic-opera.

The following April—he was nearly twenty—a new world opened before him. Shakespeare's *The Tempest* was presented at the Crystal Palace with music by Arthur Sullivan, eight years to the day after he had entered the Chapel Royal. He had composed the work as his final thesis at Leipzig and brought the score back with him. Undoubtedly the prestige of his scholarship had helped bring it to the attention of the management of the production, but Sullivan from his earliest youth had always had a way of making himself known to people, of making warm friends and keeping them, not as a social climber or business venturer, but simply as an engaging person. He was still a young man, but already much noticed in musical circles, already the gleam of hope for English music. From this time on, more and more people in high places began to expect great things from him and to raise faint and polite suggestions from time to time as to what those great things should be. For the rest of his life Sullivan felt that pressure; he saw the eyebrows significantly lifted indicating a proper direction for the candidate for Composer of England to take. The goal was oratorio, the form which Handel and Mendelssohn had made great and by which Victorian England wished forever to be remembered. To write a hymn would have been a step in the right direction.

But the next new work was a ballet, *L'Ile Enchantée*, produced at Covent Garden in 1864. Though nothing else of importance resulted from this performance, Sullivan was offered a job because of it, more significant in retrospect than the position at St. Michael's. He became organist for the theater. Now his daily existence expanded to include attendance at rehearsals and participation in performances. He learned the musician's theater from the pit up. The effect this had upon him is clear enough for us to see, but Sullivan himself, at twenty-two, could hardly have considered the theater artistically important to him. He was interested, he liked it, and it paid him a little salary; he was not averse to experimentation, but his true course lay in different waters.

His first operatic experiment never reached the stage. With the poet Chorley, who had adapted that text from Sir Walter Scott, Sullivan composed an opera called *The Sapphire Necklace*. It was never produced. His reputation remained unblemished by that embarrassment, however. That same year he composed a cantata, *Kenilworth*, for the festival at Birmingham and brought out his Irish Symphony at the Crystal Palace, fulfilling the instrumental half of the requirements for the honorary image of the English Composer.

By the time, two years later, that Sullivan reached twenty-four, he attained what must have seemed to be the perfect status for a professional composer. He was appointed professor of composition at the Royal Academy of Music. Our good-natured and most successful Irishman did not, however, enjoy teaching; no new glory was burnished on his name in that post.

In September his father died. Sullivan had always felt a deep attachment to his family and always revealed his emotions in his public work. In honor of his father he composed *In Memoriam*, which was performed almost immediately at a festival in Norwich. Following that, and returning to the accepted and expected line of production, he turned out his *Concerto for Violoncello*, which was introduced by Piatti at the Crystal Palace in London. It was at this time that Sullivan made a trip to Vienna with Grove, who was later to write a compendious *Dictionary of Music and Musicians*. This trip was made famous by their discovery of the lost manuscript score of Schubert's *Rosamunde*.

Thus Sullivan had made himself fit the image that had been lightly drawn around him by the musical society of London. He was passing just the right milestone at just the right moment in a career that would surely lead him to eternal and official honor. But at this point he suddenly, almost as an innocent diversion, agreed to compose music for a comic-opera with a libretto by F. C. Burnand: *Cox and Box*. It was written for and first produced at a late supper party in April, 1867. Those present were friends and cronies who made up a sort of artistic, informal club which met frequently to dine together, to talk about art and ideas, and to play with such novelties as this tiny little musical trick. Shortly after its first performance, *Cox and Box* was repeated at another such private affair. This performance led to one in public, and that to another. The little piece is still popular a century later and is retained in the repertory of the D'Oyly Carte Company, the only work they perform that was not written by Gilbert.

That such a superbly trained and surprisingly gifted composer of serious concert music should turn out a comic-opera—even in a private performance—was very significant. Until then, the field was overrun by slipshod popular works hastily, or at least badly, put together. But Sullivan worked with the same fine craftsmanship that he had so thoroughly assimilated in Leipzig, thus beginning the career that made him unique and great, but which he had never intended to pursue. The good gentlemen who had sent him to the continent had hoped it would happen another way, but it happened nevertheless.

Sullivan followed this success with another in December, when he brought out *Contrabandista* (libretto by Burnand) at St. George's Hall. This work was publicly reviewed and analyzed. The comment that had been made about *Cox and Box* was made again—that Sullivan's music was, if anything, too good for the libretto, thus reducing the total effect of the piece. One wonders whether the young composer yet realized that the juxtaposition of his finely wrought melodic lines with ridiculous words would seem humorous. It seems possible that he never did come to this conclusion, but took himself quite seriously when he was actually writing. He had an excellent sense of humor and fully recognized how funny his work could be in other respects. But sometimes one loses sight of this quality in the involvement of Sullivan's counterpoint and his serious harmonies.

During 1868, and for the next couple of years, Sullivan's chief sphere of action was the world of concerts. At the Worcester festival of 1869 he presented his new oratorio, *The Prodigal Son*. Sullivan had been in love, deeply in love, for nearly six years with Rachel Scott Russell. They had been together as much as possible. When they were not actually seeing each other they wrote passionate letters; their thoughts were never turned elsewhere. She watched him in every moment of the creation of music, sometimes delicately suggesting a change or complimenting him on a moment of brilliance. Every note of every piece was intimately known to her before anyone else saw it, known almost as soon as he wrote it down. Her criticism mattered very much to him; it was valid and it helped him grow artistically. His magnum opus *The Prodigal Son* had been the object of their combined attention all during its composition, but when it was first performed, although she had attended every opening of his since they had first met, she was not present. She was long separated from her husband, but to divorce him and marry Sullivan would mean social ostracism for both. Sullivan never did marry. Once when he was an old man he proposed to a young girl of twenty, but that was a quiet dream, soon wafted away in soft breezes. He was never able to break himself out of the smoky atmosphere of jovial bachelorhood that brought him such a comfortable substitute for home, such an unquestioning circle of conversational friends. A very sentimental man, this composer. The sadness of his father's death had stimulated him to composition. But perhaps the broken engagement fissured too deeply to be converted into song. He was silent for a while.

One day, late in 1869, Sullivan went to hear some music a friend of his had composed for a new play being produced by Mr. German Reed. The play's author was William Schwenck Gilbert. The two met for the first time. Each was known in his field, but Sullivan was famous. It took a year for this chance encounter to develop into something more important. During that year the war between France and Germany commenced, a war which was to recur with variations again and again until it involved the whole world. Lenin was born, Dickens died. England heard its first Wagner, and Sullivan produced his overture *Di Ballo* for the Birmingham Festival.

The first comic-opera by the team of Gilbert and Sullivan was *Thespis*.

It was a failure. We have no way of knowing how much this may have been due to the music, for only one song and one chorus remain. The rest is lost. The work was mounted in about three weeks of rehearsal, making it a hit-or-miss affair at best. It missed; it lasted for sixty-four performances and disappeared from human memory. It was four years before they tried to work together again.

Though *Thespis* failed, other music written in 1871 did not. Sullivan's famous hymn *Onward Christian Soldiers* has remained in Protestant hymnals ever since. Less well-known to us, but just as famous in its time, was his music for a production of *The Merchant of Venice* at Manchester. Gilbert shared Sullivan's attention with Tennyson, with whom the composer essayed a series of songs.

In 1872 the Prince of Wales recovered from an attack of typhus. This was the cause of national rejoicing, for which Sullivan composed a *Te Deum*, first performed at the Crystal Palace. The prince, later to become King Edward VII, became also a friend of the composer.

Sullivan was busy enough now to find it necessary to relinquish his various positions as church organist. In 1873 the Birmingham Festival presented his new oratorio *The Light of the World*. More songs, more little pieces, and more music for Shakespeare—*The Merry Wives of Windsor*—followed. It was not until 1875, the year *Carmen* first seduced Paris, that Gilbert came again into the picture.

Young Richard Carte, manager of a small musical theater, needed something to round out a double bill with Offenbach's *La Périchole*. By the most fortunate coincidence, Gilbert had a script all ready that was practically tailor-made for the situation. Carte knew that a famous name would help the theater's business, and that Sullivan's name was becoming quite famous. He suggested that Gilbert approach Sullivan with the proposal. As soon as Gilbert had read his little play to the composer, the good man accepted the proposition. In three weeks the score was composed, and the dramatic cantata, *Trial by Jury*, came out on the 25th of March. It was an instantaneous success. After 128 performances it closed, and then only because the actor Fred Sullivan, the composer's brother, playing The Learned Judge, became too ill to continue. It was revived later, then revived again and again and is just as popular now as it was before. The era of Gilbert and Sullivan, having suffered one false start, now opened with brilliance.

Sullivan, who loved fun and loved to tinker with music in the theater, still sought to create the monumental works that would make English music great. He received loud applause for the fine work in *Trial by Jury*, and Carte went ahead to lease a theater (the Opéra Comique, in London) to become the home of a new English comic-opera tradition, which long had been Carte's dream. Certainly, future works by Gilbert and Sullivan would be among the chief attractions in such a house. But Sullivan probably found more satisfaction in his appointment as Director of the new National Training School for Music—later to be renamed The Royal College of Music. He was only thirty-four; and the appointment had come down from the heights of royalty. Cambridge University created him Doctor of Music in 1876.

In 1877, however, he collaborated again with Gilbert, producing *The Sorcerer*. Now, with a major success behind them and *Thespis* forgotten, their work was more carefully planned and executed. Sullivan's choice of singers for *The Sorcerer* determined the personnel of what became the permanent D'Oyly Carte Company, and had tremendous effect in raising the general level of musicianship in the English theater.

In 1878 honor again fell over his shoulders with his appointment as British Commissioner of Music at the International Exposition in Paris, for which duty accomplished he received the cross of the Légion d'Honneur. Part of that exposition, its spidery steel tower erected by Eiffel, is still with us. But for Sullivan this was a sad year. It began with the death of his older brother Frederick. The two had been very close; Sullivan was so shaken by the loss that again he was moved to channel his grief into carefully composed music. The result was one of his most famous songs, still popular in certain recitals today: *The Lost Chord*.

By May, Carte's theater was ready for a new production. Gilbert had suggested a plot based upon that rock of Empire, the British Navy. *H.M.S. Pinafore* was such an astounding success it ran for two years at the Comique. Its music is full of the best, the happiest Sullivan, so fresh that it still pleases as thoroughly as it did at first. The composer, however, was a sick man while he wrote these carefree phrases. He was frequently in considerable pain because of his diseased kidney, and had indeed already undergone a major operation. From this time on, success built upon success while pain increased pain, until the one overcame the other.

Pinafore was pirated. The copyright laws of the United States were such that, among other things, cases of infringement had to be brought in the courts of each state separately, on different grounds, in order for an aggrieved author to win redress. Mark Twain made it a personal fight to get Congress to alter this situation. For Gilbert and Sullivan the problem was complicated by the fact that they were foreigners and therefore —according to one judge in New York—had no rights whatsoever that an American was bound to respect. The pirating got so out of hand that all kinds of unauthorized productions of their operas were playing all over the East Coast without any return to the authors. This prompted Carte to suggest that the two should go to New York and produce an authorized version of *H.M.S. Pinafore*, one that would win the public back by its perfection and its excitement. The trip was worth the effort. The legitimate

{ *149* }

show opened at the Fifth Avenue Theater in 1879 and played thereafter to packed houses. Before they left the country, Gilbert and Sullivan trained several touring troupes and sent them out to the far corners of this primitive land. Sullivan himself did some traveling, and had a good swim in the Great Salt Lake.

The composer received his second doctorate that same year, this time from Oxford University. Perhaps it was hoped that so signal an honor, especially since it reconfirmed the previous honor at Cambridge, would delicately wean him away from the low theatrical company he was keeping, and stimulate a new oratorio on more proper texts. But before that new work was born, a new opera appeared. This was *The Pirates of Penzance*, which the authors brought out themselves while they were in New York City, and which first was heard in England in makeshift costumes and uncertain form at the chilly summer resort of Paignton, on the 30th of December. This was in order to fulfill the requirements of British copyright law, the Paignton production taking place under legal conditions just a few hours before the one (which would have forced the work into the public domain had it been first), in New York.

At the Leeds Festival of 1880, when Sullivan was thirty-eight, he conducted the première of the expected oratorio, *The Martyr of Antioch*. This wholly serious work, strangely enough, had a libretto by Gilbert. It was warmly received. But in April, 1881, *Patience* made its debut, with the best music yet. The hope that a new Mendelssohn had arrived in England paled in the brilliance of the comic-opera Sullivan. He resigned his position as head of the National Training School—he had always disliked teaching—and plunged deeper into the theatrical pot. The Savoy Theater, built especially to house the Carte productions of Gilbert and Sullivan, opened in October. A year later, when *Patience* finally retired temporarily, a new opera was put before the public. It was *Iolanthe*, Gilbert's satire on the hereditary House of Peers, and Sullivan's on Wagner. The score is full of the most subtle and intricate explorations of Wagnerian techniques, composed perhaps seriously, perhaps not, but with an effect that is quite funny. The erudition of the composer is well displayed in this score, and the problem of his conflict between the serious and the humorous seems equally audible in the seriousness with which he develops his musical ideas—almost forgetting the ridiculousness of the words. While he was involved with this work his mother died. Sullivan, who had been wrapped since childhood in the warmth of a close family, was now finally alone in the world.

In 1883, at the respectable age of forty-one, Sullivan knelt and received the double touch of knighthood. Now he was fully, even officially, accepted as the Composer of England, though no title of Laureate went with it. He who had begun life playing in the streets, the son of an Irish clarinetist in a Cockney district, now hobnobbed with royalty in good, overstuffed, nineteenth-century opulence. The knighthood was supposed to achieve what the second doctorate had missed; Sullivan was supposed to forsake the profane life of the Savoy for the more sacred. And Sullivan agreed. He chafed under the frustration of hearing only polite applause at the genteel festivals, which was continually drowned out by the cheers of the mob at the theater. That mob may have consisted partly of highly respected gentry, but the total effect was annoying.

Princess Ida, therefore, suffered. She lasted nine months, but with difficulty. The night of the opening Sullivan conducted as usual, but only because two shots of morphine kept the pain of his kidney ailment down somewhat. He collapsed at the end. He had had bad times during rehearsals too, having collapsed once just five days before the première. Since two of the most important songs in the play had not then been composed, there had been considerable worry.

That was Sullivan's habit: to leave much of the composing for the last moments before an opening. Gilbert would mail him the script in bits and dribbles over the course of a few months, leaving certain sections in the rough until Sullivan could decide upon rhythmic schemes and so forth. By the time rehearsals began, most of the necessary ensembles would be ready, and perhaps some of the songs. But always there would occur one or two periods of sudden silence, then perfunctory speaking of unfinished lines that had not yet been set to music. This led to frantic work as opening dates drew near. In the case of Iolanthe, Sullivan actually composed five songs in one sleepless night, finishing in the early hours of morning. One of these was the perfectly charming "When Britain Really Ruled the Waves." To this natural tendency toward procrastination, enhanced by the method by which the two authors exchanged detailed ideas, Sullivan's disease and pain added a terrible load.

Only the determination of the producer and the lack of a new work to fill the theater kept Princess Ida going as long as it did. Finally even these failed. Sullivan was experiencing a deep depression after the production of the opera, not only because he always felt that way after an opening, but because he was sick, it had been a bad play, and the pressure of those insistent voices urging him toward the field of oratorio were becoming too much for him to bear. At last he flatly refused to compose another comic-opera with Gilbert and Carte. Revivals had to be brought in to keep the company in action.

He had looked into other possible sources of libretti. One of these was the author Bret Harte, who might have written him a "western" comic-opera—which the theater could use even today. But the project was eventually given up. When Princess Ida closed, it looked for a while as if the company would have to break up for lack of a new work. Gilbert suggested a plot about magic pills, the Lozenge Plot, which Sullivan thought revolting. Harte sent a comic sketch, but it did not please. Something really new was urgently needed.

Something new was *The Mikado*. It had a novelty, precision, and taste that surpassed all the others. Sullivan worked again at that high plateau that had produced the melodies of *Pinafore* and *Patience*, and the erudition of *Iolanthe*.

The same year, 1885, at the age of forty-three, the composer was appointed conductor of the Philharmonic Society. His life now settled into a pleasant routine: a fresh opera for the Savoy whenever it was needed, an oratorio whenever he felt the urge, and a lengthy vacation in the lakes of northern Italy or a hunting tour with the Duke of Edinburgh, or visiting Prince Wilhelm who was later to become the Kaiser of Germany. Sullivan had many friends and enjoyed their society. But the discrepancy between the glittering image of what the Composer of the Empire should be and what Sir Arthur actually thought he was somewhat roughened his naturally smooth temper.

After his oratorio, *The Golden Legend*, came a new comic-opera, *Ruddigore*, a playful satire on the extravagant melodramas that infected all stages but the Savoy's. Tardy Sullivan did a bit better than usual; the score was completed nearly a week before the opening. But all was not well between composer and playwright. Sullivan felt that he was playing an unsatisfactory role as accompanist to Gilbert's wit. He wanted to do something more serious. Nothing particular came between them, no precise point of argument turned up. They just drifted into slightly separated worlds.

Sullivan quit the Philharmonic and went traveling, stopping at Monte Carlo for a short period of relaxation. He was at odds with his collaborator on the choice of subject for a new piece. *Ruddigore* was showing some signs, visible to its worried creators, of slowing down. One day it came to Sullivan's attention that a rival production, the opera *Dorothy*, with music by Alfred Cellier, had passed its 500th performance. He was convinced that he and Gilbert were being pushed aside by upstarts and that drastic action needed to be taken. Far away, without quick reactions from his partners to check him, he decided that the Company must be dissolved and some new project thought up. He was in despair. It took all of 1887 to bring him together with Gilbert again, with a script very different from the usual—almost a tragedy within the comedy. It was *The Yeomen of the Guard*. Rivalry continued between them, but some of the music of this opera is so beautifully wedded to its words as to imply that a single creator had been at work rather than two. One of the most beautiful duets Sullivan ever composed was "I have a song to sing, O!" in the first act of *The Yeomen of the Guard*. There is a little story about it. He was having trouble setting Gilbert's words. He recognized the fact that

Gilbert had had some particular tune in mind, and went to ask the man to sing it for him. With Gilbert's first two or three notes all Sullivan's old, problematic ideas of the piece were wiped out and fresh ones sprang into being. He stopped Gilbert immediately and rushed home to compose this sweet duet.

Before rehearsals began, however, the composer's ego received its ultimate boost. There had been a command performance of *The Golden Legend*, after which the Queen herself spoke to Sir Arthur, saying, "You ought to write a grand opera—you would do it so well."

How could the obliging gentleman from Lambeth resist such a royal shove in the direction in which he had always wanted to go? From that moment his desire was insatiable. He was determined to compose a large-scale, serious opera, if not by Gilbert, by someone else. Their relations suffered severely. Sullivan complained that he could no longer stand being only "a cipher" in their work, only the accompanist, thrust into the back of the hall while Gilbert, as director, created what was to be the production on stage. This amounted to an open break between them. They exchanged acrimony by mail and could be brought together only by the most diligent, prolonged effort of D'Oyly Carte. At last Gilbert suggested the plot of a new opera in which the music would be fully as important as the words, in which by the very establishment of two characters instead of one to play the leading role, a hint of the desired equality between the creators would be made public. Thus was born *The Gondoliers*, wherein the King of Barataria is two people, not one, who share the throne. This symbolized the achievement of Sullivan's dictum that he and Gilbert should meet on an equal artistic basis, as master and master.

It was something outside this production, however, that made the reconciliation work: *Ivanhoe*, the grand opera. By working on it and *The Gondoliers* at the same time, Sullivan was happy. He composed what he thought England wanted from him, and what he loved to compose for the theater. But the rift never healed. Gilbert fought Sullivan and Carte over the way the expenses of the company were being handled, and Mrs. Carte had to bring all three factions together. For a man controlled by his sentiments as was Sullivan, it became increasingly difficult to work at all.

Ivanhoe was presented in the grand manner, in a new theater built especially for it, on the last day in January, 1891. Its composer was forty-nine, perhaps passing his prime, perhaps a little too far beyond his proper field. For a serious opera it played rather well, but its run could not be compared with the series at the Savoy. Never again did the collaborators reach the success they had had with *Patience, The Mikado, The Yeomen of the Guard,* and *The Gondoliers*. Sullivan dabbled again in incidental music for the theater, but the plays were not by Shakespeare and his music seemed less important than it had been so long before. In 1893 he worked again with his old friend, but *Utopia, Limited* was not as successful as they had hoped. In 1895 he tried reviving his *Contrabandista* with its name changed to *The Chieftain,* but it did not last. Finally in 1896 he worked for the last time on a Gilbertian libretto, *The Grand Duke.* He was fifty-four; their wars had drained whatever it was that made their works cohere. The collaboration had died.

Victoria's Diamond Jubilee brought him out once more with a ballet— *Victoria and Merrie England*—and a *Festival Te Deum.* But sickness wrenched Sullivan with such continual agony that his life was a misery. On a visit in Switzerland he fell nostalgically in love with a girl of twenty, but she wisely refused him and delicately prevented him from hurting himself over it. A few more works for the stage came, *The Beauty Stone, The Rose of Persia,* and the unfinished *Emerald Isle.*

In late November, 1900, Arthur Sullivan died. He left to England a great musical tradition in full operation plus an entirely new and unique style of opera that would identify the era as would little else save the name of its Queen. What Sullivan learned and produced has had deep effect on musical theater in general, even though he invented nothing new.

There is something else to remember—there is a choral style which we commonly associate with roast beef, snowy Christmases and the rich plush of the nineteenth century. Sullivan did not invent it, but he brought it to the perfection that made it important with fifty-six hymn tunes and many marvelous choral scenes in his operas. His style dominates his time and has provided us with a classic criterion. His prosody has never been surpassed in English music. All this might have come to pass without Sullivan, but its character would not have been the same.

One gesture from the last period of his life shows us Sullivan sharply caught up by his predicament with Gilbert, and illustrates their difference in manner. At a revival of *The Sorcerer,* the two authors were invited to take a formal bow at the end of opening night. They entered from opposite sides of the stage. There was such an ovation that Sullivan wanted to shake hands with his old friend and bury their differences. But some little detail of argument was uppermost in Gilbert's mind and not a word passed between them. It was the last time they ever met.

THE LARGER WORKS OF ARTHUR SULLIVAN

1850 Anthem: By the Waters of Babylon

1855 Song: O Israel

1862 Music for Shakespeare's *The Tempest*

1863 Wedding March for the Marriage of the Prince of Wales
Opera: The Sapphire Necklace (never produced)

1864 Cantata: Kenilworth (Birmingham)

1866 Irish Symphony (Crystal Palace)
Overture: In Memoriam (Norwich Festival)

1867 Overture: Marmion
Cox and Box
The Contrabandista

1869 Oratorio: The Prodigal Son (Worcester)

1870 Overture: Di Ballo
Music to Shakespeare's *The Merchant of Venice*
Hymn: It came upon the midnight clear

1871 Opera: Thespis (First collaboration with Gilbert)

1872 Te Deum for the Recovery of the Prince of Wales

1873 Oratorio: The Light of the World (Birmingham)

1874 Music for Shakespeare's *The Merry Wives of Windsor*

1875 Trial by Jury (Royalty Theater, Soho)
The Zoo (St. James Theater)

1877 The Sorcerer (Comique)
Music for Shakespeare's *Henry VIII* (Manchester)
Song: The Lost Chord

1878 H.M.S. Pinafore (Comique)

1879 The Pirates of Penzance (New York)

1880 Oratorio: The Martyr of Antioch (Leeds)

1881 Patience (Comique)

1882 Iolanthe (Savoy)

1884 Princess Ida (Savoy)

1885 The Mikado (Savoy)

1886 Oratorio: The Golden Legend (Leeds)

1887 Imperial Ode
Ruddigore

1888 Music to Shakespeare's *Macbeth*
The Yeomen of the Guard (Savoy)

1889 The Gondoliers (Savoy)

1891 Ivanhoe (English Opera House)

1892 Haddon Hall
Music to the play *The Foresters*

1893 Utopia, Limited (Savoy)

1894 The Chieftain (revised form of *The Contrabandista*)

1895 Music for the play *King Arthur*

1896 The Grand Duke (Savoy)

1897 Ballet: Victoria and Merrie England
Festival Te Deum

1898 The Beauty Stone

1899 The Rose of Persia

1901 The Emerald Isle (completed by Edward German, produced posthumously)

RICHARD D'OYLY CARTE

Without Richard D'Oyly Carte there would have been no great era of Gilbert and Sullivan operas. Carte's marvelous, unique and admirable combination of good taste, musical knowledge and business sense not only made their beginning possible, but also formed a solid, practical basis upon which the whole edifice could stand permanently. George Bernard Shaw's most laudatory comment about the effect of Gilbert and Sullivan's operas on the world of English theater was focused not upon the authors, but on the manager, whom he specifically complimented for making innovations in the art and practice of theater that were of primary importance. The praise was well placed.

Richard D'Oyly Carte was born in Soho, a little district in the very heart of the complex of London, on the 3rd of May, 1844. Sullivan was a two-year-old baby taking the spring sun across the river on one of the overcrowded sidewalks of Cockney Lambeth. Gilbert was already eight years old. Carte's father, also named Richard, was a partner in an instrument-making firm, Rudall, Carte and Company. This company was responsible for bringing the invention of Adolph Sax to England for the first time—the saxophone. The elder Carte was a flute player, and had always been in the music business in one way or another. In his younger days he had even operated a booking office in the northern part of England. His wife was of the old family of D'Oyly, from Wales. Her father was a clergyman who had been able to take his family on trips to the Continent from time to time, so that his daughter would grow up with a broader view of the world. This rubbed off on her child, Richard, who grew up in a family which knew of the arts and of other cultures at first hand. Their house was a meeting place for musicians, painters, poets and other artists of the city. Etchings and prints hung on the walls, finely tuned sounds filled the air. Young Richard could not help but absorb all this from the earliest moment, and thus build his excellent taste for the most complex of all the arts, the theater.

While Sullivan was singing in the Chapel Royal, Carte passed through the University School of London and went on into London University where Gilbert had preceded him. But it became more important for the young man to take a serious part in his father's business, and he had to leave the University before completing his course. With his liberal background and an intimate acquaintance from the earliest with each of the arts, this leap into the world of business cannot be viewed as a retreat. Rather, he made up for the gap in years between himself and Gilbert and Sullivan by learning his part of the later job earlier than they did theirs. All through his life he showed his mastery of the business of theater together with his deep knowledge of what the theater really meant to culture. College education could not have done much more for him in this respect.

Carte knew music well enough to play a little and to compose. In 1868, at the age of twenty-four he wrote a score for a comic-opera. But he never seriously considered himself a creator of music. His attempt to compose, however, is interesting in view of later events. Throughout his life he nourished the dream of establishing a valid tradition for opera and comic-opera in England. It was not merely a commercial notion, but a point upon which all his commercial activity was focused. He thought of it in as creative a fashion as if its establishment were an art and he the artist.

The serious labor of his career began with the establishment of an operatic and concert management agency near his father's shop. His father's previous experience certainly must have been valuable to him. In the course of time this little office grew large and important enough to handle the affairs of some of the best performers who ever visited England. The celebrated Mario, a tenor whose fame is not forgotten a century later, was Carte's client for his final tour in the British Isles. Adelina Patti and Charles Gounod, the composer of *Faust*, were also among his clients. The poet Matthew Arnold made at least part of his living giving lectures, which Carte booked. Oscar Wilde did too, on two continents—all from Carte's little office. The boundary between management of the Savoy Theater and its repertory company and that of the little agency was sufficiently vague at times. Carte would hear singers, and the singers might be quite unsure whether they were auditioning for the one organization or the other.

At an early stage in the business, he hired a girl to run the office. She was Helen Cowper-Black, or Helen Lenoir, who managed things so well that she married Carte in 1888 and took over the opera company after his death in 1901. Never did Carte's ability or luck in choosing the right personnel exhibit itself better than it did the day he hired her. This same genius—natural or studied—put Gilbert in touch with Sullivan just when each needed the other in 1875.

But that was much later. In 1870 he had suggested that Sullivan compose a comic-opera. But the composer was much too involved with finding his way in the world of oratorio for the suggestion to have effect. The following year Carte composed one himself, his second, but nothing came of it. Then he saw *Thespis*. John Hollinshead had brought Sullivan together with Gilbert for their first production. It was a terrible flop, rehearsed in a week after two weeks of preparation, and presented under chaotic conditions. But while the world stamped out of the Gaiety Theater in annoyance, Carte had the feeling that Gilbert and Sullivan had a power between them that might be crystallized into something of value, given the right conditions. He kept this thought in mind for four long years before he found a way to test it.

In 1874 he proposed that Gilbert and Sullivan collaborate on a comic-opera; but he had no money to back such a production, and neither of the proposed collaborators was in a position to begin such a work on speculation. The following year the stars formed a more propitious constellation. Carte had become business manager of a little theater in Soho, the Royalty, operated by Miss Kate Santley. It was Carte's plan to build up a repertory of comic operas, even in such a small theater, and perhaps later to turn this into an English series. He began with Offenbach's *La Périchole*, which he presented for its first performances in England. But it was too short a work to fill an evening. He needed something else. It must be English.

The year was 1875. Seeing Gilbert one day, the young impresario explained the difficult position he was in and how unfortunate it was that he could think of nothing good enough or new enough to match the French piece. Gilbert had a script which had originally been expanded from one of his *Bab Ballads* for Madame Parepa-Rosa to use on her tours with the Carl Rosa opera company. She had recently died, leaving Gilbert with his unclaimed libretto. It was a short play, *Trial by Jury*, less a play in the pure sense than a secular oratorio, a "dramatic cantata."

Carte immediately suggested that they approach Sullivan and ask him to compose the score. Not that Carl Rosa could not have done it well, but Sullivan's was a better name—and Rosa might not wish to be reminded of the sadness of his wife's death. The remembrance of *Thespis* had not yet worn off; Carte knew that the libretto was tailor-made for the fine musical technique he knew Sullivan possessed, which had been almost too good for *Thespis*. Gilbert agreed. Thus the triumphant triple career of Gilbert, Sullivan and D'Oyly Carte began, with a tiny little choral whimsy that immediately delighted London.

It was such a success that it embarrassed its partner, *La Périchole*, which Carte soon replaced with a less famous, English work. For four months the little theater in Soho had full houses—even some of "the best people"—during a run which could have gone on and on had not the leading man, Fred Sullivan, the composer's brother, taken sick. Without him the production could not well continue, for he had a superb comic technique around which he had built his characterization of The Learned Judge.

The next step was obvious. With a wholly home-grown success on his hands, Carte had no trouble interesting a few men of means to back a large company which would be devoted to the production of English comic-operas. His prospectus attracted a sufficient capital to form the Comedy Opera Company, which leased the Opéra Comique and commissioned new works. They approached three teams; Burnand and Cellier, Albery and Clay, and Gilbert and Sullivan. The first two produced nothing, but the last brought out *The Sorcerer* late in 1877. Their financial arrangements were very simple; Sullivan wrote a note to Carte stating in the most conversational terms that he and Gilbert were willing to write a two-act opera for the company in exchange for an advance of two hundred guineas (about $2,400, at present rates) against a royalty of six guineas ($70, at present rates) per performance, the agreement to cover production in London only, and to end with the end of the season. On this basis they started.

The make-up of the production of *The Sorcerer* was at the same time the general outline of what became the D'Oyly Carte Company. The cast for the first opera was chosen with an eye toward future productions, and the personalities of the people thus hired helped to determine the types of characters in later plays. The technique of rehearsal which the ultimate company developed into a firm tradition, and which is adhered to in the more serious theaters on both sides of the ocean today, began here in the Comique with Carte's implied suggestion that Gilbert and Sullivan were to be allowed absolutely free rein, with no interference in matters of script, casting, rehearsing or production, from anyone, including Carte himself and his board of directors. This policy he followed religiously throughout his association with the two creators, making not one hint or suggestion about artistic matters for a quarter of a century. For his part, Carte managed the business of the theater with an efficiency that rendered its mechanics invisible to Gilbert and Sullivan. Thus they were completely protected from the bothers and restrictions of budgetary worries and business affairs. Eventually this very fact became the reason for Gilbert's most serious argument with Carte, when Gilbert suddenly came across an expense sheet which he thought was exorbitant. But it must be remembered that Carte performed an invaluable service to both the authors by sticking to his business as he did. Insofar as their scripts allowed, the productions of the company were perfect. This was the result of Carte's good taste and excellent sense.

After *The Sorcerer* came *H.M.S. Pinafore,* which sailed along so merrily that a touring company was sent to the United States to produce an authorized version there under the personal supervision of Gilbert and

Sullivan. This was Carte's scheme for garnering some of the bags of gold that were being skimmed off by literary pirates with their imitation shows. The manager had been to America to survey the situation and had come to the conclusion that Americans would appreciate fine craftsmanship just as the English did; furthermore, once the Americans had a chance to see Gilbert and Sullivan in the original, they would be deliriously happy to see more, and less enchanted by their imitators. There were several versions of *Pinafore* going on already in New York and Philadelphia, and there was no legal way to stop them. But when the real thing was displayed at the Fifth Avenue Theater, Carte's hopes came true. The Americans flocked to see it just as if there were no competition—indeed, many who saw the pirated versions must have come to see the authorized production because they knew it would be exciting theater. Things went so very well that the authors brought out their next work not in London but in New York. It was *The Pirates of Penzance*, which they rehearsed in secrecy in order to prevent any literary pirates from stealing its ideas. The reason for all this intrigue was that the copyright law of the United States did not protect them. There was no practical way for Carte to seek redress through legal machinery.

But the success of *Pinafore* brought trouble at home. The board of directors, those who had put up the original money to start Carte's Comedy Opera Company, thought they could make more profit if they could avoid paying royalties to Gilbert and Sullivan. Figuring that at least the sets on the stage were theirs, they sent a herd of London thugs one evening to seize them and take them to a different theater where they hoped to set up a rival production. The loyal stage hands at the Comique —the cast was on stage at the time—put up a magnificent defense and eventually drove the hired army away. But the board of directors put on their rival show anyway. Carte's action was swift, once he knew his legal ground. He paid off the indebtedness to the board of directors and then dissolved the Company. Starting with an entirely clean slate, he formed, with Gilbert and Sullivan as his equal partners, the opera company that was to produce all their great successes. The agreement was very simple. Gilbert and Sullivan were to write operas whenever the Company needed them, and direct their presentation. Carte would manage the business affairs. All would share expenses and profits. The contract was to run five years.

But the climax of the early period of Gilbert and Sullivan, the period during which they worked at the Comique, was *Patience*. This was Gilbert's satire on L'Art Nouveau, in which Carte's friend Whistler and his client Oscar Wilde figured importantly. Not one to let the left hand rest while the right hand labored, Carte discussed the possibility of an American tour with Wilde, pointing out that the forthcoming opera would contribute to the artistic causes that Wilde toyed with, and might increase the size of his own audiences, were it known that he was caricatured in it. Wilde, unoffended, did undertake the tour and became, as some put it, a sandwich-man, a traveling advertisement for the opera that advertised him, a double stroke for Carte.

Patience, an immediate success, did so well that Carte decided a new theater was necessary. It was not a Company matter; he would build it with his own money and lease it to the Company at a rate lower than it was actually worth. On the 10th of October the Savoy Theater opened with the same production of *Patience* that had shown no signs of sinking at the Comique.

The Savoy was entirely new except in name. That came from the fact that Carte had built the theater on land that had once held the Savoy Palace, during the fifteenth century, the time of the Wars of the Roses. Carte's theater sat 1292 people, was decorated in cream and gold in fairly simple Italian Renaissance style—no statuary, no Venuses, Cupids and other Victorian profanities. It was the first public building to be entirely lighted by electricity—a feat made possible by the recent invention of the incandescent lamp. There were 1200 bulbs inside the house, powered by a steam generator in a separate building. Carte announced to all the world that electricity was safe and odorless, which the gas jets of the ordinary theater most certainly were not. To prove his point, he took a curtain call himself at the grand opening of the theater, holding a lighted bulb in his hand. After making a little speech which proved by word and fact that electricity so close to the human body was no more dangerous than the wire it ran through, he convinced the audience with the startling act of breaking the bulb while it was lit, which did *not* result in an explosion or fire, and did not cause anything like the catastrophe that would have happened had a gas line broken during performance. The Savoy Theater was a permanent success. Later Carte built a hotel next door, equally magnificent.

Another of his innovations was the queue. It had been the practice for the hordes of people who could not afford to get reserved seats to crush each other in turmoil as each tried to be first into the unreserved sections of the house. Carte decreed that they should stand in line and enter peaceably. The London press swore that no Englishman would knuckle down to such regimentation, but they did, and the queue is standard procedure now practically everywhere. On opening nights Carte would have tea and cakes served to those who could only stand and wait. Rudolf Bing did the same for the standees at the Metropolitan Opera House in the 1950's and 60's and invariably found his picture in the papers with compliments.

Carte was equally thoughtful of his actors and actresses, and of all the others who worked backstage and in the house. When *Patience* became profitable, he organized a picnic for everyone, with three river boats, each graced with one of the three heads of the company, Gilbert, Sullivan and D'Oyly Carte. These picnics on the river became an annual affair and served to maintain morale in a company that was drilled and drilled to the wee hours of the morning when productions were being prepared. Another thoughtful gesture: when *Iolanthe* opened in New York, the same night as the première in London, the cast received a cablegram from Carte just before they went on stage, describing the triumph of their colleagues. Needless to say, the New York opening was equally triumphant.

During the period *of Princess Ida, The Mikado* and *Ruddigore*, the two authors began to have personal difficulties that tended to stretch their working relations to a dangerous point. Carte, although he sometimes sided with Sullivan, managed to keep himself pretty well out of it. It was not his affair; their difficulties were in the realm of writing and direction, not business. On the other hand, he did have occasion to complain that Gilbert interfered with his part of the operation by demanding to be allowed to approve and disapprove every business expense. But for the time being, the major trouble was only between the two writers, leaving Carte available to mediate.

He was doing very well. In 1888 he married the girl who had been with him in the business from the beginning, Helen Lenoir. They lived in a very large, very fashionable house, full of bric-a-brac from the best sources, medallions on the walls, drawings, etchings, water-colors. His library and billiard rooms were decorated by Whistler himself. There was even an elevator—he who had built the first electrically-lit theater had the first private lift. Everything was secure and comfortable.

But not in the Company. Gilbert's acidity and Sullivan's hunger for escape began to affect business. After *Ruddigore*, it had been necessary to mount revivals of old productions, because no new opera was ready. *The Yeomen of the Guard* came and went. After it, it seemed as if the two partners would never come together on a subject for their next play. Carte stood in the middle, hearing Sullivan complain that he was being smothered by the restrictions of Gilbert's scripts and Gilbert's directing. Gilbert argued, thinking he was easing the situation by his logic, but only making things worse. Carte had to keep the peace if possible, and get the men to work again.

What finally accomplished the reconciliation was the relief Carte gave Sullivan by deciding to produce his serious opera, the beginning of what Carte hoped would be a whole new world of English grand opera. Since this gave Sullivan a way to work off his impelling desire to be the Composer for the Empire, it also made him less averse to composing another comic work with Gilbert. They decided on the plot of *The Gondoliers,* and the rift was temporarily healed.

Carte's decision was not entirely an objective one. He had always felt a bit closer to Sullivan than to Gilbert. Although his sense of humor put him on a level of understanding with the playwright, Gilbert's brusque, almost offensive manner was not as attractive as Sullivan's easy companionability. This leaning of Carte's added to the difficulty between the partners and Gilbert later accused Carte of taking sides, for emotional reasons, against him. Not that Gilbert begrudged Sullivan his chance to compose a serious opera, but he was annoyed that the composer should bend so easily under the subtle pressure of the manager.

When the expenses for the production of *The Gondoliers* were tallied, Gilbert exploded. It was April, 1890, when Gilbert, reading over the analysis, objected to the enormous costs of ten or twelve items, such as the carpenter's charges for the two boats, the dressmaker's bills, and above all, £500 for a carpet in the front of the house! He could not see why the Company should be responsible for the expenses of the building Carte owned. Carte argued that it was normal for a lessee to return a building to its owner in the condition in which he found it, and that therefore the carpets that had been worn down by the thousands who came to see Gilbert and Sullivan productions should be replaced by the Company that benefited from the sale of those thousands of tickets. Gilbert refused to accept the argument and, suspecting more hidden losses, demanded a full accounting from Carte. At this Carte, who had a temper of his own, pointed out that he himself had taken all the risks of putting up the building, had rented it at a figure below the normal rental to the Company, and had even included all the profits from concessions within the theater as part of the receipts of the producing company—a pure gift on his part, since a manager would normally keep them for his own. In short, although he had operated this theater without any help from the authors, he had been kind enough to be very generous with the distribution of profits to them. He was offended that Gilbert should demand an accounting, and told the author so in so many words. The affair burst into court, where Gilbert proved his legal point, but Carte also proved his moral one. The result was no major change in the financial operations of the Company, but the near death of its internal good will.

Because this battle, the worst in all their association, had even involved Carte, it was Helen Lenoir Carte who stepped between the combatants. Both had spoken in anger, both had uttered things neither would have said under normal circumstances. She was firm with Gilbert—she must also have been with her husband although we have no record of it. She could not prevent the court battle, but she did prevent what was still only a breach from becoming a deep enmity.

Gilbert would have nothing to do with the new theater Carte built for Sullivan's serious opera. He thought it was too far from the center of commerce, too big a venture to be successful, and he *knew* that *he* was not fitted to write grand opera librettos. As it turned out, for once, Carte was wrong and Gilbert right. *Ivanhoe* was born with royal blessing, played a while and died. The English Opera House, once so elegant, faded into relative oblivion.

The Savoy was in bad straits also. There was no new Gilbert and Sullivan work to replace *The Gondoliers*. For the first time Carte permitted a different team of authors to write for it. They brought out *The Nautch Girl*, very much in the Gilbert and Sullivan tradition, with music by Edward Solomon. It closed after 199 performances. He made a second try with *The Vicar of Bray*, again with Solomon's music. It did much better, but it was not like old times.

Finally, in 1893, came another work by the old team, *Utopia, Limited*. Gilbert refused to work on the same contractual basis as before, which had led to a court fight about expenses, but preferred a definite percentage of the receipts as his share of the profits. Carte agreed, but *Utopia* did not last long enough to make much difference.

After that came *The Grand Duke*, a failure. The collaboration had died of old age and hard living.

But the D'Oyly Carte Opera Company lived on. Old works were revived, new actors and actresses joined from time to time. For a few years the money continued to flow in and Carte continued to distribute the profits as before. On the 7th of November, 1900, at a revival of *Patience*, Carte wanted all three partners to take a bow together. He and Gilbert made it, each on canes, but Sullivan lay at home in his bed in pain; he died near the end of the month.

Carte followed him, on the third of April, 1901. He left his wife in charge of the Company, which she managed with continued success until her own death in 1913. Then his son, Rupert, took it over. He produced nothing until the end of World War I, but afterwards Rupert D'Oyly Carte rebuilt the Savoy company and refurbished the productions, bringing the famous tradition to a new peak of success. He died in 1949, and Bridget D'Oyly Carte took over, keeping the management within the family that had made the Company famous.

Not once did Richard D'Oyly Carte interfere in Gilbert's writing and directing, nor in Sullivan's composing. Not once did he suggest changing a line or softening a note of satire. He gave the two authors a perfectly maintained theatrical machine with which they could do their very best work without restrictions. Without him they would never have produced the finely constructed tradition for which we know them today. Of course, New York, the city of American theater, has no repertory company yet to criticize, but where is the D'Oyly Carte who could make such a company really great?

The only times the audiences at the Savoy were conscious of Carte's presence were at the final curtain calls of opening nights. Having checked every detail in the theater before the play began, and having spoken a word of encouragement to each and every actor, actress, stage hand, and flunky before the first curtain, the quiet man would wait until the end and then take a bow after the authors had had theirs. When the audience was silent, Carte would announce that with their kind permission, the opera would be repeated each evening until further notice. Accompanied by their applause, he would retreat into the oblivion of his job.

THE SAVOY COMPANY

Original Members

Note: This list includes Martyn Green and Henry Lytton. Although neither sang a first performance, each was very famous in the Company.

NAME	VOICE	FIRST ROLES	OTHER ROLES
Baker, Mildred	Mezzo-Soprano	Olga	Vittoria
Barnett, Alice	Contralto	Fairy Queen, Lady Jane, Ruth (*Pirates,* in New York)	
Barrington, Rutland	Baritone	Archibald Grosvenor, Capt. Corcoran, Dr. Daly, Sir Despard Murgatroyd, Giuseppe, Hildebrand, Ludwig, Mountararat, Paramount, Pooh-Bah, Sergeant of Police (in London)	Don Alhambra del Bolero, Learned Judge, Wilfred Shadbolt, Private Willis
Bell, May	Soprano	Melene	
Bentham	Tenor	Alexis	
Bernard, A.	Contralto	Inez	
Billington, Fred	Baritone	Sergeant of Police (Paignton, Engl.)	Pooh-Bah
Blackmore, H. Enes	Baritone	Sir Bailey Barre	
Bond, Jessie	Mezzo-Soprano	Lady Angela, Edith (in New York), Hebe, Mad Margaret, Melissa, Iolanthe, Phoebe, Pitti-Sing, Tessa	Constance

NAME	VOICE	FIRST ROLES	OTHER ROLES
Bond, Neva	Soprano	Isabel (in London)	
Bovill, R.	Baritone	Pish-Tush	
Bowley, G.		Bunthorne's solicitor	
Bracy, Henry	Tenor	Hilarion	
Braham, Leonora	Soprano	Ida, Patience, Phyllis, Rose Maybud, Yum-Yum	Aline
Brandram, Rosina	Contralto	Lady Blanche, Dame Carruthers, Duchess of Plaza-Toro, Dame Hannah, Kate (*Pirates*, in New York), Katisha, Lady Sophy, Baroness von Krakenfeldt	Little Buttercup, Fairy Queen, Ruth (*Pirates*), Lady Sangazure, Lady Jane
Bromley, Nellie	Soprano	Plaintiff	
Brownlow, Wallace	Baritone	Luiz, Sir Richard Cholmondeley	
Carlton		Viscount Mentone	
Chard, Kate	Soprano	Psyche	
Clifton, F.	Baritone	Bill Bobstay, Notary	
Cole, Annie	Soprano	Vittoria	
Cross, Emily	Contralto	Ruth (*Pirates*, in London)	

(*Note:* Miss Cross was called to take the role just twenty-four hours before the opening, when Miss Barnett became ill)

Denny, W. H.	Bass-Baritone	Don Alhambra del Bolero, Scaphio, Wilfred Shadbolt	
Dymott	Baritone	Bob Becket	
Everard	Contralto	Little Buttercup, Mrs. Partlet	
Farren, Nellie		Mercury	

(*Note:* At a benefit performance for Miss Farren, in 1898, W. S. Gilbert played the part of The Learned Judge in *Trial by Jury*)

{ 167 }

NAME	VOICE	FIRST ROLES	OTHER ROLES
Findlay, Josephine	Mezzo-Soprano	Zorah (*Ruddigore*)	
Fishe, Scott	Baritone	Mr. Goldbury, Prince of Monte Carlo	Mikado
Fisher, Walter	Tenor	Defendant	
Fortescue, M.	Soprano	Celia, Lady Ella	

(*Note:* She played in her first Gilbert drama as Galatea, in *Pygmalion and Galatea.* She won the part because of her remarkable beauty.)

NAME	VOICE	FIRST ROLES	OTHER ROLES
Gray, Warwick	Bass-Baritone	Scynthius	
Green, Martyn	Baritone		Archibald Grosvenor, Capt. Corcoran, Counsel for the Plaintiff, Dr. Daly, Dick Deadeye, Duke of Plaza-Toro, King Gama, Giuseppe, Sir Joseph Porter, Jack Point, Ko-Ko, Luiz, Reginald Bunthorne, Robin Oakapple, Maj.-Gen. Stanley, Strephon, Wilfred Shadbolt

(*Note:* Martyn Green joined the company at Crewe, in 1922, to play Luiz. He left in 1951 to work in the United States. He played Ko-Ko in the film version of *The Mikado.* Having lost his leg in an accident, he was unable to continue playing Gilbert and Sullivan roles, but acted as producer for a television adaptation of *The Mikado,* starring Groucho Marx as Ko-Ko, in 1960. Since then he has been active in the American legitimate theater.)

NAME	VOICE	FIRST ROLES	OTHER ROLES
Grey, Sybil	Mezzo-Soprano	Fleta, Peep-Bo, Sacharissa	
Gridley, Lawrence	Baritone	Edward Corcoran	
Grossmith, George (Junior)	Baritone	Lord Chancellor, King Gama, Jack Point, John Wellington Wells, Sir Joseph Porter, Ko-Ko, Robin Oakapple, Reginald	The Learned Judge

NAME	VOICE	FIRST ROLES	OTHER ROLES
		Bunthorne, Maj.-Gen. Stanley (*Pirates,* in London)	

(*Note:* A famous comedian, he began life as a police reporter, then found profit in music-hall singing and personal appearances in the provinces. His gift for comedy made him famous in the roles listed. He first joined Gilbert and Sullivan as a chorus member, playing a juror in *Trial by Jury.*)

NAME	VOICE	FIRST ROLES	OTHER ROLES
Gwynne, Julia	Mezzo-Soprano	Edith, Leila, Lady Saphir	
Haswell, Bowden		Calynx	
Heathcote		Chloe	
Hervey, Rose	Soprano	Kate (*Yeomen*)	
Hewson, Jones	Baritone	Herald	Col. Calverley, Luiz, Sir Marmaduke Pointdextre, Pirate King, Pish-Tush, Sir Richard Cholmondeley
Hollingsworth	Baritone	Counsel for the Plaintiff	
Hood, Marion	Soprano	Mabel (*Pirates,* in London)	
Howell-Hersee	Soprano	Phylla	
Howson, Emma	Soprano	Josephine	
Johnston, Edith		Salata	
Kelleher	Baritone	Foreman of the Jury	
Kenningham, Charles	Tenor	Ernest Dummkopf, Capt. Fitzbattleaxe	Col. Fairfax, Marco, Nanki-Poo
La Rue, Lilian	Contralto	Kate (*Pirates,* in London)	
Lawrence, Nellie	Soprano	Fiametta	Isabel
Le Hay, John	Baritone	Phantis	
Lely, Durward	Tenor	Cyril, Duke of Dunstable, Nanki-Poo, Tolloller, Richard Dauntless	Alexis

(*Note:* His real name was Lyall, and he was Scottish, born in Arbroath.)

NAME	VOICE	FIRST ROLES	OTHER ROLES
Lewis, Rudolph	Bass	Adam Goodheart	Bob Becket
Lindsay		Ruth (*Ruddigore*)	
Lugg	Bass-Baritone	Guron	Notary
Lytton, Henry A.	Baritone		Archibald Grosvenor, Capt. Corcoran, Counsel for the Plaintiff, Dr. Daly, Dick Deadeye, Duke of Plaza-Toro, King Gama, Giuseppe, Jack Point, Sir Joseph Porter, Ko-Ko, Lord Chancellor, Mikado, Pirate King, Reginald Bunthorne, Robin Oakapple, Maj.-Gen. Stanley, Wilfred Shadbolt, Strephon

(*Note:* Lytton's real name was H. A. Henri. At seventeen he joined the Company as a member of the chorus of *Princess Ida* in Glasgow in 1884, and sang his last performance as Jack Point in Dublin in 1934, a span of fifty years. He stepped in to play Robin Oakapple in the second week of the first production of *Ruddigore* when Grossmith was taken ill.)

Manners, Charles	Bass-Baritone	Private Willis	

(*Note:* With his wife, Fanny Moody, he founded the Moody-Manners Opera Company, devoted to the production of operas in English.)

May, Alice	Soprano	Aline	
McIntosh, Nancy	Soprano	Princess Zara	

(*Note:* Nancy McIntosh was born in Cleveland, Ohio, in 1874. She was in England studying singing when Gilbert heard her at a party and suggested that she be heard by Sullivan. She had never been on stage before she was cast for Princess Zara. She became Gilbert's protégée, later his adopted daughter, and his heir.)

Moore, Decima	Soprano	Casilda	

(*Note:* Casilda was her first stage role of any kind, when she was not yet seventeen. It was she, later Lady Guggisberg, who had once been known as "Delicious Decima Moore," who founded the British Women's Emergency Corps in 1914.)

{ 170 }

NAME	VOICE	FIRST ROLES	OTHER ROLES
Owen, Emmie	Soprano	Nekaya, Princess of Monte Carlo	Constance, Gianetta, Hebe, Peep-Bo
Passmore, Walter	Baritone	Duke Rudolph, Tarara	Don Alhambra del Bolero, Lord Chancellor, John Wellington Wells, Sir Joseph Porter, Jack Point, Ko-Ko, Reginald Bunthorne, Sergeant of Police, Usher
Paul, Mrs. Howard	Contralto	Lady Sangazure	
Pepper	Baritone	Usher	
Perry, Beatrice		Martha	
Perry, Florence	Mezzo-Soprano	Kalyba, Lisa	Phoebe, Yum-Yum
Pounds, Courtice	Tenor	Fairfax, Marco	Defendant
Power, George	Tenor	Frederic (*Pirates*, in London), Ralph Rackstraw	
Ralland, Herbert	Baritone	Mr. Blushington	
Rose, Jessie	Mezzo-Soprano	Bertha	Lady Angela, Edith, Hebe, Iolanthe, Phyllis, Phoebe, Pitti-Sing, Tessa, Vittoria
Russell, Scott	Tenor	Lord Dramaleigh, Dr. Tannhäuser	Leonard Meryll
Ryley, Charles	Baritone	Florian	
Shirley, W. R.	Tenor	Leonard Meryll	
Sullivan, Fred	Baritone	Learned Judge, Apollo	

(*Note:* Fred Sullivan was the composer's brother.)

Temple, G.	Baritone	Samuel (*Pirates*, in London)	
Temple, Richard	Baritone	Arac, Col. Calverley, Dick Deadeye, Sir	

{ *171* }

NAME	VOICE	FIRST ROLES	OTHER ROLES
		Marmaduke Point-dextre, Mikado, Pirate King (*Pirates,* in London), Sergeant Meryll, Strephon, Sir Roderic Murgatroyd	
Thornton, Frank		Major Murgatroyd	
Twyman		Ada	
Ulmar, Geraldine	Mezzo-Soprano	Elsie Maynard, Gianetta	Josephine, Mabel, Yum-Yum
Vincent, Ruth	Soprano	Gretchen	Aline, Casilda, Elsie Maynard, Josephine, Kate (*Yeomen*), Plaintiff
von Palmay, Ilka	Soprano	Julia Jellicoe	Elsie Maynard, Nanki-Poo

(*Note:* This Hungarian beauty was imported to play the part because her accent would help portray the character. She was given a three-year contract. *The Grand Duke* failed so soon that there was a problem finding her another part to sing. Her portrayal of Elsie, however, was quite successful. She played Nanki-Poo in Germany before she entered England.)

Warwick, Giulia	Soprano	Constance	
Wilson, Ethel		Elsa	
Workman, C. H.	Baritone	Ben Hashbaz	Duke of Plaza-Toro, Jack Point, Sir Joseph Porter, Ko-Ko, Lord Chancellor, Reginald Bunthorne, Maj.-Gen. Stanley

(*Note:* Workman went to Japan to head a touring company there in which he played all the comedy leads.)

Wyatt, Frank	Baritone	Duke of Plaza-Toro	

CHRONOLOGY OF THE ERA OF GILBERT AND SULLIVAN

YEAR	THE OUTER WORLD	MUSIC AND OPERA	GILBERT & SULLIVAN
1836	Betsy Ross died; Buffalo Bill born; Republic of Texas established	First London performance of *L'Elisir d'Amore* by Donizetti	Gilbert born, 18 November
1837	Victoria became Queen of England		
1838	Bizet born; Lorenzo da Ponte (Mozart's librettist) died		Baby Gilbert kidnapped in Naples and ransomed for 25 pounds
1839	First photographs; Cézanne born	Verdi's first opera	
1840	Daudet born	Paganini died; Tschaikovsky born	
1841	First covered wagons arrive in California; Renoir born	Dvořák born	
1842	Kropotkin born; Tennyson's first poems published	New York Philharmonic Society formed	Sullivan born, 13 May
1843	Poe's *Murders in the Rue Morgue*	Grieg born, *Die Fliegende Holländer*	
1844	Nietzsche born	Stephen Foster's first published song	
1845	Texas annexed by U.S.A.	*Tannhäuser*	
1846	Parnell born; U.S.A. at war with Mexico; Lear's *A Book of Nonsense*	*La Damnation de Faust*	

YEAR	THE OUTER WORLD	MUSIC AND OPERA	GILBERT & SULLIVAN
1847	*Wuthering Heights; Evangeline;* Johnny Appleseed died	Mendelssohn died	
1848	Marx and Engels, *The Communist Manifesto;* Gauguin born; Thoreau on *Civil Disobedience*	Foster's *O Susanna*	
1849		Chopin died	
1850	First international copyright	*Lohengrin*	
1851	*Moby Dick;* the Crystal Palace opened	*Rigoletto*	
1852	Roget's *Thesaurus; Uncle Tom's Cabin*		
1853	Van Gogh born	*Il Trovatore; La Traviata*	
1854	Battle at Balaklava; Oscar Wilde born; Thoreau's *Walden*		
1855	Whitman, *Leaves of Grass;* end of Crimean War		Sullivan's first published song
1856	Sigmund Freud born; George Bernard Shaw born	Robert Schumann died	Sullivan won first Mendelssohn Scholarship; Gilbert translated a song for Mme. Parepa
1857	The Bessemer process for steel; *Madame Bovary;* Pasteur's theory of bacilli	Elgar born; Sullivan's father made Professor of Clarinet at Royal Military School of Music	Gilbert unsuccessful in getting published
1858		Puccini born; Leoncavallo born	Sullivan to Leipzig
1859	Darwin's *Origin of Species;* John Brown raided Harpers Ferry; first successful electric light	*Faust*	

YEAR	THE OUTER WORLD	MUSIC AND OPERA	GILBERT & SULLIVAN
1860	Abraham Lincoln elected President of U.S.A.; Schopenhauer died; Chekhov born	Albeniz born	Gilbert quit government job, became barrister
1861	Civil War in U.S.A.	Melba born	Sullivan returned to London; Gilbert published first "Bab Ballad" in *Fun*
1862	Thoreau died; Turgenev, *Fathers and Sons*	Debussy born; Delius born	Sullivan's *Tempest* at the Crystal Palace
1863	Battle of Gettysburg; first showing of Impressionists in Paris	Mascagni born	
1864		Richard Strauss born; Stephen Foster died	Sullivan's *L'Ile Enchantée, Kenilworth, The Sapphire Necklace* and *Irish Symphony*
1865	Booth killed Lincoln; Kipling born; *Alice's Adventures in Wonderland*	*Tristan und Isolde*	
1866	First transatlantic cable; *Crime and Punishment*	*Mignon*	Gilbert's *Dulcamara;* Sullivan's *In Memoriam,* Concerto for Cello, and a few songs
1867	Nobel invented dynamite; Marx *Das Kapital* begun	Toscanini born; *Peer Gynt*	Gilbert married; Sullivan visited Vienna; Sullivan's *Marmion Overture, Cox and Box, The Contrabandista*
1868	Disraeli became Prime Minister	Rossini died; *Die Meistersinger*	Gilbert's *Robert le Diable;* Sullivan's song *O Fair Dove*
1869	Suez Canal opened; first railroad across U.S.A.	Berlioz died; *Das Rheingold*	Gilbert's *Ages Ago,* at a rehearsal of which he met Sullivan; Sullivan's *The Prodigal Son*

YEAR	THE OUTER WORLD	MUSIC AND OPERA	GILBERT & SULLIVAN
1870	War between France and Germany; Lenin born; Dickens died	First Wagner in England; Balfe died	Gilbert's *Our Island Home, The Princess, The Palace of Truth;* Sullivan's overture *Di Ballo*
1871	Darwin's *Descent of Man;* Communist uprising in Paris; Buchanan published *The Fleshly School of Poetry*	*Aïda* in Cairo	Gilbert's *Great Expectations, Pygmalion and Galatea;* Sullivan's *Onward Christian Soldiers, Merchant of Venice;* THESPIS
1872		Vaughan Williams born	Sullivan's *Te Deum* for the Prince of Wales' recovery
1873	Rimbaud *Une Saison en Enfer*	Caruso born; Chaliapin born	Gilbert's *The Wicked World, The Wedding March;* Sullivan's *The Light of the World;* Sullivan made Doctor of Music at Cambridge
1874		Schönberg born; *Boris Godunov; Die Fledermaus*	Sullivan's *The Merry Wives of Windsor;* Gilbert's *Topsy-Turvydom*
1875	*Anna Karenina*	*Carmen;* Bizet died; Ravel born	TRIAL BY JURY; Gilbert's *Broken Hearts*
1876	Custer's last stand; telephone patented	Bayreuth Festspielhaus opened	Sullivan appointed principal of National Training School of Music (RCM); D'Oyly Carte leased the Comique for Comedy Opera Company
1877	Selden's horseless carriage; phonograph patented		THE SORCERER; Gilbert's *On Bail*
1878		Comedy Opera Company dissolved	H.M.S. PINAFORE; Sullivan's *Henry VIII, The Lost Chord;* Gilbert, Sullivan and

YEAR	THE OUTER WORLD	MUSIC AND OPERA	GILBERT & SULLIVAN
			Carte form company; Sullivan operated on for kidney stones, Gilbert's *The Ne'er Do Weel*
1879	Einstein born; Stalin born; Beecham born; Edison patented his incandescent lamp		THE PIRATES OF PENZANCE; Gilbert and Sullivan in New York; Sullivan made Doc. Mus. at Oxford
1880	*The Brothers Karamazov;* Flaubert died	Offenbach died	Sullivan's *The Martyr of Antioch* to Gilbert's text
1881	Dostoyevsky died; Picasso born	Bartók born; Carte opened Savoy Theater; Mussorgsky died	PATIENCE; Sullivan resigned National Training School; Gilbert's *Foggerty's Fairy*
1882	Darwin died; Rossetti died; Standard Oil Company formed	*Parsifal;* Stravinski born	IOLANTHE; Gilbert's *Comedy and Tragedy*
1883	Marx died in London; Brooklyn Bridge opened; Turgenev died	Wagner died; Metropolitan Opera opened; *Lakmé*	Sullivan knighted
1884	Daimler's gasoline engine; Shaw's first play; *Huckleberry Finn*	*Manon;* Smetana died	PRINCESS IDA
1885	Hertz discovered radio transmission	*Der Zigeunerbaron;* Berg born	THE MIKADO; Sullivan conductor of the Philharmonic
1886		Liszt died	Sullivan's *The Golden Legend*
1887	Victoria's Jubilee; first Sherlock Holmes story; Edison patented kinescope	*Otello;* Jenny Lind died	RUDDIGORE; Sullivan's *Macbeth;* Sullivan left Philharmonic
1888	Blizzard in New York	Lotte Lehmann born	THE YEOMEN OF THE GUARD; Gilbert's *Brantighame Hall*
1889	The Johnstown Flood; Hitler born		THE GONDOLIERS

YEAR	THE OUTER WORLD	MUSIC AND OPERA	GILBERT & SULLIVAN
1890	Van Gogh died; *The Golden Bough*	*Cavalleria Rusticana*	The "carpet" quarrel and lawsuit
1891	The zipper patented Gauguin to Tahiti	Carnegie Hall opened; Prokofiev born; Delibes died	Sullivan's *Ivanhoe;* reconciliation between the two; Gilbert bought Grim's Dyke estate; Gilbert's *Rosencrantz and Guildenstern*
1892	Whitman died; Tennyson died	Milhaud born; *I Pagliacci*	Sullivan's *Haddon Hall, The Forester;* Gilbert's *The Mountebanks*
1893		*Falstaff* (Verdi); Gounod died; Tschaikovsky died	UTOPIA, LIMITED; Gilbert's *His Excellency*
1894		Debussy *Prélude à l'Après-midi d'un Faune*	Sullivan's *King Arthur*
1895	*The Red Badge of Courage;* Freud's study of hysteria; Diesel's engine	Hindemith born	Sullivan's *The Chieftain*
1896	Langley flew a model airplane; Roentgen discovered X-rays	*La Bohème*	THE GRAND DUKE
1897	Victoria's Diamond Jubilee; Daudet died	Brahms died	Sullivan's *Victoria and Merrie England; Festival Te Deum*
1898	Spanish-American war; Bismarck died	Gershwin born	Sullivan's *The Beauty Stone;* last meeting between Gilbert and Sullivan at the Savoy
1899	Veblen's *Theory of the Leisure Class*	Johann Strauss died	Sullivan's *The Rose of Persia*
1900	Nietzsche died; Casey Jones died	Copland born; *Tosca; Louise*	Sullivan died, 22 November
1901	Victoria died; Mann's *Buddenbrooks*	Carte died; Verdi died	*Iolanthe,* the last G & S at the Savoy for five years

YEAR	THE OUTER WORLD	MUSIC AND OPERA	GILBERT & SULLIVAN
1902		*Pelléas et Mélisande*	
1903	Wright brothers fly; Gauguin died; Whistler died; Ford Motor Company founded		
1904	Chekhov died	Dvořák died	Gilbert's *The Fairy's Dilemma*
1905	Einstein stated his theory of relativity; Russian revolution		
1906	San Francisco earthquake; Cézanne died; Ibsen died	Helen Lenoir Carte reopened the Savoy	YEOMEN revived
1907			Gilbert knighted
1908	Pound's *A Lume Spento*	Rimsky-Korsakov died	Gilbert had sold 1¾ million libretti for nearly 30,000 pounds, not counting performance rights
1909		Schönberg's first atonal piece for piano	Gilbert's *The Fallen Fairies*
1910	Mme. Curie explained radioactivity; Mark Twain died		
1911	Charlie Chaplin appeared in New York	*Der Rosenkavalier; Memphis Blues*	Gilbert died, 29 May

ROLES IN THE OPERAS OF
GILBERT AND SULLIVAN

ROLE	VOICE	DESCRIPTION	OPERA	ORIGINAL PLAYERS*
Actors	Chorus		Grand Duke and Thespis	
Actresses	Chorus		Grand Duke and Thespis	
Ada		Girl Graduate	Princess Ida	1st Twyman
Adam Good-heart, Old	Bass	Robin's faith-ful servant	Ruddigore	1st R. Lewis
Admiral *see* Joseph Porter				
Alexis	Tenor	Son of Sir Mar-maduke of the Grenadier Guards	Sorcerer	1st Bentham; Lely
Alhambra del Bolero, Don	Bass	Grand Inquisi-tor	Gondoliers	1st Denny; Bar-rington, Pass-more
Aline	Soprano	Daughter of Lady Sanga-zure, betrothed to Alexis	Sorcerer	1st May; Braham, Vincent
Ancestors	Chorus		Ruddigore	
Angela, Lady	Mezzo-Soprano	A rapturous maiden	Patience	1st Bond; Rose
Angelina *see* Plaintiff				
Annabella *see* Lady Sangazure				

* Includes other members of the D'Oyly Carte Company who played the part.

ROLE	VOICE	DESCRIPTION	OPERA	ORIGINAL PLAYERS*
Annibale		Gondolier	Gondoliers	1st Wilbraham
Antonio	Baritone	Gondolier	Gondoliers	1st Metcalf
Apollo	Baritone	An aged deity	Thespis	1st F. Sullivan
Arac	Bass-Baritone	Son of King Gama	Princess Ida	1st R. Temple
Ararat *see* Mountararat				
Archibald Grosvenor	Baritone	An idyllic poet	Patience	1st Barrington; Lytton
Associate			Trial by Jury	
Attorneys			Trial by Jury	
Bailey Barre, Sir	Baritone	One of the Flowers of Progress	Utopia	1st Blackmore
Barons	Chorus		Iolanthe	
Barristers			Trial by Jury	
Ben Hashbaz	Baritone	Costumier	Grand Duke	1st Workman
Bertha	Mezzo-Soprano	Member of Dummkopf's company	Grand Duke	1st Rose
Bill Bobstay	Baritone	Boatswain's mate	Pinafore	1st Clifton; Cummings
Blanche, Lady	Contralto	Professor of abstract science	Princess Ida	1st Brandram
Blushington, Mr.	Baritone	Of the County Council	Utopia	1st Ralland
Bob Becket	Bass	Carpenter's mate	Pinafore	1st Dymott; R. Lewis
Bolero *see* Alhambra del Bolero				
Bridesmaid *see* First Bridesmaid				
Bridesmaid, Professional *see* Zorah				
Bridesmaids, Professional	Chorus		Ruddigore	

ROLE	VOICE	DESCRIPTION	OPERA	ORIGINAL PLAYERS°
Bunthorne *see* Reginald Bunthorne				
Bunthorne's Solicitor			Patience	1st Bowley
Buttercup, Little	Contralto	Mrs. Cripps, a Portsmouth bumboat woman	Pinafore	1st Everard; Brandram
Calverley, Colonel	Baritone	Officer of the Dragoon Guards	Patience	1st R. Temple; Hewson
Calynx		Utopian Vice-Chamberlain	Utopia	1st Haswell
Captain Corcoran *see* Corcoran (*see also* Edward Corcoran)				
Carruthers, Dame	Contralto	Housekeeper to the Tower	Yeomen	1st Brandram
Casilda	Soprano	Daughter of the Duke of Plaza-Toro	Gondoliers	1st Moore; Vincent
Celia	Soprano	Fairy	Iolanthe	1st Fortescue
Chamberlains	Chorus		Grand Duke	
Chancellor *see* Lord Chancellor				
Chloe		Girl Graduate	Princess Ida	1st Heathcote
Cholmondeley *see* Richard Cholmondeley				
Chumley *see* Richard Cholmondeley				
Citizen *see* First Citizen *see* Second Citizen				
Citizens	Chorus		Yeomen	
Conrad Murgatroyd, Sir		Twelfth Baronet, a ghost	Ruddigore	1st Burbank
Constance	Soprano	Daughter of Mrs. Partlet	Sorcerer	1st Warwick; J. Bond, Owen
Contadine	Chorus	Country girls	Gondoliers	

ROLE	VOICE	DESCRIPTION	OPERA	ORIGINAL PLAYERS*
Corcoran, Captain	Baritone	Commanding H.M.S. *Pinafore*	Pinafore	1st Barrington; Lytton

(*Note:* The Captain appears again, in *Utopia, Limited,* as representative of the British Navy. He is listed as Edward Corcoran, and is a bass.)

ROLE	VOICE	DESCRIPTION	OPERA	ORIGINAL PLAYERS*
Counsel for The Plaintiff	Baritone		Trial by Jury	1st Hollingsworth; Lytton
Courtiers	Chorus		Princess Ida	
Cymon		A Thespian	Thespis	1st Wilson
Cyril	Tenor	Hilarion's friend	Princess Ida	1st Lely
Daly, Doctor	Baritone	Vicar of Ploverleigh	Sorcerer	1st Barrington; Lytton
Daphne		A Thespian	Thespis	1st Tremaine
Daughters of Maj.-Gen. Stanley	Chorus		Pirates	

(*see also* Mabel, Edith, Kate, Isabel)

ROLE	VOICE	DESCRIPTION	OPERA	ORIGINAL PLAYERS*
Daughters of the Plough			Princess Ida	

Dauntless   *see* Richard Dauntless

ROLE	VOICE	DESCRIPTION	OPERA	ORIGINAL PLAYERS*
Defendant	Tenor		Trial by Jury	1st Fisher; Pounds
Desmond Murgatroyd, Sir		Sixteenth Baronet, a ghost	Ruddigore	1st Tuer
Despard Murgatroyd, Sir	Bass-Baritone	A wicked baronet	Ruddigore	1st Barrington
Diana		An aged deity	Thespis	1st Leigh
Dick Deadeye	Bass-Baritone	Able Seaman	Pinafore	1st R. Temple; Lytton

Don Alhambra   *see* Alhambra del Bolero

Dragoons   *see* Officers of Dragoon Guards
        see Calverley, Colonel
        see Murgatroyd, Major
        see Dunstable, Lt. the Duke of

ROLE	VOICE	DESCRIPTION	OPERA	ORIGINAL PLAYERS*
Dramaleigh, Lord	Tenor or High Baritone	British Lord Chamberlain	Utopia	1st Russell
Duchess of Plaza-Toro	Contralto		Gondoliers	1st Brandram

Duke *see* Rudolph
    see Dunstable, Lt., the Duke of

ROLE	VOICE	DESCRIPTION	OPERA	ORIGINAL PLAYERS*
Duke of Plaza-Toro	Baritone	A grandee of Spain	Gondoliers	1st Wyatt; Lytton, Workman
Dukes	Chorus		Iolanthe	

Dummkopf *see* Ernest Dummkopf

ROLE	VOICE	DESCRIPTION	OPERA	ORIGINAL PLAYERS*
Dunstable, Lt., the Duke of	Tenor	Officer of the Dragoon Guards	Patience	1st Lely
Earls	Chorus		Iolanthe	
Edith	Soprano	Daughter of Maj.-Gen. Stanley	Pirates	1st (N.Y.C.) J. Bond; 1st (London) Gwynne; Rose
Edward Corcoran, Captain Sir	Bass-Baritone	Of the Royal Navy	Utopia	1st Gridley

    (*see also* Corcoran, Captain)

Edwin *see* Defendant

ROLE	VOICE	DESCRIPTION	OPERA	ORIGINAL PLAYERS*
Ella, Lady	Soprano	Rapturous maiden	Patience	1st Fortescue
Elsa	Mezzo-Soprano	Member of Dummkopf's company	Grand Duke	1st Wilson
Elsie Maynard	Soprano	A strolling singer	Yeomen	1st Ulmar; Vincent, von Palmay
Ernest Dummkopf	Tenor	Theatrical manager	Grand Duke	1st Kenningham

Executioner *see* Headsman
    (*see also* Ko-Ko)

Exploder *see* Tarara

ROLE	VOICE	DESCRIPTION	OPERA	ORIGINAL PLAYERS*
Fairfax, Colonel	Tenor	Under sentence of death	Yeomen	1st Pounds; Kenningham
Fairies	Chorus		Iolanthe	
Fairies (*see also* Celia, Leila, Fleta, Iolanthe)				
Fairy Queen	Contralto		Iolanthe	1st Barnett; Brandram
Fiametta	Soprano	Country girl	Gondoliers	1st Lawrence
First Bridesmaid			Trial by Jury	
First Citizen			Yeomen	1st Redmond
First Lord of the Admiralty *see* Joseph Porter				
First Yeoman	Tenor		Yeomen	1st Wilbraham
Fitzbattleaxe, Captain	Tenor	Of the First Life Guards	Utopia	1st Kenningham
Fleta	Speaker	Fairy	Iolanthe	1st Grey
Florian	Baritone	Hilarion's friend	Princess Ida	1st Ryley
Flowers of Progress *see* Dramaleigh, Lord; Fitzbattleaxe, Captain; Edward Corcoran, Captain Sir; Goldbury, Mr.; Bailey Barre, Sir; Blushington, Mr.				
Foreman of the Jury	Bass-Baritone		Trial by Jury	1st Kelleher
Fourth Yeoman			Yeomen	1st R. Lewis
Francesco	Tenor	Gondolier	Gondoliers	1st Rose
Frederic	Tenor	Pirate apprentice	Pirates	1st (N.Y.C.) H. Talbot; 1st (London) Power
Gama, King	Baritone	Princess Ida's father	Princess Ida	1st Grossmith; Lytton
Gentlemen	Chorus		Yeomen	
Gianetta	Soprano	Country girl	Gondoliers	1st Ulmar; Owen

{ *185* }

ROLE	VOICE	DESCRIPTION	OPERA	ORIGINAL PLAYERS°
Gilbert Murgatroyd, Sir		Eighteenth Baronet, a ghost	Ruddigore	1st Wilbraham
Giorgio	Bass-Baritone	Gondolier	Gondoliers	1st de Pledge
Girl Graduate	*see* Sacharissa, Chloe, Ada			
Girl Graduates	Chorus		Princess Ida	
Giulia	Soprano	Country girl	Gondoliers	
Giuseppe Palmieri	Baritone	Gondolier, Marco's brother	Gondoliers	1st Barrington; Lytton
Goldbury, Mr.	Baritone	Company promoter, afterward Comptroller of the Utopian Household	Utopia	1st Fishe
Gondoliers (*see also* Giuseppe, Marco)	Chorus	Gondoliers		
Goodheart	*see* Adam Goodheart, Old			
Governess	*see* Sophy, Lady			
Graduate	*see* Sacharissa, Chloe, Ada			
Graduates	Chorus	Girl graduates	Princess Ida	
Grand Duke	*see* Rudolph			
Grand Inquisitor	*see* Alhambra del Bolero			
Gretchen	Soprano	Member of Dummkopf's company	Grand Duke	1st Vincent
Grosvenor	*see* Archibald Grosvenor			
Guards	Chorus		Mikado	
Guards	*see* Dragoons			
Guron	Bass-Baritone	Son of King Gama	Princess Ida	1st Lugg
Hannah, Dame	Contralto	Rose's Aunt	Ruddigore	1st Brandram
Headsman			Yeomen	1st Richards

ROLE	VOICE	DESCRIPTION	OPERA	ORIGINAL PLAYERS*
Hebe	Mezzo-Soprano	Sir Joseph's first cousin	Pinafore	1st J. Bond; Owen, Rose
Herald	Baritone		Grand Duke	1st Hewson
Heralds	Chorus		Gondoliers	
Hilarion	Tenor	King Hildebrand's son	Princess Ida	1st Bracy
Hildebrand, King	Bass-Baritone	Hilarion's father	Princess Ida	1st Barrington
Housekeeper	see Carruthers, Dame			
Ida, Princess	Soprano	Daughter of King Gama	Princess Ida	1st Braham
Inez	Contralto	Former foster-mother of the King	Gondoliers	1st Bernard
Inquisitor	see Alhambra del Bolero			
Iolanthe	Mezzo-Soprano	Strephon's mother, a fairy	Iolanthe	1st J. Bond; Rose
Isabel	Speaker	Daughter of Maj.-Gen. Stanley	Pirates	1st (N.Y.C.) Barlow; 1st (London) N. Bond; Lawrence
Jack Point	Baritone	A strolling jester	Yeomen	1st Grossmith; Lytton, Passmore, Workman
Jailer	see Wilfred Shadbolt			
Jane, Lady	Contralto	A rapturous maiden, violoncellist	Patience	1st Barnett; Brandram
Jasper Murgatroyd, Sir		Third Baronet, a ghost	Ruddigore	1st Charles
Jester	see Jack Point			

ROLE	VOICE	DESCRIPTION	OPERA	ORIGINAL PLAYERS*
John Welling-ton Wells	Baritone	Of J. W. Wells & Company, family sorcerers	Sorcerer	1st Grossmith; Passmore
Joseph Porter, K. C. B., Sir	Baritone	First Lord of the Admiralty	Pinafore	1st Grossmith; Green, Lytton, Passmore, Workman
Josephine	Soprano	The Captain's Daughter	Pinafore	1st Howson; Ulmar, Vincent
Judge *see* Learned Judge, Scaphio, Phantis				
Julia Jellicoe	Soprano	English Come-dienne	Grand Duke	1st von Palmay
Jupiter		Chief of the aged deities	Thespis	1st Maclean
Jurymen	Chorus	Trial by Jury		
Kalyba, Princess	Soprano	Younger daugh-ter of King Paramount	Utopia	1st F. Perry
Kate	Soprano	Niece to Dame Carruthers	Yeomen	1st Hervey; Vincent
Kate	Mezzo-Soprano	Daughter of Maj.-Gen. Stanley	Pirates	1st (N.Y.C.) Brandram; 1st (London) La Rue
Katisha	Contralto	An elderly lady in love with Nanki-Poo	Mikado	1st Brandram
King *see* Pirate King, Gama, Hildebrand, Paramount				
Ko-Ko	Baritone	Lord High Ex-ecutioner of Titipu	Mikado	1st Grossmith; Green, Lytton, Passmore, Workman
Lawyer *see* Bunthorne's Solicitor, Counsel for the Plaintiff				
Learned Judge	Baritone		Trial by Jury	1st F. Sullivan; Barrington, Grossmith

{ *188* }

ROLE	VOICE	DESCRIPTION	OPERA	ORIGINAL PLAYERS*
Leila	Mezzo-Soprano	Fairy	Iolanthe	1st Gwynne
Leonard Meryll	Tenor	Son of the Sergeant	Yeomen	1st Shirley; Russell
Lieutenant the Duke of Dunstable *see* Dunstable				
Lionel Murgatroyd, Sir		Sixth Baronet, a ghost	Ruddigore	1st Trevor
Lisa	Soprano	A soubrette	Grand Duke	1st F. Perry
Little Buttercup *see* Buttercup				
Lord Chancellor	Baritone	Phyllis' guardian	Iolanthe	1st Grossmith; Passmore, Workman
Ludwig	Baritone	Leading Comedian	Grand Duke	1st Barrington
Luiz	Tenor	Attendant to the Duke	Gondoliers	1st Brownlow; Hewson, Green
Mabel	Soprano	Daughter of Maj.-Gen. Stanley	Pirates	1st (N.Y.C.) B. Roosevelt; 1st (London) Hood; Ulmar
Mad Margaret	Mezzo-Soprano		Ruddigore	1st J. Bond
Maidens *see* Rapturous Maidens, Bridesmaids				
Major-General Stanley *see* Stanley				
Marco Palmieri	Tenor	Gondolier, Giuseppe's brother	Gondoliers	1st Pounds; Kenningham
Margaret *see* Mad Margaret				
Marines	Silent		Pinafore	
Marmaduke Pointdextre, Sir	Bass-Baritone	Elderly baronet	Sorcerer	1st R. Temple; Hewson
Marquises	Chorus		Iolanthe	
Mars		An aged deity	Thespis	1st Wood

{ *189* }

ROLE	VOICE	DESCRIPTION	OPERA	ORIGINAL PLAYERS*
Martha		Member of Dummkopf's company	Grand Duke	1st B. Perry
Melene	Soprano	Utopian Maiden	Utopia	1st Bell
Melissa	Mezzo-Soprano	Lady Blanche's daughter	Princess Ida	1st J. Bond
Men at Arms	Chorus		Gondoliers	
Mentone, Viscount			Grand Duke	1st Carlton
Mercury		A god	Thespis	1st Farren
Mervyn Murgatroyd, Sir		Twentieth Baronet, a ghost	Ruddigore	1st Cox
Meryll, Sergeant	Bass-Baritone	Of the Yeomen of the Guard	Yeomen	1st R. Temple
Meryll *(see also* Leonard Meryll, Phoebe Meryll)				
Mikado of Japan	Bass-Baritone		Mikado	1st R. Temple; Fishe, Lytton
Monte Carlo, Prince of	Baritone		Grand Duke	1st Fishe
Monte Carlo, Princess of	Soprano	Betrothed to Rudolph	Grand Duke	1st Owen
Mountararat, Earl of	Bass-Baritone		Iolanthe	1st Barrington
Mrs. Cripps *see* Buttercup				
Murgatroyd, Major		Officer of the Dragoon Guards	Patience	1st Thornton
Murgatroyd *see* Conrad, Desmond, Despard, Gilbert, Jasper, Lionel, Mervyn, Roderick, Rupert, Ruthven				
Nanki-Poo	Tenor	Son of the Mikado, disguised as a wandering minstrel	Mikado	1st Lely; Kenningham

{ *190* }

ROLE	VOICE	DESCRIPTION	OPERA	ORIGINAL PLAYERS°
Nekaya, Princess	Soprano	Younger daughter of King Paramount	Utopia	1st Owen
Nicemis		A Thespian	Thespis	1st Loseby
Nobles	Chorus		Grand Duke Mikado	
Notary (*see also* Tannhäuser, Doctor)	Bass		Sorcerer	1st Clifton; Lugg
Oakapple *see* Robin Oakapple				
Officers	Chorus		Ruddigore	
Officers of Dragoon Guards	Chorus		Patience	
Olga		Member of Dummkopf's company	Grand Duke	1st Baker
Pages	Silent		Gondoliers	
Palmieri *see* Giuseppe, Marco				
Paramount the First	Baritone	King of Utopia	Utopia	1st Barrington
Partlet, Mrs.	Contralto	A pew-opener	Sorcerer	1st Everard
Patience	Soprano	A dairy-maid	Patience	1st Braham
Peep-Bo	Soprano or Mezzo-Soprano	Ward of Ko-Ko	Mikado	1st Grey; Owen
Peers	Chorus		Iolanthe	
Phantis	Bass-Baritone	Judge of the Utopian Supreme Court	Utopia	1st Le Hay
Phoebe Meryll	Mezzo-Soprano	Sgt. Meryll's daughter	Yeomen	1st J. Bond; F. Perry, Rose
Phylla	Soprano	Utopian maiden	Utopia	1st Howell-Hersee; Easton
Phyllis	Soprano	Ward in Chancery, in love with Strephon	Iolanthe	1st Braham; Rose

{ *191* }

ROLE	VOICE	DESCRIPTION	OPERA	ORIGINAL PLAYERS*
Pirate King	Bass-Baritone		Pirates	1st (N.Y.C.) Broccolini; 1st (London) R. Temple; Hewson; Lytton
Pirates	Chorus		Pirates	
Pish-Tush	Baritone	A noble lord	Mikado	1st Bovill; Hewson
Pitti-Sing	Mezzo-Soprano	Ward of Ko-Ko	Mikado	1st J. Bond; Rose
Plaintiff	Soprano		Trial by Jury	1st Bromley; Vincent
Plaza-Toro *see* Duke of Plaza-Toro				
Point *see* Jack Point				
Police	Chorus		Pirates	
Police Sergeant *see* Sergeant of Police				
Pooh-Bah	Bass-Baritone	Lord High Everything Else	Mikado	1st Barrington; Billington
Preposteros		A Thespian	Thespis	1st Payne
Pretteia		A Thespian	Thespis	1st Berend
Prince *see* Nanki-Poo, Hilarion, Monte Carlo				
Private Willis *see* Willis, Private				
Professional Bridesmaids (*see also* Zorah, Ruth)	Chorus		Ruddigore	
Professor of Abstract Science *see* Blanche, Lady				
Professor of Humanities *see* Psyche, Lady				
Psyche, Lady	Soprano	Professor of Humanities	Princess Ida	1st Chard
Public	Chorus		Trial by Jury	
Public Exploder *see* Tarara				
Queen *see* Fairy Queen				

ROLE	VOICE	DESCRIPTION	OPERA	ORIGINAL PLAYERS*
Ralph Rackstraw	Tenor	Able seaman	Pinafore	1st Power
Rapturous Maidens (*see also* Angela, Saphir, Ella, Jane)	Chorus		Patience	
Reginald Bunthorne	Baritone	A fleshly poet	Patience	1st Grossmith; Green, Lytton, Passmore, Workman
Richard Cholmondeley, Sir	Baritone	Lieutenant of the Tower	Yeomen	1st Brownlow; Hewson
Richard Dauntless	Tenor	Foster brother of Robin Oakapple and a Man-o'-war's man	Ruddigore	1st Lely
Robin Oakapple	Baritone	Sir Ruthven Murgatroyd disguised as a young farmer	Ruddigore	1st Grossmith; Lytton

(*Note:* Lytton took over the part during the second week, when Grossmith was taken ill.)

ROLE	VOICE	DESCRIPTION	OPERA	ORIGINAL PLAYERS*
Roderic Murgatroyd, Sir	Bass-Baritone	Twenty-first baronet, a ghost	Ruddigore	1st Temple
Rose Maybud	Soprano	A village maiden	Ruddigore	1st Braham
Rudolph	Baritone	Grand Duke of Pfennig-Halbpfennig	Grand Duke	1st Passmore
Rupert Murgatroyd, Sir	Bass-Baritone	First Baronet, a ghost	Ruddigore	1st Price
Ruth	Contralto	Pirate maid of all work	Pirates	1st (N.Y.C.) Barnett; 1st (London) Cross; Brandram

{ 193 }

ROLE	VOICE	DESCRIPTION	OPERA	ORIGINAL PLAYERS*
Ruth		Professional Bridesmaid	Ruddigore	1st Lindsay
Ruthven Murgatroyd, Sir	*see* Robin Oakapple			
Sacharissa	Soprano	Girl Graduate	Princess Ida	1st Grey
Sailors	Chorus		Pinafore	
Salata		Utopian maiden	Utopia	1st Johnston
Samuel	Baritone	Pirate King's lieutenant	Pirates	1st (N.Y.C.) Cook; 1st (London) G. Temple; Cummings
Sangazure, Lady	Contralto	Lady of ancient lineage	Sorcerer	1st Paul; Brandram
Saphir, Lady	Mezzo-Soprano	A rapturous maiden	Patience	1st Gwynne
Scaphio	Baritone	Judge of the Utopian Supreme Court	Utopia	1st Denny
School Girls	Chorus		Mikado	
(*see also* Yum-Yum, Pitti-Sing, Peep-Bo)				
Scynthius	Bass-Baritone	Son of King Gama	Princess Ida	1st Gray
Second Citizen			Yeomen	1st Boyd
Second Yeoman	Baritone		Yeomen	1st Medcalf
Sergeant of Marines			Pinafore	1st H. Talbot
Sergeant of Police	Bass-Baritone		Pirates	1st (N.Y.C.) Clifton; 1st (Paignton) Billington; 1st (London) Barrington; Passmore
Shadbolt	*see* Wilfred Shadbolt			
Sillimon		A Thespian	Thespis	1st Taylor
Singer	*see* Elsie Maynard *see* Nanki-Poo			

ROLE	VOICE	DESCRIPTION	OPERA	ORIGINAL PLAYERS°
Sisters, Cousins, Aunts	Chorus	Of the First Lord of the Admiralty	Pinafore	
Soldiers	Chorus		Princess Ida	
Solicitor *see* Bunthorne's Solicitor				
Sophy, Lady	Contralto	English gouvernante	Utopia	1st Brandram
Sorcerer *see* John Wellington Wells				
Soubrette *see* Lisa				
Sparkeion		A Thespian	Thespis	1st Clary
Stanley, Maj.-Gen.	Baritone		Pirates	1st (N.Y.C.) J. H. Ryley; 1st (Paignton) R. Mansfield; 1st (London) Grossmith; Green, Lytton, Workman
Strephon	Baritone	A young man half fairy, half mortal	Iolanthe	1st R. Temple; Lytton
Stupidas		A Thespian	Thespis	1st Payne
Tannhäuser, Dr.	Tenor	Notary	Grand Duke	1st Russell
Tarara	Baritone	Public Exploder	Utopia	1st Passmore
Tessa	Mezzo-Soprano	Country girl	Gondoliers	1st J. Bond; Rose
Thespians *see cast of the opera* Thespis				
Thespis		Chief actor	Thespis	1st Toole
Third Yeoman			Yeomen	1st Merton
Three little maids *see* Yum-Yum, Pitti-Sing, Peep-Bo				
Timidon		A Thespian	Thespis	1st Marshall
Tipseion		A Thespian	Thespis	1st Soutar
Tolloller, Earl of	Tenor		Iolanthe	1st Lely

ROLE	VOICE	DESCRIPTION	OPERA	ORIGINAL PLAYERS*
Tom Tucker		Midshipmite	Pinafore	
Trainbearer			Iolanthe	
Usher	Bass-Baritone		Trial by Jury	1st Pepper; Passmore
Vicar *see* Daly, Doctor				
Villagers	Chorus		Ruddigore	
Villagers	Chorus		Sorcerer	
Viscount *see* Mentone				
Viscounts	Chorus		Iolanthe	
Vittoria	Mezzo-Soprano	Country girl	Gondoliers	1st Cole; Rose, Baker
von Kraken-feldt, Baroness	Contralto	Betrothed to Rudolph	Grand Duke	1st Brandram
Wilfred Shad-bolt	Bass	Head Jailer and Assistant Tormentor	Yeomen	1st Denny; Barrington, Lytton
Willis, Private	Bass	Of the Grenadier Guards	Iolanthe	1st Manners; Barrington
Yeomen (*see also* First Yeoman, Second Yeoman)				
Yeomen of the Guard	Chorus		Yeomen	
Yum-Yum	Soprano	Ward of Ko-Ko	Mikado	1st Braham; F. Perry, Ulmar
Zara, Princess	Soprano	Eldest daughter of Paramount	Utopia	1st McIntosh
Zorah	Soprano	Professional bridesmaid	Ruddigore	1st Findlay
Zorah (*see also* Mrs. Partlet)				

FIRST LINES AND FAMOUS LINES
FROM THE OPERAS

LINE	SINGER	OPERA	ACT
A British tar is a soaring soul (*Glee*)	Ralph, Boatswain's Mate, Carpenter's Mate, Chorus	Pinafore	I
A company promoter this	Zara	Utopia	I (*in finale*)
A complicated gentleman allow me to present	Zara	Utopia	I (*in finale*)
A is happy, B is not *see* See how the fates			
A King of autocratic power	Paramount	Utopia	I
A lady fair, of lineage high	Psyche	Princess Ida	II
A laughing boy but yesterday	Sgt. Meryll	Yeomen	I
A magnet hung in a hardware shop	Archibald Grosvenor	Patience	II
A maiden fair to see (*Ballad*)	Ralph, Chorus	Pinafore	I
A man who would woo a fair maid (*Trio*)	Elsie, Phoebe, Fairfax	Yeomen	II
A many years ago	Buttercup	Pinafore	II
A more humane Mikado never (*Precedes* My object all sublime)	Mikado, Chorus	Mikado	II
A nice dilemma we have here	Learned Judge, Counsel, Defendant, Plaintiff, Usher, Foreman of the Jury	Trial by Jury	
A policeman's lot is not a happy one *see* When a felon's not engaged in his employment			

LINE	SINGER	OPERA	ACT
A rollicking band of pirates we	Sergeant, Pirates, Police, Chorus	Pirates	II
A shepherd I	Strephon, Ensemble	Iolanthe	I
A tenor, all singers above	Fitzbattleaxe	Utopia	II
A wandering minstrel I	Nanki-Poo, Chorus	Mikado	I
A woman's college! maddest folly going! (*Recitative preceding* They intend to send a wire)	Florian	Ida	II
A wonderful joy our eyes to bless	Goldbury	Utopia	II
Admiral's song *see* I am the monarch of the sea			
After much debate internal	Duke	Patience	II (*in finale*)
After sailing to this island	Tessa, Gianetta	Gondoliers	II
Ah! gallant soldier, brave and true	Zara, Fitzbattleaxe	Utopia	I
Ah, well-beloved *see* O rapture, when alone together			
Alas! I waver to and fro (*Trio*)	Phoebe, Leonard, Sgt. Meryll	Yeomen	I
Alas! that lovers thus should meet	Aline, Dr. Daly	Sorcerer	II
All frenzied with despair I rave	Cholmondeley, Ensemble	Yeomen	I (*in finale*)
All hail great judge!	Chorus	Trial by Jury	
All in all since that fond meeting *see* None shall part us from each other			
All is prepared (*Recitative*)	Mabel, Frederic	Pirates	II
All shall equal be *see* For everyone who feels inclined			
All the legal furies seize you!	Learned Judge	Trial by Jury	
Alone, and yet alive! (*Recitative for* Hearts do not break)			
Alone and unobserved *see* Am I alone			
Although of native maids the cream	Nekaya, Kalyba	Utopia	I

LINE	SINGER	OPERA	ACT
Am I alone and unobserved?	Bunthorne	Patience	I

(*Recitative for* If you're anxious for to shine)

An ultra-poetical, super-aesthetical   *see* When I go out of door

| And a good judge, too | Chorus | Trial by Jury | |

(*Appears first in the song* When I, good friends, was called to the bar; *Appears second in finale* Oh, joy unbounded)

And everyone will say as you walk your mystic way   *see* If you're anxious for to shine

Ape and the lady   *see* A lady fair of lineage high

Art is wrong and Nature right   *see* Whatever you are—be that

As in a month you've got to die	Pooh-Bah	Mikado	I
			(*in finale*)
As pure and blameless peasant	Robin	Ruddigore	I
As some day it may happen	Ko-Ko, Nobles	Mikado	I
Away! away! My heart's on fire!	Ruth, Pirate King,	Pirates	II
(*Trio*)	Frederic		

Away we go   *see* Then away we go to an island fair

Barcarole   *see* Over the bright blue sea

| Behold the Lord High Execu-tioner | Noblemen | Mikado | I |

Better far to live   *see* Oh, better far

Beware! beware! beware!   *see* Painted emblems of a race

Big, big D—   *see* I am the Captain of the Pinafore

Blameless dances   *see* I was once a very abandoned person

Blue blood!   *see* Spurn not the nobly born

| Bold-faced ranger (perfect stranger) | Lady Sophy | Utopia | I |

Bolero   *see* Dance a cachucha

Bow, bow, to his daughter-in-law elect!   *see* Miya Sama

Braid the raven hair	Pitti-Sing, Chorus	Mikado	II
			(*opening*)
Bridegroom and bride!	Chorus	Gondoliers	I

Bridesmaids' chorus   *see* Comes the broken flower

LINE	SINGER	OPERA	ACT
Brightly dawns our wedding day *(Madrigal)*	Yum-Yum, Pitti-Sing, Nanki-Poo, Go-To	Mikado	II

Bunthorne's entrance   *see* In a doleful train

Bunthorne's poem   *see* Oh, Hollow, hollow, hollow!

| Buon' giorno, signorine! | Marco, Giuseppe, Chorus of girls | Gondoliers | I |

Buttercup's song   *see* I'm called Little Buttercup

Cachucha   *see* Dance a cachucha

Can't guess!   *see* Oh, why am I moody and sad?

Captain's song   *see* I am the Captain of the Pinafore

| Carefully on tiptoe stealing | Ensemble | Pinafore | II |

Chattering chorus   *see* How beautifully blue the sky

| Cheerily carols the lark (*Scena preceding* To a garden full of posies) | Margaret | Ruddigore | I |

| Climbing over rocky mountain | Edith, Kate, Daughters of the Major-General | Pirates | I |

(*Note: This chorus was first used in* Thespis, *and is one of the two musical numbers remaining from that opera.*)

Come, friends, who plough the sea   *see* With cat-like tread, upon our prey we steal

(*Note: The tune for these words is now known as* Hail, hail, the gang's all here!)

Come, mighty Must!	Blanche	Ida	II
Comes the broken flower	Bridesmaids	Trial by Jury	
Comes the pretty young bride	Women	Yeomen	II (*in finale*)

Conceive me if you can   *see* When I go out of door

Couplets   *see* Didst thou not, oh, Leonard Meryll

| Dance a cachucha, fandango, bolero | Chorus | Gondoliers | II |

Dark danger hangs upon the deed!   *see* Alas! I waver to and fro!

Darwinian man   *see* A lady fair, of lineage high

LINE	SINGER	OPERA	ACT
Dear friends, take pity on my lot	Constance	Sorcerer	II

Death is the only true un-
raveller
  (*Last line of the recitative before* Try we life, long)

Death to the invader!	Chorus	Ida	III (*opening*)

Defer, defer, to the Lord High Executioner! *see* Behold the Lord High Executioner

Didst thou not, oh, Leonard Meryll (*Couplets*)	1st and 2nd Yeo-men, Chorus	Yeomen	I

Divorce is nearly obsolete in England *see* Society has quite forsaken

Do not forget you've married me! *see* Now, Marco dear

Eagle high in cloudland soaring	Chorus unaccom-panied	Utopia	II
Eat, drink, and be gay (*Tea-cup brindisi*)	Marmaduke, Chorus	Sorcerer	I

Elegiacs *see* Comes the pretty young bride

Elliptical billiard balls *see* My object all sublime

Elopement *see* Carefully on tiptoe stealing

English girls *see* A wonderful joy our eyes to bless

Entrance of the Mikado *see* Miya sama

Entrance of the peers *see* Loudly let the trumpet bray

Etiquette lesson *see* I am a courtier grave and serious

Every day, as the days roll on
  (*Zorah's solo in* Fair is Rose)

Every maid is the maid for me! *see* I am a maiden, cold and stately

Everybody says I'm such a disagreeable man *see* If you give me your attention

Everyone is now a fairy *see* Soon as we may

Exactly so! *see* True love must single-hearted be

Expressive glances (*Trio*)	Hilarion, Cyril, Florian	Ida	I

Fading is the taper waist *see* Silvered is the raven hair

LINE	SINGER	OPERA	ACT
Fagan for a father *see* Fold your flapping wings			
Faint heart never won fair lady *see* If you go in			
Fair is Rose as the bright May-day	Bridesmaids	Ruddigore	I *(opening)*
Fair moon, to thee I sing	Capt. Corcoran	Pinafore	II
Fandango *see* Dance a cachucha			
Fare thee well, attractive stranger	Ensemble	Iolanthe	I
Farewell, my own (*Octette*)	Ralph, Josephine, Joseph Porter, Boatswain, Dick Deadeye, Hebe, Buttercup, Chorus	Pinafore	II
Farewell! Thou hadst my heart	Rose	Ruddigore	I
Finale *see* Kind sir, you cannot have the heart		Gondoliers	I
see Now let the loyal lieges gather round		Gondoliers	II
Finale *see* For a month to dwell		Ida	I
see Oh! joy, our chief is saved		Ida	II
see With joy abiding		Ida	III
Finale *see* When darkly looms the day		Iolanthe	I
see Soon as we may		Iolanthe	II
Finale *see* With aspect stern		Mikado	I
see For he's gone and married Yum-Yum		Mikado	II
Finale *see* Let the merry cymbals sound		Patience	I
see After much debate internal		Patience	II
Finale *see* For he's the captain of the *Pinafore*		Pinafore	II
Finale *see* Having been a wicked baronet a week		Ruddigore	II
Finale *see* Sprites of earth and air		Sorcerer	I
see Or I or he must die!		Sorcerer	II
Finale *see* Oh, joy unbounded		Trial by Jury	
Finale *see* Although your royal summons to appear		Utopia	I
see There's a little group of isles		Utopia	II
Finale *see* Comes the pretty young bride		Yeomen	II
First, we polish off some batches *see* Rising early in the morning			
First you're born—and I'll be bound	Paramount	Utopia	I

LINE	SINGER	OPERA	ACT
Five years have flown since I took wing	Zara, Chorus	Utopia	I
Fold your flapping wings (*Note: This song was taken out after the opening of the opera because of critical disapproval.*)	Strephon	Iolanthe	II
For a month to dwell (*Trio*)	Arac, Guron, Scynthius	Ida	I (*in finale*)
For English girls are good as gold *see* Although of native maids the cream			
For every one who feels inclined	Marco, Giuseppe, Chorus	Gondoliers	I (*in finale*)
For he's going to marry Yum-Yum (*Note: Appears again as finale of Act II*)	Pitti-Sing, Chorus	Mikado	I (*in finale*)
For he's the captain of the Pinafore (*see also* I am the Captain of the Pinafore)	Capt. Corcoran, Chorus	Pinafore	II (*in finale*)
For I am blithe and I am gay *see* I cannot tell what this love may be			
For now I'm a judge *see* When I, good friends, was called to the bar			
For riches and rank I do not long (*Ballad*)	Phyllis	Iolanthe	I
For the merriest fellows are we, tra-la	Antonio, Chorus	Gondoliers	I
Free from his fetters grim (*Ballad*)	Fairfax	Yeomen	II
From bias free of every kind *see* Now, jurymen hear my advice			
From charms intramural *see* When thoroughly tired			
From every kind of man obedience I expect (*see also* Miya sama)	Mikado, Katisha, Chorus	Mikado	II
From the briny sea (*Precedes* I shipped, d'ye see)	Bridesmaids	Ruddigore	I
From the sunny Spanish shore	Duke, Duchess of Plaza-Toro, Casilda, Luiz	Gondoliers	I
Gaily tripping, lightly skipping	Sisters, Cousins, Aunts	Pinafore	I

LINE	SINGER	OPERA	ACT

Gavotte
(*Occurs after* When the buds are blossoming; *see also* I am a courtier grave and serious.)

| Gentle Jane was as good as gold (*One of Grosvenor's poems*) | Archibald | Patience | II |

| Gently, gently (*Trio*) | Hilarion, Cyril, Florian | Ida | II |

Ghosts' chorus   *see* Painted emblems of a race

| Go away, madam | Lord Chancellor | Iolanthe | I (*in finale*) |

| Go, breaking heart | Lady Ella | Patience | I |

| Good morrow, good lover! | Phyllis | Iolanthe | I |

| Good morrow, good mother! | Strephon | Iolanthe | I |

Hail, hail, the gang's all here
(*The tune of this song was taken from Sullivan's tune for* Come, friends, who plough the sea.)

| Hail, Poetry, thou heaven-born maid! | Ensemble | Pirates | I (*in finale*) |

| Hail the bride of seventeen summers | Bridesmaids | Ruddigore | I (*in finale*) |

| Hail! the valiant fellow | Chorus | Yeomen | II |

| Happily coupled are we | Rose, Richard | Ruddigore | II |

| Hark, the hour of ten is sounding | Chorus | Trial by Jury | (*opening*) |

| Hate me! I drop my H's | Lady Sangazure, John Wellington Wells | Sorcerer | II |

Haughty, humble, coy or free   *see* I am a maiden, cold and stately

| Having been a wicked baronet a week | Robin, Rose, Richard, Despard, Margaret | Ruddigore | II (*finale*) |

He is an Englishman!   *see* I, humble, poor and lowly born

| He loves! (*Ballad*) | Iolanthe | Iolanthe | II |

He was a little boy   *see* Long years ago, fourteen maybe

He will have to be contented   *see* If Saphir I choose to marry

LINE	SINGER	OPERA	ACT
He yields! He answers to our call!	Ghosts	Ruddigore	II
Headache song *see* When you're lying awake			
Hearts do not break	Katisha	Mikado	II
Heighdy! heighdy! *see* I have a song to sing, O!			
Henceforward, of a verity	Paramount	Utopia	I (*in finale*)
Here far away from all the world	Sparkeion, Nicemis	Thespis	I
Here is a case unprecedented (*Quintet*)	Marco, Giuseppe, Casilda, Gianetta, Tessa	Gondoliers	II
Here we are, at the risk of our lives	Girls	Gondoliers	II
Here's a how-de-do! (*Trio*)	Yum-Yum, Ko-Ko, Nanki-Poo	Mikado	II
Here's a man of jollity	Chorus	Yeomen	I
Here's a pretty kettle of fish! *see* Strephon's a Member of Parliament			
Here's a pretty mess *see* Here's a how-de-do			
Here's a state of things *see* Here's a how-de-do			
Hereupon we're both agreed	Jack Point, Wilfred Shadbolt	Yeomen	II
He's going to marry Yum-Yum *see* For he's going to marry Yum-Yum			
Hey, but I'm doleful, willow willow waly! *see* Prithee, pretty maiden			
Hip, hip, hurrah! *see* Now hearken to my strict command			
His sisters and his cousins and his aunts *see* I am the monarch of the sea			
Hold, monsters! (*Recitative and chorus*)	Mabel, Samuel, Major-General, Daughters, Pirates	Pirates	I
Hornpipe (*The hornpipe was added after the song* I shipped, d'ye see)			
How beautifully blue the sky! (*Chattering chorus*)	Mabel, Daughters of the Maj.-Gen., Frederic	Pirates	I

LINE	SINGER	OPERA	ACT
How fair! how modest! how discreet!	Chorus	Utopia	I
(*Precedes* Although of native maids the cream)			
How say you, maiden, will you wed	Elsie, Jack Point, Lieutenant	Yeomen	I
(*Trio*)			
Hunger, I beg to state *see* Merrily ring the luncheon bell			
Hush, hush, not a word!	Major-General,	Pirates	II
(*Recitative, Solo, Chorus*)	Frederic, Pirates, Police		
I am a courtier grave and serious	Duke, Duchess of Plaza-Toro, Casilda,	Gondoliers	II
(*Gavotte*)	Marco, Giuseppe		
I am a maiden, cold and stately	Hilarion, Cyril,	Ida	II
(*Trio*)	Florian		
I am so proud *see* Trio about Execution			
I am the Captain of the *Pinafore*	Captain Corcoran	Pinafore	I
(*see also* For he's the captain of the *Pinafore*)			
I am the monarch of the sea	Joseph Porter, Chorus	Pinafore	I
(*Followed by* When I was a lad)			
I am the moon, the lamp of night	Nicemis	Thespis	I
I am the very model of a modern Major-General	Stanley, Daughters, Pirates	Pirates	I
I built upon a rock	Ida	Ida	III
I cannot tell what this love may be	Patience	Patience	I
I can't think why! *see* If you give me your attention			
I have a song to sing, O!	Elsie, Jack Point, Chorus	Yeomen	I
(*Also sung at end of opera by Jack Point*)			
I hear the soft note of the echoing voice	Angela, Saphir, Ella, Calverley,	Patience	I
(*Sextet*)	Dunstable, Major Murgatroyd		
I heard one day *see* Trio about Execution			

LINE	SINGER	OPERA	ACT
I, humble, poor and lowly born	Ralph, Josephine, Chorus	Pinafore	II
I know a youth who loves a little maid	Rose, Robin	Ruddigore	I
I love him—I love him	Plaintiff, Defendant	Trial by Jury	
I never use a big, big D— *see* I am the Captain of the *Pinafore*			
I once knew a chap who discharged a function	Thespis	Thespis	I
I once was a very abandoned person	Despard, Mad Margaret	Ruddigore	II
I once was as meek as a newborn lamb	Robin, Adam Goodheart	Ruddigore	II *(opening)*
I polished up the handle of the big front door *see* When I was a lad			
I shipped, d'ye see, in a Revenue sloop (*Ballad*)	Richard	Ruddigore	I
I smoke like a furnace—I'm always in liquor *see* I love him, I love him			
I stole the prince and I brought him here	Don Alhambra	Gondoliers	I
I the tree and thou the flower *see* None shall part us from each other			
I was a love-sick boy! *see* When first my old, old love I knew			
I will marry her myself! *see* All the legal furies seize you			
I would kiss you fondly thus *see* Were you not to Ko-Ko plighted			
Ida was a twelvemonth old (*Ballad*)	Hilarion	Ida	I
If love is a thorn *see* I cannot tell what this love may be			
If Saphir I choose to marry (*Quintet*)	Col. Calverley, Major Murgatroyd, Angela, Saphir, Duke of Dunstable	Patience	II
If somebody there chanced to be (*Ballad*)	Rose	Ruddigore	I
If there be pardon in your breast	Patience, Chorus	Patience	I *(in finale)*

LINE	SINGER	OPERA	ACT
If you ask us how we live	Leila	Iolanthe	I
If you give me your attention, I will tell you what I am	Gama	Ida	I
If you go in (Trio)	Lord Chancellor, Mountararat, Tolloller	Iolanthe	II
If you think that, when banded in unity (Trio)	Scaphio, Phantis, Paramount	Utopia	II
If you walk down Piccadilly with a poppy or a lily to shine	see If you're anxious for		
If you want a receipt for that popular mystery	Calverley	Patience	I
If you want to know who we are	Noblemen	Mikado	I (opening)
If you wish in the world to advance	see My boy, you may take it from me		
If we're weak enough to tarry	Strephon, Phyllis	Iolanthe	II
If you're anxious for to shine in the high aesthetic line	Reginald Bun-thorne	Patience	I
I'm called Little Buttercup	Buttercup	Pinafore	I
I'm Captain Corcoran, K. C. B.	Edward Corcoran	Utopia	I (in finale)
I'm very much pained to refuse	see Of all the young ladies I know		
In a contemplative fashion (Quartet)	Marco, Giuseppe, Gianetta, Tessa	Gondoliers	II

(Note: Sullivan considered this quartet the very best example of his use of several themes at once for symbolic-comic effect.)

In a doleful train (Also a solo by Lady Jane in Act II)	Ladies	Patience	I
In a set and formal measure	see Thank you, gallant gondolieri		
In babyhood upon her lap I lay	Strephon	Iolanthe	I (in finale)
In bygone days I had thy love (Ballad)	Rose	Ruddigore	II
In enterprise of martial kind	Duke of Plaza-Toro, Duchess, Casilda, Luiz	Gondoliers	I

LINE	SINGER	OPERA	ACT
In every mental lore	Scaphio, Phantis, Chorus	Utopia	I
In good Queen Bess's time *see* When Britain really ruled the waves			
In lazy languor—motionless	Utopian maidens	Utopia	I *(opening)*
In sailing o'er life's ocean wide	Richard, Robin, Rose	Ruddigore	I
In the autumn of our life	Yeomen	Yeomen	I
In the reign of James the Second	Counsel	Trial by Jury	
In vain to us you plead	Leila, Celia	Iolanthe	II
Incantation *see* Sprites of earth and air			
Is life a boon? *(Ballad)*	Fairfax	Yeomen	I
It clearly knew the deference due to a man of pedigree *see* The criminal cried			
It may not be, for so the fates decide	Lord Chancellor	Iolanthe	II
It's clear that medieval art alone retains its zest *(Trio)*	Duke, Major, Colonel	Patience	II
It's love that makes the world go round! *see* If you go in			
It's understood, I think, all round *(Quartet)*	Fitzbattleaxe, Zara, Scaphio, Phantis	Utopia	I
I've got a little list *see* As some day it may happen			
I've jibe and joke *(Recitative and song)*	Jack Point	Yeomen	I
I've wisdom from the East and from the West *see* I've jibe and joke			
Judge's autobiography *see* When I, good friends, was called to the bar			
Kind Captain, I've important information	Dick Deadeye, Captain Corcoran	Pinafore	II
Kind sir, you cannot have the heart	Gianetta	Gondoliers	I *(finale)*
Kissing duet *see* Were you not to Ko-Ko plighted			
Kissing song *see* Would you know the kind of maid			

LINE	SINGER	OPERA	ACT
Legend of Sir Rupert Murgatroyd *see* Sir Rupert Murgatroyd			
Leonard Merylll	Chorus	Yeomen	I *(finale)*
Let all your doubts take wing	Scaphio, Phantis	Utopia	I
Let the merry cymbals sound	Ensemble	Patience	I *(in finale)*
Let us fly to a far-off land *(Aria; part of the Incantation scene)*	Aline	Sorcerer	I
Life Guards chorus *see* Five years have flown			
Like a ghost his vigil keeping	Wilfred, Jack Point, Chorus	Yeomen	II
List and learn, ye dainty roses	Contadine	Gondoliers	I *(opening)*
Literary merit meets with proper recognition *see* Society has quite forsaken			
Little maid of Arcadee *(Note: This song, plus the chorus* Climbing over Rocky Mountain, *are all that remain of the music of* Thespis)	Sparkeion	Thespis	II
Long years ago—fourteen, maybe	Patience, Angela	Patience	I
Lord Chancellors were cheap as sprats *see* There lived a king			
Loudly let the trumpet bray! *(The procession of the Peers)*	Chorus	Iolanthe	I
Love feeds on hope, they say, or love will die	Angela, Chorus	Patience	I *(opening)*
Love feeds on many kinds of food, I know *(Ballad)*	Alexis	Sorcerer	I
Love is a plaintive song *(Ballad)*	Patience	Patience	II
Madrigal *see* When the buds are blossoming; Brightly dawns our wedding day			
Magnet song *see* A Magnet hung in a hardware shop			
Major-General's biography *see* I am the very model of a modern Major-General			
Man is Nature's sole mistake *see* Man will swear and Man will storm			

LINE	SINGER	OPERA	ACT
Man will swear and Man will storm	Psyche	Ida	I

(*Part of the scene beginning* Towards the empyrean heights)

March of the Mikado's troops   *see* Miya sama

| Marriage with deceased wife's sister | Fairy Queen | Iolanthe | I |

(*One of the parliamentary blisters to be pricked by Strephon. It was a point of law that came up in Parliament annually for many years in the late 1800's.*)

Matter, matter, matter, matter
(*Burden of the original patter song. See* My eyes are fully open to my awful situation.)

| Merrily ring the luncheon bell | Chorus | Ida | II |

Merry maiden and the tar   *see* Kind captain, I've important information

Mighty maiden with a mission	Chorus	Ida	II
Mighty old Mars, the god of war	Timidon	Thespis	I
Miya sama	Chorus	Mikado	II

(*Note: This is the first line of an actual war-song of the Imperial Army of Japan, as sung in 1868. Sullivan changed only the last four measures of the music. The translation of the entire passage is as follows:*
Oh my prince, oh my prince,
What is that fluttering in the wind
  Before your imperial horse?
Know ye not it is the imperial banner
  Of silken brocade,
Signal for the punishment of rebels?)

| Monster, monster, dread our fury | Jury | Trial by Jury | |

Most politely   *see* Perhaps if you address the lady

| My boy, you may take it from me | Robin | Ruddigore | I |

My brain it teems   *see* Trio about Execution

| My eyes are fully open to my awful situation | Robin, Despard, Mad Margaret | Ruddigore | II |

(*The Patter Trio*)
(*Note: The final lines of this trio are as follows:*
This particularly rapid, unintelligible patter
Isn't generally heard, and if it is it doesn't matter!)

LINE	SINGER	OPERA	ACT
My gallant crew, good morning	Captain Corcoran, Chorus	Pinafore	I

(*Recitative before* I am the Captain of the Pinafore)

My heart says *see* In sailing o'er life's ocean wide			

My object all sublime	Mikado	Mikado	II

(*Part of the song beginning* A more humane Mikado never.)
(*Note: Gilbert decided to delete this song in final rehearsals, but the cast pleaded to have it reinstated.*)

My papa he keeps three horses (*Game song*)	Girls	Gondoliers	I
Mystic poet, hear our prayer!	Angela, Chorus	Patience	I
'Neath this blow	Mountararat, Tolloller	Iolanthe	I

Never? Hardly ever!   *see* I am the Captain of the Pinafore

Never mind the why and wherefore	Joseph Porter, Captain Corcoran, Josephine	Pinafore	II
Night has spread her pall once more	Chorus	Yeomen	II (*opening*)

Nightmare song   *see* When you're lying awake

No, I'll be brave! (*Recitative, solo, chorus*)	Mabel, Sergeant, Police	Pirates	II

None but the brave deserve the fair   *see* If you go in

None shall part us from each other	Phyllis, Strephon	Iolanthe	I

Nonsense, yes, perhaps; but oh, what precious nonsense!
(*Lady Saphir says this after hearing Bunthorne's poem,* Patience, Act I.)

Nothing whatever to grumble at   *see* Whene'er I poke sarcastic joke

Now for the gay Sally Lunn   *see* Now to the banquet we press

Now for the pirates' lair! (*Recitative and trio*)	Frederic, Ruth, Pirate King	Pirates	II
Now hearken to my strict command	Hildebrand, Chorus	Ida	I
Now is not this ridiculous *See* In a doleful train	Dragoons	Patience	I

LINE	SINGER	OPERA	ACT
Now, Jurymen, hear my advice	Usher, Chorus	Trial by Jury	
Now let the loyal lieges gather round (*Recitative*)	Don Alhambra del Bolero	Gondoliers	II (*in finale*)
Now, Marco dear	Tessa, Gianetta	Gondoliers	I (*in finale*)
Now to the banquet we press	Ensemble	Sorcerer	I & II
Now what can that have been	Chorus	Yeomen	II
Now wouldn't you like to rule the roast	Melissa, Blanche	Ida	II
Octette *see* Farewell, my own			
O, don't the days seem lank and long *see* Whene'er I poke sarcastic joke			
O make way for the Wise Men!	Chorus	Utopia	I
O my darling, O my pet *see* Now, Marco dear			
O rapture, when alone together (*Recitative and duet*)	Casilda, Luiz	Gondoliers	I
O'er the season vernal	Plaintiff	Trial by Jury	
Of all the young ladies I know	Tolloller	Iolanthe	I
Of happiness the very pith	Chorus	Gondoliers	II (*opening*)
Oh! a private buffoon is a light-hearted loon	Jack Point	Yeomen	II
Oh, admirable art!	Zara, Fitzbattleaxe	Utopia	I
Oh, better far to live and die	Pirate King, Pirates	Pirates	I
Oh, Captain Shaw *see* Oh, foolish fay			
Oh dainty triolet *see* Expressive glances			
Oh, dry the glistening tear	Mabel, Daughters of the Major-General	Pirates	II (*opening*)
Oh, false one, you have deceived me! (*Recitative and duet*)	Frederic, Ruth	Pirates	I
Oh fool, that fleest my hallowed joys!	Katisha	Mikado	I (*in finale*)
Oh, foolish fay	Fairy Queen, Fairies	Iolanthe	II

LINE	SINGER	OPERA	ACT
Oh, Fortune, to my aching heart be kind	Maidens	Patience	I *(in finale)*
Oh, gentlemen, listen, I pray	Defendant	Trial by Jury	
Oh, goddess wise *(Aria)*	Ida	Ida	II
Oh, happy the lily when kissed by the bee	Rose, Richard	Ruddigore	I *(in finale)*

(Note: Taken up in the finale of the second act by chorus.)

Oh, happy young heart! *(Aria)*	Aline	Sorcerer	I
Oh, Hollow, hollow, hollow *(A spoken poem)*	Reginald Bunthorne	Patience	I

Oh, I love the jolly rattle of an ordeal by battle   *see* When anger spreads his wing

Oh, I'm the celestial drudge	Mercury	Thespis	I
Oh, is there not one maiden breast	Frederic, Mabel, Daughters of the Major-General	Pirates	I
Oh joy, oh rapture unforeseen *(Ensemble)*	Josephine, Ralph, Chorus	Pinafore	I

(Also used in Act II, as a quartet by the above plus Dick Deadeye.)

Oh! joy, our chief is saved	Chorus	Ida	II *(finale)*
Oh, joy unbounded	Ensemble	Trial by Jury	
Oh joyous boon! oh, mad delight	Aline, Dr. Daly, Ensemble	Sorcerer	II

Oh, kiss me, kiss me, kiss me, kiss me   *see* Would you know the kind of a maid

Oh list while we a love confess	Ensemble	Patience	I *(in finale)*
Oh love, true love—unworldly, abiding!	Alexis, Aline	Sorcerer	I *(finale)*
Oh, maiden, rich	Chorus	Utopia	I

Oh make way for the Wise Men!   *see* O make way for the Wise Men!

Oh, many a man, in Friendship's name   *see* Tho' p'r'aps I may incur your blame

LINE	SINGER	OPERA	ACT
Oh men of dark and dismal fate (*Recitative and solo*)	Major-General, Ensemble	Pirates	I (*in finale*)
Oh, Mercy, Thou whose smile has shown *see* The prisoner comes to meet his doom			
Oh my darling, Oh my pet *see* Now, Marco dear			
Oh! My name is John Welling- ton Wells	John Wellington Wells	Sorcerer	I
Oh, my voice is sad and low	Dr. Daly	Sorcerer	II
Oh never, never, never, since I joined the human race	Learned Judge, Jury, Bridesmaids	Trial by Jury	
Oh, never shall I forget the cry *see* The criminal cried			
Oh, philosophers may sing of the troubles of a king *see* Rising early in the morning			
Oh, Sergeant Meryll, is it true	Yeomen	Yeomen	I (*in finale*)
Oh, the rapture unrestrained	Lady Sophy, Paramount	Utopia	II
Oh, 'tis a glorious thing, I ween *see* Then one of us will be a queen			
Oh to be wafted away (*One of his poems*)	Reginald	Patience	I
Oh, why am I moody and sad?	Despard, Chorus	Ruddigore	I
Olympus is now in a terrible muddle	Mercury	Thespis	II
On a tree by a river a little tom-tit	Ko-Ko	Mikado	II
On the day when I was wedded	Duchess of Plaza- Toro	Gondoliers	II
Oncely, twicely *see* I am a courtier grave and serious			
Or I or he must die!	Ensemble, John Wellington Wells	Sorcerer	II (*in finale*)
Our great Mikado, virtuous man	Pish-Tush, Chorus	Mikado	I
Over the bright blue sea (*Barcarole*)	Girls' Chorus	Pinafore	I
Painted emblems of a race (*Precedes* When the night wind howls)	Chorus of Ancestors	Ruddigore	II

LINE	SINGER	OPERA	ACT

Parley-voo   *see* I shipped, d'ye see, on a Revenue sloop)

Patter songs   *see* My eyes are fully open to my awful situation; I am the very model of a modern Major-General; When you're lying awake with a dismal headache.

Perhaps if you address the lady	Gama, Hildebrand	Ida	I
Phoebus am I, with golden ray	Sparkeion	Thespis	I

Pity, pity me   *see* Alas! that lovers thus should meet

Poem   *see* Oh Hollow, hollow, hollow; Gentle Jane was as good as gold; Teasing Tom was a very bad boy

Policemen's chorus   *see* When the foeman bares his steel

Poor little man! Poor little maid!   *see* I know a youth who loves a little maid

Poor wandering one!	Mabel, Daughters of the Major-General	Pirates	I

Portraits' chorus   *see* Painted emblems of a race

Pour, oh pour the pirate sherry!	Samuel, Pirates	Pirates	I *(opening)*
Pray, what authors should she read	Melissa	Ida	II

(*Part of* Towards the empyrean heights)

Prithee, pretty maiden, prithee tell me true	Patience, Archibald Grosvenor	Patience	I

Procession heralding the Mikado   *see* Miya sama

Punishment fit the crime   *see* My object all sublime

Quaff the nectar—cull the roses	Chorus	Utopia	I

(*Entrance of King Paramount*)

Quintet   *see* If Saphir I choose to marry

Rapture, rapture!	Dame Carruthers, Sergeant Meryll	Yeomen	II
Refrain, audacious tar	Josephine, Ralph	Pinafore	I
Ring forth, ye bells	Chorus	Sorcerer	I *(opening)*
Rising early in the morning	Giuseppe, Chorus	Gondoliers	II

Sad is that woman's lot who, year by year
(*Recitative for* Silvered is the raven hair)

LINE	SINGER	OPERA	ACT

Said I to myself—said I   *see* When I went to the Bar as a very young man

Scena   *see* The hours creep on apace

Search throughout the pano- rama	Chorus	Ida	I *(opening)*
See how the Fates their gifts allot (*Glee*)	Pitti-Sing, Katisha, Ko-Ko, Pooh-Bah, Mikado	Mikado	II

Sextet   *see* I hear the soft note

She is such a smart little craft
  (*Refrain after* Happily coupled are we)

Sighing softly to the river (*Ballad*)	Major-General Stanley, Ensemble	Pirates	II *(in finale)*
Silvered is the raven hair	Lady Jane	Patience	II

  (*Note: This song was later published by Chappell with a different text
  (by Conway), beginning,* In the twilight of our love. *The publisher was
  unwilling to risk criticism by publishing Gilbert's "offensive" lines outside the opera.*)

Sing "Bah to you"   *see* So go to him

Sing hey, lackaday   *see* There grew a little flower

Sing hey, the merry maiden and the tar   *see* Kind Captain, I've important
information

Sing "Hey to you"   *see* So go to him

Sing high, sing low   *see* For everyone who feels inclined

Sing, hoity, toity! Sorry for some!   *see* Now wouldn't you like to rule the roast

Sing me your song, O!   *see* I have a song to sing, O!

Sing "Pooh to you"   *see* So go to him

Sir Rupert Murgatroyd (*Legend*)	Dame Hannah	Ruddigore	I

Sisters, Cousins and Aunts   *see* I am the monarch of the sea

Sit with downcast eye   *see* Braid the raven hair

Small titles and orders	Duke and Duchess of Plaza-Toro	Gondoliers	II
So go to him and say to him	Reginald and Jane	Patience	II
So please you, Sir, we much regret	Yum-Yum, Peep- Bo, Pitti-Sing, Pooh-Bah, Chorus	Mikado	I

LINE	SINGER	OPERA	ACT
Society has quite forsaken all her wicked courses	Paramount, Flowers of Progress	Utopia	II
Soldiers of our Queen *see* The soldiers of our Queen			
Some seven men form an association	Goldbury	Utopia	I *(in finale)*
Some years ago, no doubt you know	Hildebrand	Ida	II *(in finale)*
Soon as we may	Ensemble	Iolanthe	II *(in finale)*
Sorry her lot who loves too well *(Ballad)*	Josephine	Pinafore	I
Sprites of earth and air *(Incantation)*	John Wellington Wells, Chorus	Sorcerer	I
Spurn not the nobly born *(Ballad)*	Tolloller	Iolanthe	I
Stay, Frederic, stay!	Mabel, Frederic	Pirates	II
Stay, we must not lose our senses *(Recitative and chorus)*	Frederic, Pirates, Daughters of the Major-General	Pirates	I
Stop, ladies, pray! *(Recitative and chorus)*	Frederic, Edith, Kate, Daughters of the Major-General	Pirates	I
(see also Oh, is there not one maiden breast)			
Strange adventure! Maiden wedded *(Quartet)*	Fairfax, Sergeant Meryll, Dame Carruthers, Kate	Yeomen	II
Strephon's a Member of Parliament	Chorus	Iolanthe	II
Subjected to your heavenly gaze	Paramount, Lady Sophy	Utopia	I
Sweet and low as accents holy *see* Words of love too loudly spoken			
Take a pair of sparkling eyes	Marco	Gondoliers	II
Take a wretched thief *see* Fold your flapping wings			
Taken from the county jail	Ko-Ko	Mikado	I
Tantantara! Tzing! Boom! *see* Loudly let the trumpet bray			
Taradiddle, taradiddle, tol-lol-lay *see* The lady of my love			

LINE	SINGER	OPERA	ACT
Teasing Tom was a very bad boy (*One of his poems*)	Archibald	Patience	II
Temptation, oh, temptation *see* How say you, maiden			
Thank you, gallant gondolieri!	Gianetta, Tessa, Chorus	Gondoliers	I
That's a kind of mother that is usually spurious *see* The lady of my love			
The battle's roar is over	Richard, Rose	Ruddigore	I
The criminal cried, as he dropped him down	Ko-Ko, Pitti-Sing, Pooh-Bah, Chorus	Mikado	II
The flowers that bloom in the spring (*Duet with ensemble*)	Nanki-Poo, Ko-Ko, Pitti-Sing, Yum-Yum, Pooh-Bah	Mikado	II
The hour of gladness is dead and gone	Katisha	Mikado	I (*in finale*)
The hours creep on apace (*Scena*)	Josephine	Pinafore	II
The lady of my love has caught me	Strephon, Fairies	Iolanthe	I
The Law is the true embodiment	Lord Chancellor, Chorus	Iolanthe	I
The nightingale sighed for the moon's bright ray (*Madrigal*)	Ralph, Chorus	Pinafore	I
The prisoner comes to meet his doom	Elsie, Chorus	Yeomen	I (*in finale*)
The royal prince was by the king entrusted (*Recitative*)	Inez	Gondoliers	II (*in finale*)
The ruler of the Queen's Navee *see* I am the monarch of the sea			
The screw may twist and the rack may turn *see* When our gallant Norman foes			
The soldiers of our Queen	Dragoons	Patience	I
The sun, whose rays are all ablaze	Yum-Yum	Mikado	II
The woman of the wisest wit (*Quintet*)	Psyche, Melissa, Hilarion, Cyril, Florian	Ida	II

{ *219* }

LINE	SINGER	OPERA	ACT
The world is but a broken toy (*Quartet*)	Ida, Hilarion, Cyril, Florian	Ida	II
Then away we go to an island fair	Chorus	Gondoliers	I (*in finale*)
Then, Frederic, let your escort lion-hearted (*Recitative*)	Frederic, Major-General Stanley	Pirates	II
Then hail, O king of a golden land	Chorus	Gondoliers	II (*in finale*)
Then one of us will be a queen (*Quartet*)	Marco, Giuseppe, Gianetta, Tessa	Gondoliers	I (*in finale*)
There grew a little flower (*Ballad*)	Dame Hannah	Ruddigore	II
There is beauty in the bellow of the blast	Ko-Ko, Katisha	Mikado	II
There lived a king, as I've been told	Alhambra, Marco, Giuseppe	Gondoliers	II
There was a time	Casilda, Luiz	Gondoliers	I
There's a little group of isles beyond the wave	Zara, Chorus	Utopia	II (*finale*)
They intend to send a wire to the moon	Hilarion	Ida	II
Things are seldom what they seem	Buttercup, Capt. Corcoran	Pinafore	II
This helmet, I suppose	Arac	Ida	III
This is our duty plain	Chorus	Ida	III
This the autumn of our life *see* In the autumn of our life			
Tho' p'r'aps I may incur your blame (*Quartet*)	Phyllis, Tolloller, Mountararat, Private Willis	Iolanthe	II
Thou hast the power thy vaunted love (*Ballad*)	Alexis	Sorcerer	II
Thou the tree and I the flower *see* None shall part us from each other			
Though tear and long-drawn sigh	Elsie	Yeomen	I

LINE	SINGER	OPERA	ACT

Though the views of the House have diverged   *see* Of all the young ladies I know

Three little maids from school   Yum-Yum, Pitti-Sing, Peep-Bo   Mikado   I
(*Composed on the 21st of December, 1884; the very first part of the score to be composed.*)

Time was when Love and I were well acquainted   Dr. Daly   Sorcerer   I
(*Ballad*)

Tink-a-tank, tink-a-tank   *see* When first my old, old love I knew

'Tis done, I am a bride
(*Recitative for* Though tear and long-drawn sigh)

'Tis said that joy in full perfection   Phoebe, Elsie, Dame Carruthers   Yeomen   II (*in finale*)
(*Trio*)

To a garden full of posies   Mad Margaret   Ruddigore   I
(*Ballad*)

To fit the wit of a bit of a chit   *see* Some years ago, no doubt you know

To let the punishment fit the crime   *see* My object all sublime

To sit in solemn silence in a dull, dark dock   *see* Trio about Execution

To thy fraternal care   Wilfred, Fairfax, Phoebe   Yeomen   I (*in finale*)
(*Trio*)

To work and think, my dear   Sillimon   Thespis   II

To you I give my heart so rich   Phyllis, Ensemble   Iolanthe   I

Towards the empyrean heights   Girl graduates   Ida   II (*opening*)

Tower warders, under orders   Chorus   Yeomen   I
(*Entrance of the Yeomen*)

Trio about Execution   Ko-Ko, Pooh-Bah, Pish-Tush   Mikado   I

Trio of schoolgirls   *see* Three little maids from school

True love must single-hearted be   Patience   Patience   I (*in finale*)

Try we life-long, we can never   Duke and Duchess of Plaza-Toro, Casilda, Luiz, Inquisitor   Gondoliers   I
(*Quintet*)

LINE	SINGER	OPERA	ACT
Turn, oh turn in this direction	Maidens	Patience	II
Twenty lovesick maidens we	Rapturous maidens	Patience	I (*opening*)
Twenty years ago *see* Ida was a twelvemonth old			
Up in the air, sky-high *see* Soon as we may			
Upon our sea-girt land	Chorus	Utopia	II
Warders are ye? Whom do ye ward? (*Follows* Night has spread her pall)	Dame Carruthers	Yeomen	II
Watch and ward *see* When our gallant Norman foes			
We are dainty little fairies	Celia	Iolanthe	I (*opening*)
We are gentlemen of Japan *see* If you want to know who we are			
We are warriors three	Arac, Guron, Scynthius	Ida	I
We polish the Regalia and the Coronation Plate *see* Rising early in the morning			
We sail the ocean blue	Sailors	Pinafore	I (*opening*)
Welcome, gentry	Bridesmaids	Ruddigore	I
Welcome joy, adieu to sadness!	Marmaduke, Lady Sangazure	Sorcerer	I
We're called gondolieri	Marco, Giuseppe	Gondoliers	I
Were I thy bride (*Ballad*)	Phoebe	Yeomen	I
Were you not to Ko-Ko plighted	Yum-Yum, Nanki-Poo	Mikado	I
What is he but I *see* Fold your flapping wings			
What, never? *see* I am the Captain of the Pinafore			
What ought we to do	Edith, Kate, Daughters of the Major-General	Pirates	I
What these may be, Utopians all	Zara	Utopia	I (*in finale*)

LINE	SINGER	OPERA	ACT
Whatever you are—be that (*Quartet*)	Nekaya, Kalyba, Dramaleigh, Goldbury	Utopia	II
When a felon's not engaged in his employment	Sergeant, Police	Pirates	II
When a merry maiden marries	Tessa	Gondoliers	I
When a wooer goes a-wooing (*Quartet*)	Elsie, Phoebe, Fairfax, Jack Point	Yeomen	II
When all night long a chap remains	Private Willis	Iolanthe	II (*opening*)
When anger spreads his wing	Soldiers	Ida	III
When, as the fruit of warlike deeds	Daphne	Thespis	I
When Britain really ruled the waves	Mountararat	Iolanthe	II
When Britain sounds the trump of war	Zara	Utopia	I (*in finale*)
When but a maid of fifteen year	Lady Sophy	Utopia	II
When darkly looms the day (*Quartet*)	Strephon, Iolanthe, Mountararat, Tolloller, Chorus	Iolanthe	I (*in finale*)
When every one is somebodee	*see* There lived a king		
When first my old, old love I knew	Defendant	Trial by Jury	
When Frederic was a little lad	Ruth	Pirates	I
When he is here	Constance	Sorcerer	I
When I first put this uniform on	Col. Calverley	Patience	I
When I go out of door	Bunthorne, Grosvenor	Patience	II
When I, good friends, was called to the Bar	Learned Judge, Chorus	Trial by Jury	
When I was a lad I served a term	Joseph Porter, Chorus	Pinafore	I
When I went to the Bar as a very young man	Lord Chancellor	Iolanthe	I

LINE	SINGER	OPERA	ACT
When I'm a bad Bart *see* As pure and blameless peasant			
When love is alive and hope is dead! *see* Sorry her lot			
When maiden loves, she sits and sighs	Phoebe	Yeomen	I *(opening)*
When our gallant Norman foes	Dame Carruthers, Yeomen	Yeomen	I
When the buds are blossoming *(Madrigal)*	Rose, Chorus	Ruddigore	I
When the foeman bares his steel	Sergeant, Mabel, Edith, Stanley, Daughters of the Major-General, Policemen	Pirates	II
When the night wind howls	Roderic and Chorus	Ruddigore	II
When thoroughly tired	Bucks and Blades	Ruddigore	I
When you had left our pirate fold *(Solo, trio, chant)*	Ruth, Frederic, Pirate King	Pirates	II
When you're lying awake with a dismal headache	Lord Chancellor	Iolanthe	II
Whene'er I poke sarcastic joke	Gama	Ida	III
While mighty Jove goes down below	Thespis	Thespis	I
Who can tell? *see* Will Prince Hilarion's hopes be sadly blighted?			
Whom thou hast chained must wear his chain	Hilarion	Ida	II *(in finale)*
Will Prince Hilarion's hopes be sadly blighted?	Florian, Chorus	Ida	I *(opening)*
Willow, titwillow, titwillow *see* On a tree by a river			
Willow willow waly *see* Prithee, pretty maiden			
With a sense of deep emotion *(Aria)*	Counsel	Trial by Jury	
With aspect stern	Ensemble	Mikado	I *(finale)*
With cat-like tread, upon our prey we steal	Samuel, Pirates, Police	Pirates	II

{ 224 }

LINE	SINGER	OPERA	ACT
With ducal pomp and ducal pride	Chorus	Gondoliers	II
With fury deep we burn	Scaphio, Phantis	Utopia	II
With happiness my soul is cloyed *see* 'Tis said that joy in full perfection			
With heart and with voice	Girls	Sorcerer	I
With joy abiding	Ida, Hilarion, Chorus	Ida	III (*finale*)
With nothing whatever to grumble at *see* Whene'er I poke sarcastic joke			
With wily brain upon the spot	Scaphio, Phantis, Tarara	Utopia	II
Within this breast there beats a heart	Richard	Ruddigore	I
Woman's heart is one with woman's hand! *see* Kind sir, you cannot have the heart			
Words of love too loudly spoken	Zara, Fitzbattleaxe	Utopia	II
Would you know the kind of maid	Cyril	Ida	II
You hold yourself like this *see* It's clear that medieval art			
You understand?	Despard, Richard	Ruddigore	I
You'll lay your head *see* Now, Marco dear			
Young man, despair	Pooh-Bah, Nanki-Poo, Pish-Tush	Mikado	I
Your maiden hearts, ah, do not steel	Duke of Dunstable	Patience	I (*in finale*)
You're Diana, I'm Apollo (*Quartet*)	Sparkeion, Daphne, Nicemis, Thespis	Thespis	II
Youth must have its fling *see* So please you, sir, we much regret			

THEMES AND TEXTS OF
THE FAMOUS MUSICAL NUMBERS

TRIAL BY JURY
Song: Defendant

Oh, gen - tle - men, lis - ten, I pray, Though I own that my

heart has been ran - ging, Of na - ture the laws I o -

bey, For na - ture is con - stan - tly chan - ging.

Oh, gentlemen, listen, I pray,
　Though I own that my heart has been ranging,
Of nature the laws I obey,
　For nature is constantly changing.
The moon in her phases is found,
　The time and the wind and the weather,
The months in succession come round,
　And you don't find two Mondays together.
Consider the moral, I pray,
　Nor bring a young fellow to sorrow,
Who loves this young lady to-day,
　And loves that young lady to-morrow.

Note: The hyphenation of syllables in the lyrics with the music accords with singing practice rather than dictionary usage. In the musical themes, flagged notes are connected by beams as in instrumental music so that the rhythmic patterns will be more readily apparent.

{ 226 }

BRIDESMAIDS: Consider the moral, etc.

DEFENDANT: You cannot eat breakfast all day,
           Nor is it the act of a sinner,
      When breakfast is taken away,
           To turn his attention to dinner;
   And it's not in the range of belief,
           To look upon him as a glutton,
  Who, when he is tired of beef,
           Determines to tackle the mutton.
       But this I am willing to say,
           If it will appease her sorrow,
    I'll marry this lady to-day,
           And I'll marry the other to-morrow!

BRIDESMAIDS: But this he is willing to say, etc.

THE SORCERER
Song: Mr. Wells

My   name   is   John   Wel - ling - ton   Wells, _____   I'm   a

dea - ler   in   ma - gic   and   spells, _____

My name is John Wellington Wells,
I'm a dealer in magic and spells,
     In blessings and curses
     And ever-filled purses,
In prophecies, witches, and knells.

If you want a proud foe to "make tracks"—
If you'd melt a rich uncle in wax—
     You've but to look in
     On the resident Djinn,
Number seventy, Simmery Axe!

We've a first-rate assortment of magic;
     And for raising a posthumous shade
With effects that are comic or tragic,
     There's no cheaper house in the trade.
Love-philtre—we've quantities of it;
     And for knowledge if any one burns,
We're keeping a very small prophet, a prophet
     Who brings us unbounded returns:

For he can prophesy
With a wink *of* his eye,
Peep with security
Into futurity,
Sum up your history,
Clear up a mystery,
Humour proclivity
For a nativity—for a nativity;
He has answers oracular,
Bogies spectacular,
Tetrapods tragical,
Mirrors so magical,
Facts astronomical,
Solemn or comical,
And, if you want it, he
Makes a reduction on taking a quantity!
        Oh!

If any one anything lacks,
He'll find it all ready in stacks,
    If he'll only look in
    On the resident Djinn,
Number seventy, Simmery Axe!

    He can raise you hosts
                Of ghosts,
And that without reflectors;
    And creepy things
                With wings,
And gaunt and grisly spectres.
    He can fill you crowds
                Of shrouds,
And horrify you vastly;
    He can rack your brains
                With chains,
And gibberings grim and ghastly!

    Then, if you plan it, he
    Changes organity,
    With an urbanity,
    Full of Satanity,
    Vexes humanity
    With an inanity
    Fatal to vanity—
Driving your foes to the verge of insanity!

    Barring tautology,
    In demonology,
    'Lectro-biology,

Mystic nosology,
Spirit philology,
High-class astrology,
Such is his knowledge, he
Isn't the man to require an apology!

Oh!
My name is John Wellington Wells,
I'm a dealer in magic and spells,
In blessings and curses
And ever-filled purses,
In prophecies, witches, and knells.

If any one anything lacks,
He'll find it all ready in stacks,
If he'll only look in
On the resident Djinn,
Number seventy, Simmery Axe!

H. M. S. PINAFORE
Opening chorus

We — sail the o - cean blue, And our sau - cy ship's a

beau - ty;

SAILORS:
We sail the ocean blue,
And our saucy ship's a beauty;
We're sober men and true,
And attentive to our duty.
When the balls whistle free
O'er the bright blue sea,
We stand to our guns all day;
When at anchor we ride
On the Portsmouth tide,
We've plenty of time to play.

RECIT.

BUTTERCUP: Hail, men-o'-war's men—safeguards of your nation.
Here is an end, at last, of all privation;
You've got your pay—spare all you can afford
To welcome Little Buttercup on board.

H. M. S. PINAFORE

Aria: Buttercup

I'm   called Lit‑tle   But‑ter‑cup   dear Lit‑tle   But‑ter‑cup,

Though I could   ne‑ver tell   why,

ARIA

I'm called Little Buttercup—dear Little Buttercup
Though I could never tell why,
But still I'm called Buttercup—poor little Buttercup,
Sweet Little Buttercup I!

I've snuff and tobaccy, and excellent jacky,
I've scissors, and watches, and knives;
I've ribbons and laces to set off the faces
Of pretty young sweethearts and wives.

I've treacle and toffee, I've tea and I've coffee,
Soft tommy and succulent chops;
I've chickens and conies, and pretty polonies,
And excellent peppermint drops.

Then buy of your Buttercup—dear Little Buttercup;
Sailors should never be shy;
So, buy of your Buttercup—poor Little Buttercup;
Come, of your Buttercup buy!

H. M. S. PINAFORE

Song: Captain Corcoran and Chorus

CAPT.:	I am the Captain of the *Pinafore;*
ALL:	And a right good captain, too!
CAPT.:	You're very, very good,
	And be it understood,
	I command a right good crew,
ALL:	We're very, very good,
	And be it understood,
	He commands a right good crew.
CAPT.:	Though related to a peer,
	I can hand, reef, and steer,
	Or ship a selvagee;
	I am never known to quail
	At the fury of a gale,

Captain

I am the Cap - tain of the Pi - na - fore;

Chorus

And a

right good cap - tain, too!

And I'm never, never sick at sea!

ALL: What, never?

CAPT.: No, never!

ALL: What, *never?*

CAPT.: Hardly ever!

ALL: He's hardly ever sick at sea!

Then give three cheers, and one cheer **more**,

For the hardy Captain of the *Pinafore!*

CAPT.: I do my best to satisfy you all—

ALL: And with you we're quite content.

CAPT.: You're exceedingly polite,

And I think it only right

To return the compliment.

ALL: We're exceedingly polite,

And he thinks it's only right

To return the compliment.

CAPT.: Bad language or abuse,

I never, never use,

Whatever the emergency;

Though "Bother it" I may

Occasionally say,

I never use a big, big D—

ALL: What, never?

CAPT.: No, never!

ALL: What, *never?*

{ *231* }

CAPT.:   Hardly ever!
ALL: Hardly ever swears a big, big D—
         Then give three cheers, and one cheer more,
         For the well-bred Captain of the *Pinafore!*

H. M. S. PINAFORE
Song: Sir Joseph Porter, Cousin Hebe, Chorus

I am the   mo - narch   of   the   sea,   The ru - ler

of   the Queen's Na - vee,   Whose   praise Great   Bri - tain

loud - ly chants. And   we   are his sis-ters, and his cou-sins, and his aunts,

I am the monarch of the sea,
The ruler of the Queen's Navee,
Whose praise Great Britain loudly chants.

COUSIN HEBE: And we are his sisters, and his cousins
                and his aunts!
REL.:   And we are his sisters, and his cousins, and
                his aunts!
SIR JOSEPH: When at anchor here I ride,
                My bosom swells with pride,
                And I snap my fingers at a foeman's taunts;
COUSIN HEBE: And so do his sisters, and his cousins, and
                his aunts!
ALL: And so do his sisters, and his cousins, and
                his aunts!
SIR JOSEPH: But when the breezes blow,
                I generally go below,
                And seek the seclusion that a cabin grants;
COUSIN HEBE: And so do his sisters, and his cousins, and
                his aunts!
ALL: And so do his sisters, and his cousins, and
                his aunts!
                His sisters and his cousins,
                Whom he reckons up by dozens,
                And his aunts!

H. M. S. PINAFORE

Song: Sir Joseph Porter and Chorus

When I was a lad I served a term As of -fice boy to an at -

tor -ney's firm. I cleaned the win-dows and I swept the floor, And I

po-lished up the han -dle of the big front door.

When I was a lad I served a term
As office boy to an attorney's firm.
I cleaned the windows and I swept the floor,
And I polished up the handle of the big front door.
    I polished up that handle so carefullee
    That now I am the Ruler of the Queen's Navee!

CHORUS: He polished, etc.

SIR JOSEPH: As office boy I made such a mark
That they gave me the post of a junior clerk.
I served the writs with a smile so bland,
And I copied all the letters in a big round hand—
    I copied all the letters in a hand so free,
    That now I am the Ruler of the Queen's Navee!

CHORUS: He copied, etc.

SIR JOSEPH: In serving writs I made such a name
That an articled clerk I soon became;
I wore clean collars and a bran'-new suit
For the pass examination at the Institute,
    And that pass examination did so well for me,
    That now I am the Ruler of the Queen's Navee!

CHORUS: And that pass examination, etc.

SIR JOSEPH: Of legal knowledge I acquired such a grip
That they took me into the partnership.
And that junior partnership, I ween,
Was the only ship that I ever had seen.
    But that kind of ship so suited me,
    That now I am the Ruler of the Queen's Navee!

CHORUS: But that kind, etc.

SIR JOSEPH: I grew so rich that I was sent
By a pocket borough into Parliament.
I always voted at my party's call,
And I never thought of thinking for myself at all.
I thought so little, they rewarded me
By making me the Ruler of the Queen's Navee!

CHORUS: He thought so little, etc.

SIR JOSEPH: Now landsmen all, whoever you may be,
If you want to rise to the top of the tree,
If your soul isn't fettered to an office stool,
Be careful to be guided by this golden rule—
Stick close to your desks and never go to sea,
And you all may be Rulers of the Queen's Navee!

CHORUS: Stick close, etc.

H. M. S. PINAFORE
Legend: Buttercup

A ma - ny years a - go, When I was young and

char - ming, As some of you may know, I

prac - tised ba - by - far - ming.

A many years ago,
When I was young and charming,
As some of you may know,
I practised baby-farming.

ALL: Now this is most alarming!
When she was young and charming,
She practised baby-farming,
A many years ago.

BUT.: Two tender babes I nussed:
One was of low condition,

The other, upper crust,
 A regular patrician.

ALL: Now, this is the position:
 One was of low condition,
 The other a patrician,
  A many years ago.

BUT.: Oh, bitter is my cup!
  However could I do it?
 I mixed those children up,
  And not a creature knew it!

ALL: However could you do it?
 Some day, no doubt, you'll rue it,
 Although no creature knew it,
  So many years ago.

BUT.: In time each little waif
  Forsook his foster-mother,
 The well-born babe was Ralph—
  Your captain was the other!!!

ALL: They left their foster-mother,
 The one was Ralph, our brother,
 Our captain was the other,
  A many years ago.

THE PIRATES OF PENZANCE
Song: Mabel and Chorus

Poor wan - d'ring one! _____ Though thou hast
sure - ly strayed, Take heart of grace,
Thy steps re - trace, Poor wan - d'ring one! _____

Poor wandering one!
Though thou hast surely strayed,
 Take heart of grace,
 Thy steps retrace,

{ 235 }

Poor wandering one!
Poor wandering one!
If such poor love as mine
   Can help thee find
   True peace of mind—
Why, take it, it is thine!
     Take heart, fair days will shine;
     Take any heart—take mine!

ALL: Take heart; no danger lowers;
         Take any heart—but ours!

THE PIRATES OF PENZANCE
Song: Major-General Stanley and Chorus

I am the ve- ry mo-del of a mo-dern Ma- jor Gi- ne - ral; I've

in - for - ma - tion veg -e - ta- ble, a - ni-mal and mi - ne- ral,

I am the very model of a modern Major-Gineral;
I've information vegetable, animal, and mineral,
I know the kings of England, and I quote the fights historical,
From Marathon to Waterloo, in order categorical;
I'm very well acquainted too with matters mathematical,
I understand equations, both the simple and quadratical,
About binomial theorem I'm teeming with a lot o' news—
With many cheerful facts about the square of the hypotenuse.

ALL: With many cheerful facts, etc.

GEN.: I'm very good at integral and differential calculus,
      I know the scientific names of beings animalculous;
      In short, in matters vegetable, animal, and mineral,
      I am the very model of a modern Major-Gineral.

ALL: In short, in matters vegetable, animal, and mineral,
      He is the very model of a modern Major-Gineral.

GEN.: I know our mythic history, King Arthur's and Sir Caradoc's,
      I answer hard acrostics, I've a pretty taste for paradox,
      I quote in elegiacs all the crimes of Heliogabalus,
      In conics I can floor peculiarities parabolous.
      I can tell undoubted Raphaels from Gerard Dows and Zoffanies,
      I know the croaking chorus from the *Frogs* of Aristophanes,

Then I can hum a fugue of which I've heard the music's din afore,
And whistle all the airs from that infernal nonsense *Pinafore*.

ALL: And whistle all the airs, etc.

GEN.: Then I can write a washing bill in Babylonic cuneiform,
And tell you every detail of Caractacus's uniform;
In short, in matters vegetable, animal, and mineral,
I am the very model of a modern Major-Gineral.

ALL: In short, in matters vegetable, animal, and mineral,
He is the very model of a modern Major-Gineral.

GEN.: In fact, when I know what is meant by "mamelon" and "ravelin,"
When I can tell at sight a Mauser rifle from a javelin,
When such affairs as sorties and surprises I'm more wary at,
And when I know precisely what is meant by "commissariat,"
When I have learnt what progress has been made in modern gunnery,
When I know more of tactics than a novice in a nunnery:
In short, when I've a smattering of elemental strategy,
You'll say a better Major-Gineral has never *sat* a gee—

ALL: You'll say a better, etc.

GEN.: For my military knowledge, though I'm plucky and adventury,
Has only been brought down to the beginning of the century;
But still in matters vegetable, animal, and mineral,
I am the very model of a modern Major-Gineral.

ALL: But still in matters vegetable, animal, and mineral,
He is the very model of a modern Major-Gineral.

THE PIRATES OF PENZANCE
Song: Sergeant, Chorus of Police, Mabel, Edith

SERG.: When the foeman bares his steel,
Tarantara! tarantara!
We uncomfortable feel,
Tarantara!
And we find the wisest thing,
Tarantara! tarantara!
Is to slap our chests and sing
Tarantara!
For when threatened with emeutes,
Tarantara! tarantara!
And your heart is in your boots,
Tarantara!
There is nothing brings it round,
Tarantara! tarantara!
Like the trumpet's martial sound,
Tarantara! tarantara!
Tarantara-ra-ra-ra-ra!

ALL: Tarantara-ra-ra-ra-ra!

MABEL: Go, ye heroes, go to glory,
           Though ye die in combat gory,
           Ye shall live in song and story.
               Go to immortality!
           Go to death, and go to slaughter;
           Die, and every Cornish daughter
           With her tears your grave shall water.
              Go, ye heroes, go and die!

EDITH: Go, ye heroes, go and die!

POLICE: Though to us it's evident,
                Tarantara! tarantara!
        These intentions are well meant,
                Tarantara!
        Such expressions don't appear,
                Tarantara! tarantara!
        Calculated men to cheer,
                Tarantara!
        Who are going to meet their fate
        In a highly nervous state,
                Tarantara!
        Still to us it's evident

These intentions are well meant.
    Tarantara!

EDITH: Go and do your best endeavour,
    And before all links we sever,
    We will say farewell for ever.
      Go to glory and the grave!

GIRLS: For your foes are fierce and ruthless,
    False, unmerciful, and truthless.
    Young and tender, old and toothless,
      All in vain their mercy crave.

SERG.: We observe too great a stress,
    On the risks that on us press,
    And of reference a lack
    To our chance of coming back.
    Still, perhaps it would be wise
    Not to carp or criticise,
    For it's very evident
    These attentions are well meant.

ALL: Yes, to them it's evident
    Our attentions are well meant.
      Tarantara-ra-ra-ra-ra!

Go, ye heroes, go to glory, etc.

THE PIRATES OF PENZANCE
Song: Sergeant and Chorus

SERG.: When a felon's not engaged in his employment—
ALL: His employment,
SERG.: Or maturing his felonious little plans—
ALL: Little plans,
SERG.: His capacity for innocent enjoyment—
ALL: 'Cent enjoyment
SERG.: Is just as great as any honest man's—
ALL: Honest man's.
SERG.: Our feelings we with difficulty smother—
ALL: 'Culty smother
SERG.: When constabulary duty's to be done—
ALL: To be done.
SERG.: Ah, take one consideration with another—
ALL: With another,
SERG.: A policeman's lot is not a happy one.
ALL: When constabulary duty's to be done—
      To be done,
   The policeman's lot is not a happy one.

SERG.: When the enterprising burglar's not a-burgling—
ALL: Not a-burgling,

When a fe-lon's not en-gaged in his em-

ploy-ment Or ma-tu-ring his fe-lo-nious lit-tle

His em-ploy-ment,

plans

Lit - tle plans,

SERG.: When the cut-throat isn't occupied in crime—
ALL: 'Pied in crime,
SERG.: He loves to hear the little brook a-gurgling—
ALL: Brook a-gurgling,
SERG.: And listen to the merry village chime—
ALL: Village chime.
SERG.: When the coster's finished jumping on his mother—
ALL: On his mother,
SERG.: He loves to lie a-basking in the sun—
ALL: In the sun.
SERG.: Ah, take one consideration with another—
ALL: With another,
SERG.: The policeman's lot is not a happy one.

{ 240 }

ALL: When constabulary duty's to be done—
To be done,
The policeman's lot is not a happy one—
Happy one.

PATIENCE
Opening chorus

Twen - ty love - sick mai - dens we, ——

Love - sick all a - gainst our will. ——.

Twenty love-sick maidens we,
Love-sick all against our will.
Twenty years hence we shall be
Twenty love-sick maidens still.
Twenty love-sick maidens we,
And we die for love of thee.

ANGELA: Love feeds on hope, they say, or love will die—

ALL: Ah, miserie!

ANGELA: Yet my love lives, although no hope have I!

ALL: Ah, miserie!

ANGELA: Alas, poor heart, go hide thyself away—
To weeping concords tune thy roundelay
Ah, miserie!

CHORUS: All our love is all for one,
Yet that love he heedeth not.
He is coy and cares for none,
Sad and sorry is our lot!
Ah, miserie!

ELLA: Go, breaking heart,
Go, dream of love requited;
Go, foolish heart,
Go, dream of lovers plighted;
Go, madcap heart,
Go, dream of never waking;
And in thy dream
Forget that thou art breaking!

CHORUS: Ah, miserie!

ELLA: Forget that thou art breaking!

CHORUS: Twenty love-sick maidens, etc.

PATIENCE
Song: Bunthorne

If you're an-xious for to shine in the high aes-the-tic line— as a

man   of   cul - ture   rare,

RECIT.

Am I alone,
        And unobserved? I am!
Then let me own
        I'm an æsthetic sham!

This air severe
        Is but a mere
                Veneer!

This cynic smile
        Is but a wile
                Of guile!

This costume chaste
        Is but good taste
                Misplaced!

Let me confess!
A languid love for lilies does *not* blight me!
Lank limbs and haggard cheeks do *not* delight me!
        I do *not* care for dirty greens
                By any means.
                I do *not* long for all one sees
                        That's Japanese.
        I am *not* fond of uttering platitudes
                In stained-glass attitudes.
        In short, my mediævalism's affectation,
        Born of a morbid love of admiration!

{ 242 }

SONG

If you're anxious for to shine in the high æsthetic line as a man of culture rare,
You must get up all the germs of the transcendental terms, and plant them everywhere.
You must lie upon the daisies and discourse in novel phrases of your complicated state of mind,
The meaning doesn't matter if it's only idle chatter of a transcendental kind.
    And every one will say,
    As you walk your mystic way,
"If this young man expresses himself in terms too deep for *me*,
Why, what a very singularly deep young man this deep young man must be!"

Be eloquent in praise of the very dull old days which have long since passed away,
And convince 'em, if you can, that the reign of good Queen Anne was Culture's palmiest day.
Of course you will pooh-pooh whatever's fresh and new, and declare it's crude and mean,
For Art stopped short in the cultivated court of the Empress Josephine.
    And every one will say,
    As you walk your mystic way,
"If that's not good enough for him which is good enough for *me*,
Why, what a very cultivated kind of youth this kind of youth must be!"

Then a sentimental passion of a vegetable fashion must excite your languid spleen,
An attachment *à la* Plato for a bashful young potato, or a not-too-French French bean!
Though the Philistines may jostle, you will rank as an apostle in the high æsthetic band,
If you walk down Piccadilly with a poppy or a lily in your mediæval hand.
    And every one will say,
    As you walk your flowery way,
"If he's content with a vegetable love which would certainly not suit *me*,
Why, what a most particularly pure young man this pure young man must be!"

PATIENCE

Duet: Patience and Grosvenor

Pri- thee, pret -ty mai - den   pri - thee, tell me true,

(Hey,   but I'm dole - ful,   wil - low wil - low wa - ly)

GROS.: Prithee, pretty maiden—prithee, tell me true,
  (Hey, but I'm doleful, willow willow waly)
Have you e'er a lover a-dangling after you?
    Hey willow waly O!
      I would fain discover
      If you have a lover?
    Hey willow waly O!

PAT.: Gentle sir, my heart is frolicsome and free—
  (Hey, but he's doleful, willow willow waly!)
Nobody I care for comes a-courting me—
    Hey willow waly O!
      Nobody I care for
      Comes a-courting—therefore,
    Hey willow waly O!

GROS.: Prithee, pretty maiden, will you marry me?
  (Hey, but I'm hopeful, willow willow waly!)
I may say, at once, I'm a man of propertee—
    Hey willow waly O!
      Money, I despise it;
      Many people prize it,
    Hey willow waly O!

PAT.: Gentle sir, although to marry I design—
  (Hey, but he's hopeful, willow willow waly!)
As yet I do not know you, and so I must decline.
    Hey willow waly O!
      To other maidens go you—
      As yet I do not know you,
    Hey willow waly O!

IOLANTHE
Song: Private Willis

When all night long a chap re-mains On

sen-try-go, to chase mo-no-to-ny

When all night long a chap remains
  On sentry-go, to chase monotony
He exercises of his brains,
  That is, assuming that he's got any.

{ 244 }

Though never nurtured in the lap
   Of luxury, yet I admonish you,
I am an intellectual chap,
   And think of things that would astonish you.
      I often think it's comical—Fal, lal, la!
       How Nature always does contrive—Fal, lal, la!
        That every boy and every gal
         That's born into the world alive
        Is either a little Liberal
         Or else a little Conservative!
          Fal, lal, la!

When in that House M.P.'s divide,
   If they've a brain and cerebellum, too,
They've got to leave that brain outside,
   And vote just as their leaders tell 'em to.
But then the prospect of a lot
   Of dull M.P.'s in close proximity,
All thinking for themselves, is what
   No man can face with equanimity.
       Then let's rejoice with loud Fal la—Fal lal la!
       That Nature always does contrive—Fal lal la!
        That every boy and every gal
         That's born into the world alive
        Is either a little Liberal
         Or else a little Conservative!
          Fal lal la!

IOLANTHE
Song: Lord Mountararat

When   Bri - tain real - ly   ruled   the waves (In

good Queen Bess - 's —   time)

    When Britain really ruled the waves—
      (In good Queen Bess's time)
    The House of Peers made no pretence
    To intellectual eminence,
      Or scholarship sublime;
    Yet Britain won her proudest bays
    In good Queen Bess's glorious days!

CHORUS: Yes, Britain won, etc.

LORD MOUNT.: When Wellington thrashed Bonaparte,
                   As every child can tell,
               The House of Peers, throughout the war,
               Did nothing in particular,
                   And did it very well:
               Yet Britain set the world ablaze
               In good King George's glorious days!

CHORUS: Yes, Britain set, etc.

LORD MOUNT.: And while the House of Peers withholds
                   Its legislative hand,
               And noble statesmen do not itch
               To interfere with matters which
                   They do not understand,
               As bright will shine Great Britain's rays
               As in King George's glorious days!

CHORUS: As bright will shine, etc.

IOLANTHE
Song: Fairy Queen

Oh, foo - lish   fay,   Think you, be - cause   His brave ar -

ray My bo - som   thaws,   I'd di - so - bey Our fai - ry

laws?

                   Oh, foolish fay,
                       Think you, because
                   His brave array
                       My bosom thaws,
                   I'd disobey
                       Our fairy laws?
                   Because I fly
                       In realms above,

{ 246 }

> In tendency
>> To fall in love,
> Resemble I
>> The amorous dove?

(*Aside.*) Oh, amorous dove!
>> Type of Ovidius Naso!
>>> This heart of mine
>>> Is soft as thine,
>>> Although I dare not say so!

CHORUS: Oh, amorous dove, etc.

QUEEN: On fire that glows
>> With heat intense
> I turn the hose
>> Of common sense,
> And out it goes
>> At small expense!
> We must maintain
>> Our fairy law;
> That is the main
>> On which to draw—
> In that we gain
>> A Captain Shaw!

(*Aside.*) Oh, Captain Shaw!
>> Type of true love kept under!
>>> Could thy Brigade
>>> With cold cascade
>>> Quench my great love, I wonder!

CHORUS: Oh, Captain Shaw! etc.

THE MIKADO

Song: Nanki-Poo

A   wan - d'ring min - strel   I,   A   thing   of

shreds _____ and   pat - ches,

> A wand'ring minstrel I,
>> A thing of shreds and patches,
>> Of ballads, songs and snatches,
> And dreamy lullaby!

My catalogue is long,
  Through every passion ranging,
  And to your humours changing
I tune my supple song!

        Are you in sentimental mood?
          I'll sigh with you,
            Oh, sorrow, sorrow!
        On maiden's coldness do you brood?
          I'll do so, too—
            Oh, sorrow, sorrow!
        I'll charm your willing ears
        With songs of lovers' fears,
        While sympathetic tears
          My cheeks bedew—
            Oh, sorrow, sorrow!

But if patriotic sentiment is wanted,
  I've patriotic ballads cut and dried;
For where'er our country's banner may be planted,
  All other local banners are defied!
Our warriors, in serried ranks assembled,
  Never quail—or they conceal it if they do—
And I shouldn't be surprised if nations trembled
  Before the mighty troops of Titipu!

CHORUS: We shouldn't be surprised, etc.

NANK.:   And if you call for a song of the sea,
            We'll heave the capstan round,
         With a yeo heave ho, for the wind is free,
         Her anchor's a-trip and her helm's a-lee,
            Hurrah for the homeward bound!

CHORUS: Yeo-ho—heave ho—
            Hurrah for the homeward bound!

NANK.:   To lay aloft in a howling breeze
            May tickle a landsman's taste,
         But the happiest hour a sailor sees
            Is when he's down
            At an inland town,
         With his Nancy on his knees, yeo ho!
            And his arm around her waist!

CHORUS: Then man the capstan—off we go,
            As the fiddler swings us round,
         With a yeo heave ho,
         And a rumbelow,
            Hurrah for the homeward bound!

NANK.:   A wandering minstrel I, etc.

{ 248 }

THE MIKADO
Trio: Yum-yum, Peep-Bo, Pitti-Sing

Three   lit -tle   maids from school are   we,   Pert   as   a

school - girl   well   can   be,

THE THREE:	Three little maids from school are we,
	Pert as a school-girl well can be,
	Filled to the brim with girlish glee,
	Three little maids from school!
YUM-YUM:	Everything is a source of fun. (*Chuckle.*)
PEEP-BO:	Nobody's safe, for we care for none! (*Chuckle.*)
PITTI-SING:	Life is a joke that's just begun! (*Chuckle.*)
THE THREE:	Three little maids from school!
ALL (*dancing*):	Three little maids who, all unwary,
	Come from a ladies' seminary,
	Freed from its genius tutelary—
THE THREE (*suddenly demure*):	
	Three little maids from school!
YUM-YUM:	One little maid is a bride, Yum-Yum—
PEEP-BO:	Two little maids in attendance come—
PITTI-SING:	Three little maids is the total sum.
THE THREE:	Three little maids from school!
YUM-YUM:	From three little maids take one away.
PEEP-BO:	Two little maids remain, and they—
PITTI-SING:	Won't have to wait very long, they say—
THE THREE:	Three little maids from school!
ALL (*dancing*):	Three little maids who, all unwary,
	Come from a ladies' seminary,
	Freed from its genius tutelary—
THE THREE (*suddenly demure*):	
	Three little maids from school!

THE MIKADO
Song: Yum-Yum

The sun, whose rays
Are all ablaze
    With ever-living glory,
Does not deny
His majesty—
    He scorns to tell a story!

{ *249* }

The sun, whose rays Are all a-blaze With e-ver-li-ving glo-ry,

Does not de-ny His ma-jes-ty He scorns to tell a sto-ry!

He don't exclaim,
"I blush for shame,
  So kindly be indulgent."
But, fierce and bold,
In fiery gold,
  He glories all effulgent!

I mean to rule the earth,
  As he the sky—
We really know our worth,
  The sun and I!

Observe his flame,
That placid dame,
  The moon's Celestial Highness:
There's not a trace
Upon her face
  Of diffidence or shyness:
She borrows light
That, through the night,
  Mankind may all acclaim her!
And, truth to tell,
She lights up well,
  So I, for one, don't blame her!

Ah, pray make no mistake,
  We are not shy;
We're very wide awake,
  The moon and I!

THE MIKADO
Trio: Yum-Yum, Nanki-Poo, and Ko-Ko

YUM.:   Here's a how-de-do!
                     If I marry you,
                When your time has come to perish,
                Then the maiden whom you cherish
                     Must be slaughtered, too!
                     Here's a how-de-do!

{ *250* }

Yum-Yum

Here's a how - de - do! If I mar - ry

you, When your time has come to pe - rish,

Then the mai - den whom you che - rish

NANK.:

Here's a pretty mess!
In a month, or less,
I must die without a wedding!
Let the bitter tears I'm shedding
Witness my distress,
Here's a pretty mess!

KO.:

Here's a state of things!
To her life she clings!
Matrimonial devotion
Doesn't seem to suit her notion—
Burial it brings!
Here's a state of things!

ENSEMBLE

YUM-YUM *and* NANKI-POO	KO-KO
With a passion that's intense I worship and adore, But the laws of common sense We oughtn't to ignore. If what he says is true, 'Tis death to marry you! Here's a pretty state of things! Here's a pretty how-de-do!	With a passion that's intense You worship and adore, But the laws of common sense You oughtn't to ignore. If what I say is true, 'Tis death to marry you! Here's a pretty state of things! Here's a pretty how-de-do!

THE MIKADO
March: March of the Mikado's Troops

Chorus

Mi - ya sa - ma, mi - ya sa - ma, On n'm-ma no ma - yé ni

Miya sama, miya sama,
On n'm-ma no mayé ni

{ *251* }

Pira-Pira suru no wa
Nan gia na
Toko tonyaré tonyaré na?

THE MIKADO
Duet: Mikado and Katisha

Mikado

From eve - ry kind of man O - be - dience I _ ex - pect;

MIK.:　From every kind of man
　　　　Obedience I expect;
　　　　I'm the Emperor of Japan—

KAT.:　And I'm his daughter-in-law elect!
　　　　He'll marry his son
　　　　(He's only got one)
　　　　To his daughter-in-law elect.

MIK.:　My morals have been declared
　　　　Particularly correct;

KAT.:　But they're nothing at all, compared
　　　　With those of his daughter-in-law elect!
　　　　Bow—Bow—
　　　　To his daughter-in-law elect!

ALL:　　　Bow—Bow—
　　　　To his daughter-in-law elect.

MIK.:　In a fatherly kind of way
　　　　I govern each tribe and sect,
　　　　All cheerfully own my sway—

KAT.:　Except his daughter-in-law elect!
　　　　As tough as a bone,
　　　　With a will of her own,
　　　　Is his daughter-in-law elect!

MIK.:　My nature is love and light—
　　　　My freedom from all defect—

KAT.:　Is insignificant quite,
　　　　Compared with his daughter-in-law elect!
　　　　Bow—Bow—
　　　　To his daughter-in-law elect!

ALL:　　　Bow—Bow—
　　　　To his daughter-in-law elect!

{ 252 }

THE MIKADO

Song: Mikado

My   ob - ject all   su - blime ——   I

shall   a - chieve   in   time

MIK.:   A more humane Mikado never
Did in Japan exist,
To nobody second,
I'm certainly reckoned
A true philanthropist.
It is my very humane endeavour
To make, to some extent,
Each evil liver
A running river
Of harmless merriment.

My object all sublime
I shall achieve in time—
To let the punishment fit the crime—
The punishment fit the crime;
And make each prisoner pent
Unwillingly represent
A source of innocent merriment!
Of innocent merriment!

All prosy dull society sinners,
Who chatter and bleat and bore,
Are sent to hear sermons
From mystical Germans
Who preach from ten till four.
The amateur tenor, whose vocal villainies
All desire to shirk,
Shall, during off-hours,
Exhibit his powers
To Madame Tussaud's waxwork.

The lady who dyes a chemical yellow
Or stains her grey hair puce,
Or pinches her figger,
Is painted with vigour
And permanent walnut juice.

The idiot who, in railway carriages,
    Scribbles on window-panes,
        We only suffer
        To ride on a buffer
    In Parliamentary trains.

        My object all sublime, etc.

CHORUS: His object all sublime, etc.

MIK.:   The advertising quack who wearies
    With tales of countless cures,
        His teeth, I've enacted,
        Shall all be extracted
    By terrified amateurs.
The music-hall singer attends a series
    Of masses and fugues and "ops"
        By Bach, interwoven
        With Spohr and Beethoven,
    At classical Monday Pops.

The billiard sharp whom any one catches,
    His doom's extremely hard—
        He's made to dwell—
        In a dungeon cell
    On a spot that's always barred.
And there he plays extravagant matches
    In fitless finger-stalls
        On a cloth untrue,
        With a twisted cue
    And elliptical billiard balls!

        My object all sublime, etc.

CHORUS: His object all sublime, etc.

THE MIKADO
Duet: Nanki-Poo and Ko-Ko

The   flo - wers that bloom in the spring,   Tra - la,   Breathe

pro - mise of   mer - ry   sun - shine

NANK.: The flowers that bloom in the spring,
         Tra la,
  Breathe promise of merry sunshine—
As we merrily dance and we sing,
         Tra la,
We welcome the hope that they bring,
         Tra la,
  Of a summer of roses and wine.
    And that's what we mean when we say that a thing
    Is welcome as flowers that bloom in the spring.
         Tra la la la la la, etc.

ALL: Tra la la la la, etc.

KO.:   The flowers that bloom in the spring,
         Tra la,
  Have nothing to do with the case.
I've got to take under my wing,
         Tra la,
A most unattractive old thing,
         Tra la,
  With a caricature of a face
  And that's what I mean when I say, or I sing,
  "Oh, bother the flowers that bloom in the spring."
         Tra la la la la la, etc.

ALL: Tra la la la la, Tra la la la la, etc.

THE MIKADO
Song: Ko-Ko

On a tree by a river a little tom-tit
    Sang, "Willow, titwillow, titwillow!"
And I said to him, "Dicky-bird, why do you sit
    Singing 'Willow, titwillow, titwillow'?"
"Is it weakness of intellect, birdie?" I cried,
"Or a rather tough worm in your little inside?"
With a shake of his poor little head, he replied,
    "Oh, willow, titwillow, titwillow!"

He slapped at his chest, as he sat on that bough,
   Singing "Willow, titwillow, titwillow!"
And a cold perspiration bespangled his brow,
   Oh, willow, titwillow, titwillow!
He sobbed and he sighed, and a gurgle he gave,
Then he plunged himself into the billowy wave,
And an echo arose from the suicide's grave—
   "Oh, willow, titwillow, titwillow!"

Now I feel just as sure as I'm sure that my name
   Isn't Willow, titwillow, titwillow,
That 'twas blighted affection that made him exclaim
   "Oh, willow, titwillow, titwillow!"
And if you remain callous and obdurate, I
Shall perish as he did, and you will know why,
Though I probably shall not exclaim as I die,
   "Oh, willow, titwillow, titwillow!"

RUDDIGORE

Song: Sir Roderic

When the night wind howls   in the chim-ney cowls,   and the

bat   in the moon - light   flies,

When the night wind howls in the chimney cowls, and the bat in the
   moonlight flies,
And inky clouds, like funeral shrouds, sail over the midnight skies—
When the footpads quail at the night-bird's wail, and black dogs bay
   at the moon,
Then is the spectres' holiday—then is the ghosts' high-noon!

CHORUS: Ha! ha!
                Then is the ghosts' high-noon!

SIR ROD.: As the sob of the breeze sweeps over the trees, and the mists lie low
        on the fen,
      From grey tomb-stones are gathered the bones that once were women
        and men,
      And away they go, with a mop and a mow, to the revel that ends too
        soon,
      For cockcrow limits our holiday—the dead of the night's high-noon!

CHORUS: Ha! ha!
                    The dead of the night's high-noon!

SIR ROD.: And then each ghost with his ladye-toast to their church-yard beds
            takes flight,
          With a kiss, perhaps, on her lantern chaps, and a grisly grim "good-
            night";
          Till the welcome knell of the midnight bell rings forth its jolliest tune,
          And ushers in our next high holiday—the dead of the night's high-
            noon!

CHORUS: Ha! ha!
                    The dead of the night's high-noon!

THE YEOMEN OF THE GUARD
Duet: Elsie and Jack Point

I have a song to· sing, O! _____

Sing me your song, O! _____

It is sung to the moon By a love-lorn_ loon, Who

fled from the moc - king throng, O!

POINT: I have a song to sing, O!

ELSIE: Sing me your song, O!

POINT: It is sung to the moon
                                By a love-lorn loon,
                        Who fled from the mocking throng, O!
                    It's a song of a merryman, moping mum,
                    Whose soul was sad, and whose glance was glum,
                    Who sipped no sup, and who craved no crumb,
                        As he sighed for the love of a ladye.

{ 257 }

Heighdy! heighdy!
Misery me, lackadaydee!
He sipped no sup, and he craved no crumb,
As he sighed for the love of a ladye.

ELSIE: I have a song to sing, O!

POINT: What is your song, O?

ELSIE:

It is sung with the ring
Of the songs maids sing
Who love with a love life-long, O!
It's the song of a merrymaid, peerly proud,
Who loved a lord and who laughed aloud
At the moan of the merryman, moping mum,
Whose soul was sad, and whose glance was glum,
Who sipped no sup, and who craved no crumb,
As he sighed for the love of a ladye.
Heighdy! heighdy!
Misery me, lackadaydee!
He sipped no sup, etc.

POINT: I have a song to sing, O!

ELSIE: Sing me your song, O!

POINT:

It is sung to the knell
Of a churchyard bell,
And a doleful dirge, ding dong, O!
It's a song of a popinjay, bravely born,
Who turned up his noble nose with scorn
At the humble merrymaid, peerly proud,
Who loved a lord, and who laughed aloud
At the moan of a merryman, moping mum,
Whose soul was sad, and whose glance was glum,
Who sipped no sup, and who craved no crumb,
As he sighed for the love of a ladye.

BOTH:

Heighdy! heighdy!
Misery me, lackadaydee!
He sipped no sup, etc.

ELSIE: I have a song to sing, O!

POINT: Sing me your song, O!

ELSIE:

It is sung with a sigh
And a tear in the eye,
For it tells of a righted wrong, O!
It's a song of the merrymaid, once so gay,
Who turned on her heel and tripped away
From the peacock popinjay, bravely born,

{ 258 }

Who turned up his noble nose with scorn
At the humble heart that he did not prize:
So she begged on her knees, with downcast eyes,
For the love of the merryman, moping mum,
Whose soul was sad, and whose glance was glum,
Who sipped no sup, and who craved no crumb,
    As he sighed for the love of a ladye.

BOTH: Heighdy! heighdy!
                        Misery me, lackadaydee!
His pains were o'er, and he sighed no more,
    For he lived in the love of a ladye.

THE GONDOLIERS
Song: Marco

(Original key G♭.)

      Take a pair of sparkling eyes,
         Hidden, ever and anon,
            In a merciful eclipse—
    Do not heed their mild surprise—
         Having passed the Rubicon,
            Take a pair of rosy lips;
    Take a figure trimly planned—
         Such as admiration whets
            (Be particular in this);
    Take a tender little hand,
         Fringed with dainty fingerettes,
            Press it—in parenthesis;—
    Ah! Take all these, you lucky man—
    Take and keep them, if you can!

    Take a pretty little cot—
         Quite a miniature affair—
            Hung about with trellised vine,
    Furnish it upon the spot
         With the treasures rich and rare
            I've endeavoured to define.

Live to love and love to live—
You will ripen at your ease,
Growing on the sunny side—
Fate has nothing more to give.
You're a dainty man to please
If you are not satisfied.
Ah! Take my counsel, happy man;
Act upon it, if you can!

THE GONDOLIERS
Chorus and dance

Dance a — ca - chu - cha, fan - dan - go, bo - le - ro,

Xe - res we'll drink Man - za - nil - la, Mon - te - ro —

Dance a cachucha, fandango, bolero,
Xeres we'll drink—Manzanilla, Montero—
Wine, when it runs in abundance, enhances
The reckless delight of that wildest of dances!
To the pretty pitter-pitter-patter,
And the clitter-clitter-clitter-clatter—
Clitter—clitter—clatter,
Pitter—pitter—patter,
Patter, patter, patter, patter, we'll dance.
Old Xeres we'll drink—Manzanilla, Montero;
For wine, when it runs in abundance, enhances
The reckless delight of that wildest of dances!

THE GONDOLIERS
Gavotte: Duke, Duchess, Marco, Giuseppe, Casilda

I — am a cour - tier grave and se - rious Who — is a -

bout to kiss your hand:

DUKE: I am a courtier grave and serious
Who is about to kiss your hand:
Try to combine a pose imperious
With a demeanour nobly bland.

MAR. *and* GIU.: Let us combine a pose imperious
With a demeanour nobly bland.

(MARCO *and* GIUSEPPE *endeavour to carry out his instructions.*)

DUKE: That's, if anything, *too* unbending—
Too aggressively stiff and grand;

(*They suddenly modify their attitudes.*)

Now to the other extreme you're tending—
Don't be so deucedly condescending!

DUCH. *and* CAS.: Now to the other extreme you're tending—
Don't be so dreadfully condescending!

MAR. *and* GIU.: Oh, hard to please some noblemen seem!
At first, if anything, *too* unbending;
Off we go to the other extreme—
Too confoundedly condescending!

DUKE: Now a gavotte perform sedately—
Offer your hand with conscious pride;
Take an attitude not too stately,
Still sufficiently dignified.

MAR. *and* GIU.: Now for an attitude not too stately,
Still sufficiently dignified.

(*They endeavour to carry out his instructions.*)

DUKE (*beating time*):

Oncely, twicely—oncely, twicely—
Bow impressively ere you glide.
(*They do so.*)

Capital both—you've caught it nicely!
That is the style of thing precisely!

DUCH. *and* CAS.: Capital both—they've caught it nicely!
That is the style of thing precisely!

MAR. *and* GIU.: Oh, sweet to earn a nobleman's praise!
Capital both—we've caught it nicely!
Supposing he's right in what he says,
This is the style of thing precisely!

{ *261* }

BIBLIOGRAPHY

AUTHOR	TITLE	PAGES	PUBLISHER	DATE
Baily, Leslie	The Gilbert and Sullivan Book	443	Cassell, London	1952
	same, *revised*	475	Coward-McCann, New York	1957
Bassuk, Albert O.	How to Present the Gilbert and Sullivan Operas		Bass, New York	1934
Bond, Jessie	The Life and Reminiscences of Jessie Bond, the Old Savoyard	243	Lane, London	1930
Bradstock, Lillian	Pooh-Bah and the Rest of Gilbert and Sullivan, A Story Version	260	Figurehead, London	1933
Browne, Edith	William Schwenck Gilbert		Lane, New York	1907
Cellier, F. A.	Gilbert, Sullivan and D'Oyly Carte, Reminiscences of the Savoy		Pitman, London	1914
	same		Reprinted, New York	1927
Cox-Ife, William	Training the Gilbert and Sullivan Chorus	98	Chappell, New York	1956
———	How to Sing Both Gilbert and Sullivan	155	Chappell, London	1959
Dark, Sidney	William Schwenck Gilbert, His Life and Letters		Methuen, London	1923
Darlington, W. A.	The World of Gilbert and Sullivan	209	Crowell, New York	1950
Dunhill, T. F.	Sullivan's Comic Operas, a Critical Appreciation		Arnold, London	1928

AUTHOR	TITLE	PAGES	PUBLISHER	DATE
Dunn, George E.	A Gilbert and Sullivan Dictionary		Allen & Unwin, London	1936

(*A most valuable book, defining all the foreign words, strange references, and esoteric remarks that appear in the libretti*)

AUTHOR	TITLE	PAGES	PUBLISHER	DATE
Findon, B. W.	Sir Arthur Sullivan, his Life and Music	214	Nisbet, London	1904
Fitzgerald, Percy	The Operas of Gilbert and Sullivan	248	Lippincott, Philadelphia	1894
————	The Savoy Opera and the Savoyards	248	Chatto and Windus, London	1894
Fitz-Gerald, Shafto	The Story of the Savoy Opera	239	Paul, London	1924
	Reprinted		Appleton, New York	1925
Godwin, A. H.	Gilbert and Sullivan, a Critical Appreciation		Dent, London	1926
Goldberg, Isaac	Gilbert and Sullivan, a Handbook to the Famous Operettas		Little Blue Books, Girard, Kansas	1935
————	Sir William Schwenck Gilbert, a Study in Modern Satire		Stratford, Boston	1913
————	The Story of Gilbert and Sullivan, or The Compleat Savoyard		Simon and Schuster, New York	1928

(*Best source of activity in the United States*)

AUTHOR	TITLE	PAGES	PUBLISHER	DATE
Halton, F. J.	The Gilbert and Sullivan Operas, a Concordance		Bass, New York	1935
Hewitt, Tony	The School Gilbert and Sullivan	48	Albyn, Edinburgh	1949
Joseph, Arthur	Gilbert and Sullivan	64	Parrish, London	1951
Lambton, Gervase	Gilbertian Characters and a Discourse on William Schwenck Gilbert's Philosophy	118	Allen, London	1931
Lawrence, Arthur	Sir Arthur Sullivan, Life Story, Letters and Reminiscences	340	Stone, Chicago	1900

BIBLIOGRAPHY

AUTHOR	TITLE	PAGES	PUBLISHER	DATE
Lytton, H. A.	The Secrets of a Savoyard		Jarrolds, London	1922
	Revised as A Wandering Minstrel	287	*the same*	1933
Pearson, Hesketh	Gilbert, His Life and Strife	276	Methuen, London	1957
	Reprinted		Harper, New York	1958

(*An excellent book, which brings out some of the subtler reasons for Gilbert's attitudes and actions*)

AUTHOR	TITLE	PAGES	PUBLISHER	DATE
——	Gilbert and Sullivan, a Biography	319	Hamilton, London	1935
Purdy, Claire Lee	Gilbert and Sullivan, Masters of Mirth and Melody	276	Messner, New York	1947
Rickett, Edmund and Hoogland, B.	Let's Do Some Gilbert and Sullivan, a Practical Production Handbook	238	Coward-McCann, New York	1940
Searle, Townley	Sir William Schwenck Gilbert, a Topsy-Turvy Adventure		Alexander-Ouseley, London	1931

(*Containing a bibliography*)

AUTHOR	TITLE	PAGES	PUBLISHER	DATE
Sullivan, Herbert	Sir Arthur Sullivan, his Life, Letters, and Diaries		Cassell, London	1927
Walbrook, Henry	Gilbert and Sullivan Opera, a History and a Comment	154	White, London	1922
Williamson, Audrey	Gilbert and Sullivan Opera, a New Assessment	292	Macmillan, New York	1953

(*With illustrations in color*)

AUTHOR	TITLE	PAGES	PUBLISHER	DATE
Wood, Roger	A D'Oyly Carte Album	66	Black, London	1953
	Reprinted		Pitman, New York	1954

(*A photographic essay, with pictures of recent Savoy productions*)

AUTHOR	TITLE	PAGES	PUBLISHER	DATE
Wyndam, H. S.	Arthur Seymour Sullivan	285	Paul, Trench & Traubner, London	1926